Editor in Chief: Tom Whitfield
Editor, layout, design: Angela K. Durden

ISBN: 978-1-950729-22-7
Blue Room Books
BlueRoomBooks.com

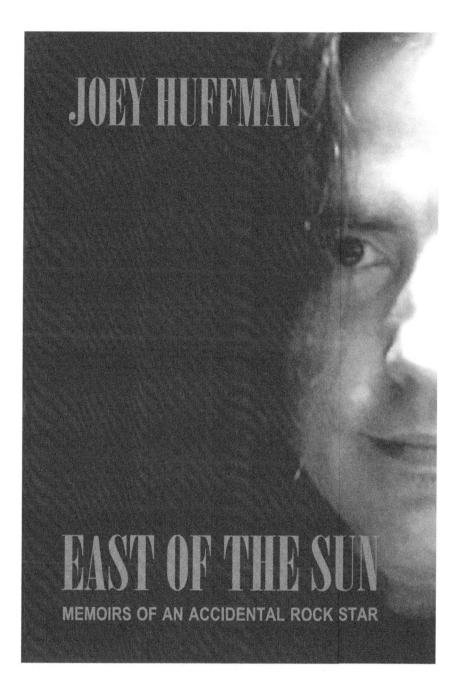

Dedicated to:

My children Whitney and Joey:
I love you more than you know.

Charles and Chuck Huffman:
Dad and Brother

And all the many artists, techs, songwriters, musicians,
roadies, caterers, hotel staff, bus drivers, and venues
I had the pleasure to know.

Foreword

It's September 2013, Joey and I are standing backstage in either Mississippi or Louisiana (it all runs together, it all looks the same). There's a deli tray and we decided to do this thing that we do where we try weird food combinations.

Cinnamon toast, strawberry jelly, Tabasco, and Dijon mustard? 1/5 stars in my book, Joey said that it was the best thing he had ever eaten. Years later, I'm not sure if he was serious or not.

Get the picture?

On this day the question was, "Does ranch dressing make an acceptable dipping sauce for pineapple?" The answer, we both declared, was "not suitable". Then Joey looked at me and said seven words that I'll never forget: "I think I have a brain tumor." I told him there was no way he had a brain tumor, and then it was showtime.

A few weeks go by and everyone is home. It's late afternoon and my phone rings, I see that it's Kimberly (Joey's then-girlfriend), so I immediately answer. The news was in: The headaches and other assorted issues Joey was having at the time were caused by — well, you guessed it — a brain tumor. For years, I would tell him he got it just to spite me.

Fast forward a few months, Christmas is rapidly approaching, and I get a phone call from Joey. "I need someone to take me Christmas shopping," he tells me.

I respond with something to the effect of "Man, it's three and a half hours each way, I'm not driving seven hours to take you to Target."

"I have a brain tumor, you motherfucker."

And that settled it.

The next morning I headed to Atlanta to take him Christmas shopping. That story is in this book. I cried when I read it for the first time. He's right, I didn't have time to come over to Atlanta, but I found time. It was the only choice to make at the time, damn the consequences.

You see, everyone talks about the meaning of Christmas. Some people have never felt it, some people think they've felt it, and others *know* they've felt it. It's a wild energy, generally untapped. Anyone can watch "It's a Wonderful Life" with their family and say that they get it, but that's not it. It's nowhere near the same vibrational level as when your best friend thinks that this may be his last Christmas and you yourself think this may be your best friend's last Christmas.

To this day, I've never felt a spirit quite like that and perhaps never will again.

I met Joey in 2011. He gave me his phone number and told me that having it was like entering a contract to answer his calls both day and night. At that moment we quickly began to become best friends. There's a decent age gap there, but we could tell we were similar. I honestly didn't know just how similar until I read this book, the most realistic one I've ever read about life on the road.

But everything about our friendship now makes sense.

I love you, brother. No matter how many Diet Mountain Dews you've spilled on me before the show (you say you don't remember any of that, but it happened...a lot); no matter how many times you forget my birthday (it only happened once, but it was my twenty-first, so fuck you); and no matter how many times you tell me "Yeah, I'd probably ask her to move back in" in regards to the toxic girlfriend I absolutely should NOT have moved back in with.

(In her defense, I was toxic too. We flew to Las Vegas to break up, stayed that way for a year and a half, then she came back into my life and wanted to move back in, and anyone in my circle would have said to avoid her like the plague. But, it was one AM in Nevada and all I had was Joey, we were both drinking heavily and, as he'll tell you himself, he doesn't always have the best moral compass.)

Joey, you're the Dragon to my Nighthawk, congrats on landing East of the Sun and becoming:

The Legend...

The Forrest Gump of Rock & Roll...

The Human Rain Delay...

And, most importantly, the best damn Accidental Rock Star anyone could ever ask for.

Your best friend,
Izzy Miller

1995: Rock & Roll Hall of Fame

Soul Asylum: Karl Mueller *(far left)***, Joey Huffman**
*(second from left)***, and Dave Pirner** *(far right)*
with Lou Reed *(singing)*

CONCERT FOR THE ROCK & ROLL HALL OF FAME

September 2, 1995, the Rock & Roll Hall of Fame celebrated its official opening with a gigantic all-star concert at Cleveland Municipal Stadium. It was the last show in that stadium before it was demolished in 1996 — and this Accidental Rock Star was on the stage with Soul Asylum, Iggy Pop, and Lou Reed in front of sixty thousand people. It was heavenly.

Featuring Rock & Roll Hall of Famers paying tribute to legends and highlighting their own work, the fast-paced and fun show was televised live around the world by Home Box Office. Performers, including future Hall of Famers, played on a two-sided circular stage that rotated to allow one group to set up while the other was in the spotlight. There's a third stage for solo acoustic performances by Dr. John, Jackson Browne, Ann and Nancy Wilson of Heart, and others.

The concert brought more talent under one roof than at any concert before. Other artists included Bruce Springsteen, Bob Dylan, Bon Jovi, Chuck Berry, Little Richard, Aretha Franklin, Johnny Cash, Booker T. and the M.G.'s, Melissa Etheridge, Eric Burdon, John Mellencamp, Jerry Lee Lewis, Sam Moore, Natalie Merchant, Al Green, George Clinton and the P-Funk All-Stars, Robbie Robertson, The Allman Brothers Band, The Pretenders, Martha and the Vandellas, John Fogerty, Bruce Hornsby, Boz Scaggs, Slash, Gin Blossoms, Sheryl Crow, The Kinks, and James Brown. There's a story in a little bit about James Brown and my wife that you'll find fun.

One of the most electrifying combinations was delivered by alternative rockers Soul Asylum with punk pioneers Lou Reed and Iggy Pop. Pop joined Soul Asylum on Back Door Man, the Willie Dixon Blues tune first performed by Howlin' Wolf and later popularized by The Doors. Our band, though, gave the tune a hard, aggressive edge, and Pop, in top punk form, pranced around the stage like a punkish Mick Jagger.

Reed used his performance to pay tribute to Velvet Underground guitarist Sterling Morrison, 53, who died on August 30, two days before the concert, of non-Hodgkin's lymphoma. He performed Sweet Jane in collaboration with Soul Asylum as a way to memorialize his friend. In a newspaper interview (if memory serves, it was The Austin Chronicle), Reed said he didn't attend Sterling's funeral, choosing instead to dedicate a song to him from the stage of the Rock & Roll Hall of Fame so his name would be heard by millions.

Lou simply wanted to play Sweet Jane for Sterling one last time. And he did.

Former WMMS deejay, Columbia Records exec, and LJT Entertainment founder Kid Leo started the evening's proceedings with a pre-concert cheer, paying tribute to the Clevelanders who rallied to bring the Hall of Fame to the city. He says This is the home of Rock & Roll. Bar none, above all, Cleveland is the home of Rock & Roll.

That's right, kids: Cleveland rocks.

Day Before Concert

Sometimes you just have to be there to make history. So there I was. In Cleveland, Ohio. With Soul Asylum. To play The Concert for The Rock & Roll Hall of Fame to celebrate its grand opening.

With my head shuffling memories with promises of the coming day, I woke in my room at the Renaissance Cleveland Hotel where I'd checked in the night before. I turned on the TV to watch the news. Remember when you could get the entire news cycle with actual real facts in thirty minutes on CNN's Headline News? Those were the days, right? Lobby call for rehearsal was at 1:00 p.m., which was fine with me because sometimes I just like to sit around and think. And right now, I was thinking about the gig.

Soul Asylum had been rehearsing Back Door Man and Sweet Jane at our soundchecks for about a month. We knew them backward and forward. But today would be the first time we'd get to play them with the artists and we were looking forward to it.

But first things first.

My wife Kim was flying in from Atlanta later that evening. I called to make sure she knew what the plan was. After arriving and until I got back from rehearsal, she should hang tight until she heard from me. I was hoping to get back early enough for us to have a nice dinner. Plus, I'd been touring with Soul Asylum since March with only short breaks, so I was really looking forward to seeing her.

Excited and nervous, I got to lobby call early. The place was a madhouse with people racing around in controlled chaos. It seemed as if every artist playing the show was staying at the hotel. I saw a few familiar faces and gave them a nod.

Went outside to wait for the van. Said good morning to Dave Pirner and Bill Sullivan. We chatted about the show and what a major task it had to be. We were in awe. The rest of the band showed up and we headed to the venue.

Cleveland Municipal Stadium (next page, undated photo) was so enormous we saw it well before arriving. Beside the stadium were what looked like office and other functional types of buildings. Backstage was just a huge, paved area with a chain link fence and so jammed with what seemed like a thousand tour buses that we couldn't pull in. We were let off at a gate and walked about a quarter mile to get to the stage. Because we flew in, we didn't have a tour bus, so our dressing rooms were in one of the office buildings yet another quarter mile further.

Unusual for a television shoot, our dressing room was well-stocked, including a bottle of Absolut and cranberry juice. But this gig was more about the music than the HBO production. Beth, our very own PA, showed up to chaperone us to stage, but much to her dismay we decided we needed another drink, so got busy mixing them. If you really want to upset TV personnel, being late and dragging your feet is the perfect way to do it.

Beth impatiently waited for us to pour drinks, then barked Come on, we're late; that means my ass, not yours.

Only been there twenty minutes and we're already making friends. I offered to mix her one to kill the bug up her ass, but she ignored me and led the way to a smaller dressing room — it was more like a holding cell — to wait until they were ready for us.

Bill Sullivan posted our bail and we had thirty minutes to check our gear and get soundcheck done. Everything was working, so we started running through Sweet Jane for soundcheck and onstage volume adjusting so we'd hear each other. The stage was alive with activity. We were supposed to do Iggy first, but he was snaking some of the female riggers.

Running late, finally Lou showed up, took his guitar out of the case and didn't even bother tuning it. Just plugged in, turned it up, and said Okay, I'm ready.

We began Sweet Jane and when Lou began singing, I got the shivers. He's a legend and we're backing him up. What an honor. You couldn't have met a nicer guy. The music world lost an intellectual badass when he died October 27, 2013.

Next up was Iggy Pop. We were performing Back Door Man with him but we're being sneaky and putting a chorus of I Wanna Be Your Dog [written by Dave Alexander, Iggy Pop, Ron Asheton, and Scott Asheton] in the middle of the song. Iggy was awesome as always. Both Lou and Iggy thanked the band, but it was definitely our pleasure.

We headed back to the hotel where I hoped to find Kim. I was not disappointed. Suitcase open on the luggage stand, her perfume wafting in the air — my favorite: Halston Eau De Cologne Spray. And there she was, on the bed, on top of the covers, sound asleep. I thought about waking her up but just cuddled up and held her. She let out a moan as if she approved and I fell asleep, too.

We woke up a little later. She kissed me soft and slow. I missed her so much that kiss made my heart ache. We kissed for a long time then got intimate. It was very gentle and filled a hole in my heart and soul I didn't realize was there or so big. Afterward we held each other for a while, then she went to take a shower leaving me to bask in the afterglow.

Kim had called the concierge and asked for a recommendation for a good place to eat. Somewhere locals would go, she said, and made reservations at The Marble Room Steaks and Raw Bar. We were seated at 8:30. I had prime rib and Kim a filet mignon. Delicious. We had no room for dessert. Actually, our dessert would be in the room, soooo…

Off we went back to the hotel and up to our room. She giggled and fell back on the bed. I took that as an invitation and pounced on top of her. I gave her long and deliberate kisses. When she touched me, I felt chills all over my body and we made love again until we were sweating and content. My foot touched hers. We were quiet and uttered not one syllable for a quarter of an hour. I broke the silence by saying I love you. She reciprocated the feeling.

After a shower, I dried and wrapped the towel around my waist. Called the front desk and arranged for a wake-up call for 8:00 a.m. Kim had already put on a silk robe I bought her at Victoria's Secret. We crawled under the covers to get warm. The air conditioner kept the room at a constant temperature of seventy degrees. We held each other close to stay warm. After that we drifted off to sleep with the TV as our backdrop.

A ringing phone cracked the peacefulness. I picked it up and said hello, but no one was on the other end. Thoughts cleared and I remembered it was the wake-up call. Then memory came flooding back and I remembered what I was doing today. I ordered breakfast for two and let Kim sleep, then gently woke her when the food came. I poured her a cup of coffee with extra sugar and Half and Half. Then I poured myself a cup.

The day sheet had been slipped underneath the door sometime during the night. Gave it a quick look. Lobby call: 10:00 a.m. Stage call: 11:00 a.m. for camera blocking and lighting.

Kim and I climbed into the van and waited for the rest of the degenerates to arrive. Lou Reed and his girlfriend Laurie Anderson caught a ride with us, too. Everyone showed up on time and, after a head count, Bill Sullivan gave the runner the green light.

Lou Reed was a quiet guy. When he talked to his girlfriend, Laurie, he almost whispered. He wasn't Rock Star Quiet as in I'm too good to talk to you. He's a shy, complicated, deep man. He was polite and well-mannered and would engage in conversation if you talked to him first. It'd certainly take more than a day at a gig to get to know him and be his friend.

He seemed nervous. I don't know how long it had been since he played for a crowd this big but it seemed to be heavy on his mind. We arrive at the venue and are greeted by fans on the other side of a chain link fence shouting *Loooooouuuu*. I did my best Harry Caray impression and said Remember they're saying Lou not *boooooo*. Apparently, he wasn't a Cubs fan because he looked at me like I was talking crazy. We were early so we went for breakfast at Craft Services, which is just TV/film vernacular for Catering.

The director needed us onstage to block camera angles, determine how to light the scene, and rehearse with the musicians and crew to determine lighting and other adjustments that needed to be made before broadcasting live on HBO.

We played Sweet Jane with Lou about fifteen times before the director was satisfied. Pretty much the same thing with Iggy. We kids were getting cranky. Afternoon came and that meant Cocktail Time! The director set us free and with much rejoicing we hiked to the dressing room and had our cocktails in Solo cups so we would be ready to go when the runner showed up to take us back to the hotel.

Back at our room, and with a little time to kill, I had sex on the brain, but Kim was hungry. So, we ordered room service. I got the Club Sandwich — The Yardstick By Which All Other Food Is Measured — and she had a Caesar Salad with grilled chicken. We laid down and took a nap. She woke and kissed me on the forehead. I heard the shower turn on and bathroom door close and laid in bed thinking about the show. How fortunate was I to be here in Cleveland with all these talented people? It's almost too much to process. I blocked from mind that it was being simultaneously broadcast live on HBO.

Kim had been shopping for this event. She bought three different outfits. She modeled them for me, and I made comments and told her what I liked. But it didn't matter, she always chose what she was in the mood for. She chose a black knee-high party dress with spaghetti straps and a neckline low enough to feature her outstanding endowments. Then it was time to play my favorite game called Which Shoe? How it works is this:

Kim shows me two pairs. I must choose one. She pulls out another pair and I must now pick between the pair I chose and the new pair. I picked the black fuck-me pumps and she wore them.

Lobby call was a bigger madhouse than before. We couldn't even squeeze into the bar to get a drink. Soon our troupe were all in the lobby and we headed to the venue. The driver got us as close as possible. We unloaded and walked to the dressing room where I mixed drinks for Danny, Dave, and me.

The big news and gossip? James Brown was here. Everybody wanted to meet him, but he was holed up in his tour bus and not taking visitors. When Kim heard, she asked which tour bus was his. Helpfully, Dave pointed it out. She says she's going to see Mr. Brown and walked out of the dressing room making a beeline toward the Godfather of Soul's tour bus.

She knocked on the door.

Someone answers and tells her to wait.

Thirty seconds later in she goes.

Dave's jaw drops.

He couldn't believe what his lying eyes had just told him. How did Kim, Joey's wife, get an audience with James Brown? But things are not always how they seem. What Dave didn't know was that Kim had danced on James Brown's Future Shock TV series where she and her partner Drew were the only white couple. Kim even went on tour with Mr. Brown for a leg.

Kim and James had a nice half-hour visit and when the door opened, there she was, hugging him and gave him a kiss on the cheek. Yep, that's my wife, my grin said to Dave. From that day on everybody had a new respect for Kim.

The hospitality tent next to the stage was as big as any circus tent. Everyone that's anyone was in there. I got to meet Johnny Cash and June Carter Cash. They were very nice. June had a rock on her finger that looked as big as the Hope Diamond. I also met Bon Jovi and Little Richard. I'd already met Bruce Springsteen but had to remind him from where. I was overwhelmed. Way too many beautiful and talented people to digest.

The band was on for 8:00 p.m. Minder Beth started gathering us up around 6:30. She'd get two of us, tell us to sit, stay. Then she'd find another and come back to the rendezvous location and the others would be gone. I'm sure we irritated her to no end, but she had the bad attitude first. She finally rounded up everybody and escorted us to that small holding cell backstage. Lou and Laurie were there with us and out of the blue Kim, in her most charming Southern accent, asked Laurie Would you take a picture of me and my husband?

Laurie looked confused but lifted up her camera and took a few shots. Kim thanked her. Usually in a situation like that you have your own camera and ask someone to use it to take a picture of you. Did Lou and Laurie later look through their pictures and come to ours and say Who the fuck is this?

But back to the matter at hand.

John Fogerty was finishing up his set with Fortunate Son. Next was the Classic Performances video of Otis Redding. When that started showing we needed to get to the back of the rotating stage and take our places. Lou Reed was on first.

I was getting the nervous jitters like always before I play. That same nervousness was on Lou's face. I left my drink in the holding cell while Kim watched in the VIP area at stage right.

The video ends and Lou Reed is announced. The stage rotates around. When it locked into place, drummer Sterling Campbell counted off Sweet Jane, the band began playing, and all that nervousness left me as it did Lou because he was at home again and enjoying the moment.

When the song was over Lou took a bow and exited stage right as Iggy Pop came in at stage left. Sterling counted off Back Door Man as Iggy grabbed the microphone and greeted the crowd with Hello, Fuckers! He was in rare form.

When we got to I Wanna Be Your Dog, he got quite animated. On this part of the song all required of me is to bang out eighth notes while playing an octave and a fifth. I was banging that piano so hard I pulled up a fingernail that began bleeding. I looked up in the VIP area to get Kim's attention but all I saw was Bon Jovi shaking his head. I don't believe he's a punk rock fan.

The show ran late. Wish I could've met more people. It was just too much. I found Kim and all she talked about was meeting Bon Jovi. He was a celebrity crush of hers. Feeling a bit ignored, pettily I asked Hey, did you know I played tonight? She said she did. Naturally I had to show her I got hurt at work so, playing that sympathy card, I held out my right ring finger and peeled back my fingernail.

Girls don't like stuff like that and Kim's a girl and she shouted Don't do that, you're freaking me out.

I know; it's kind of freaking me out, too.

Does it hurt?

[Is that sympathy from her?] What do you think?

I followed that up with Did you even see me play or were you sitting in Bon Jovi's lap? (Joey, Joey, Joey, you just had to stir that jealousy pot.)

That's mean! she chastised.

I know, let's go to the dressing room and make some drinks because, as we all know, alcohol makes everybody forget, right?

But Kim wanted wine and there was none, so we went to the dressing room while Bill Sullivan found the runner and I found a bottle of Absolut.

Don't get so drunk you won't be able to mingle at the hotel, Joey. But I have to be drunk to mingle, you should know that, Kim. But you promised not to drink too much, Joey; this is my vacation so don't ruin it by becoming a liability.

Now, I'm not a people person. I'm fine being alone. Doesn't help with the networking much, but what can I do? On the other hand, Kim is a people person and great at networking. Still, she was right.

I'd promised not to drink too much, so I made that vodka and cranberry last a couple of hours. Before too long Bill Sullivan says the runner's waiting.

Bill, what a wonderful tour manager you are, someday you will make some man a great wife.

Fuck you, Joey.

Thirty minutes later we're back at the hotel. It wasn't crowded like before but that's because the concert was not yet over. As people finish their slots at the concert, the bar gets progressively more crowded. I spied an empty high-top table in the corner toward the back of the bar. Let people come to us. The plan was brilliant.

Kim, do you need to go to the room and change? I'd like to go to the room and freshen up a bit, if that's okay. Sure, meet me at that high-top table over there near the back; I'll be comfortable there because it's not in the middle of the fray but you can see the entire bar from that vantage point. Okay, I'll be right back; I love you. I love you, too.

I went directly to that table and ordered a double Absolut and cranberry and a Chardonnay. Surveying the lay of the land, I spotted someone walking toward me. I didn't recognize him at first but when he got closer, I recognized my old friend Kelvin Holly and stood to give him a hug. He's in town playing with Little Richard; he's had that gig for a few years. I told him I was here with Soul Asylum backing up Iggy Pop and Lou Reed. I asked about mutual friends from Alabama. Some were doing well, others not so much.

Almost instantly, it seemed, Kim was by my side. She'd changed out of the dress into jeans and a long-sleeve, boat-neck top with blue, maroon, and tan stripes of varying sizes. The sleeves were baggy, but I liked that. She's still wearing the fuck-me pumps. She looked amazing. But she'd look good in a burlap sack. I introduced her to Kelvin, and they chatted for a bit. Watching her I was again reminded Kim is definitely a people person and can talk to anyone.

Kelvin had to go to his room and change. We say goodbye then watched the room. We didn't see anyone we knew for awhile, then people started trickling in and Dave and Karl stepped into the bar looking for a drink. They saw us and came over and had a seat. Dave says the show's running late and won't be over until 2:00 a.m. We were getting bored.

Dave, can you ruin my day?

Alas, I cannot, Joey.

Kenny Aronoff, John Mellencamp's drummer, walked in. I point him out to Kim. I wanted to talk but didn't want to bother him. Besides, I was comfortable hiding at a table in a back corner. Next thing I see is Kim walking straight toward Kenny. When she reached him they began to talk. Then they shook hands. Then she's pointing straight at me and they're walking our way. I was so embarrassed. Kenny introduces himself.

Hey, look, I'm so sorry my wife bothered you. No trouble at all, he says. Can I buy you a drink, Kenny? I'll have a Corona with a lime twist, thank you.

I waved down our server and ordered Kenny's drink, another for myself and another Chardonnay for Kim. We make a toast and clink glasses then drink. Kenny hung around and talked to Dave, Karl, and me. Soon he had to run but it was a real pleasure to meet him.

Dave bought the next round of drinks. I was getting a good buzz on and I think Kim was on a wobbler as well. We sat in the corner for a long time and saw a few musicians that supported the major stars but none of the big names came in.

It was 2:00 a.m. and the bar was about shut down. We were tired after such a busy day. Kim wanted to go to the room and lay down. So did I. So we do. It's nice and cold. I took off my clothes and ran to get under the covers. Kim joined me and I wrapped my arms around her to get warm. She'd taken her clothes off, too. Oooo…always a good sign, right? We start kissing and caressing each other. It felt really good. We made love and fell asleep in each other's arms where I felt safe and secure.

Kim had to catch a 2:30 p.m. flight back to Atlanta. After breakfast and coffee, she got a shower, leaving me alone with my thoughts. Kim had to go back home and me to Columbia, Maryland, later that day to play the Merriweather Post Pavilion. A two-week break in the tour started September 7th so I'd get to go home and see her again soon. Still, I hated to see her leave.

Bags packed by noon, we went for a drink in the bar then had the concierge hail a cab. I didn't want her to leave. I was holding onto her hands and giving her kisses on her forehead. I was being very affectionate. But soon it was that time. We walked outside and I put her in a cab to the airport.

Call me when you get home safe, Kim. Goodbye, Joey!

Then the cab pulled out taking her away from me. I waved until I couldn't see the cab anymore.

Keith Richards Chronicles!

1988

Dates & Cities
& Venues

11/24	Fox Theatre, Atlanta, GA
11/25	New Daisy Theatre Nightclub, Memphis, TN
11/27	Constitution Hall, Washington D.C.
11/29	Beacon Theatre, New York, NY
12/01	Tower Theatre, Philadelphia, PA
12/02	Tower Theatre, Philadelphia, PA
12/04	Orpheum Theatre, Boston, MA
12/05	Orpheum Theatre, Boston, MA
12/07	Music Hall, Cleveland, OH
12/08	Fox Theatre, Detroit, MI
12/10	Aragon Ballroom, Chicago, IL
12/13	Henry J. Kaiser Arena, Oakland, CA
12/14	Universal Amphitheatre, Los Angeles, CA
12/15	Hollywood Palladium, Los Angeles, CA
12/17	Brendan Byrne Arena, East Rutherford, NJ

KEITH RICHARDS CHRONICLES: 1 OF 4

Sunday, November 20, 1988

Tony Russell, Keith Richards' tour manager, called. How much would I charge to come untangle the keyboard nightmare they were having with Ivan Neville's setup? Ivan, Aaron Neville's son, is a great player. I learned a lot watching him but he didn't know anything about getting together a rig for a national tour. Hoping they could afford it because my money was tight, I say two hundred fifty. There's a pause. I panic: I've asked for too much.

The voice on the other end of the phone says they'd pay five hundred if I'd come to rehearsal right now and try to fix the keyboard issue. Apparently, I shot myself in the foot about the price. They probably would have paid double or triple that. Live and learn.

I raced to the Atlanta Lakewood rehearsal warehouse and walk in close to 9:00 p.m. Nobody's playing anything. The band's crouched around a table at the back of the room drinking wine and passing a joint. Tony says Thanks for coming down and helping; keyboards are stage right.

Walking to the keyboards, I'm trying to see Keith, but with smoke from weed and cigarettes and the crowd around the table, I couldn't pick him out.

Ivan's rig was pretty much a shambles. The Hammond B3 and Yamaha piano keyboard were fine, but he couldn't access the rack of sound modules he needed since he only had a MIDI cable. He had a sampling module and a couple of others as well as a Roland D-550. I absorbed the keyboard situation quickly and knew exactly how to fix it: I'd just set it up like my rig.

I motioned Tony over to keyboard world. Told him I'm confident I can fix it but needed to buy a couple of things including a MIDI patchbay and MIDI cables. Cost: Less than four hundred.

He smiled and handed over five bills and says to get what was needed in the morning; don't forget the receipt; report back here with the gear at noon.

It made me feel like part of something really cool.

Monday, November 21, 1988

Early the next day I went to American Music and got a MIDI patchbay and many MIDI cables of different lengths — you can never have too many. Back at Lakewood the place seemed deserted. Tony was there, as were backline techs, but no sign of the band. I asked when rehearsal was, and he says noon. That was right now. Tony saw my panic and quickly explained noon doesn't really mean noon. It means whatever time Keith gets up and feels like rehearsing. Apparently, nobody was in a hurry to do anything much.

Did I want to meet the backline crew? I did. Tony made the introductions: Drum tech Artie Smith. Alan Rogan, Keith's exclusive guitar tech. And Royden *Chuch* (pronounced like Chooch) Magee was tech for everybody else. He'd been Ronnie Wood's guitar tech as far back as the Faces were a band and had been with Ronnie from the very beginning. Chuch was a very likeable guy but, alas, he'd pass of a heart attack during a Rolling Stones tour rehearsal in 2002.

Rogan, on the other hand, was an egocentric troublemaker. Later I found out that he'd —

Worked for only the best guitarists!

Been everywhere!

Knew everything!

And let you know it!

After meeting the crew, I went to keyboard world and started arranging Ivan's rig. A MIDI patchbay is a lot like the old-fashioned telephone switchboard. The operator takes incoming calls and connects them to outgoing calls. I used the piano as the master controller. Connecting the piano to the patchbay gave it the ability to talk to (trigger) any or all modules in the rack. The general idea is to have one preset for each song. It's very basic stuff.

First: MIDI patchbay is installed into the rack.

Second: Wire MIDI input and output cables.

Third: Wire up everything else.

Fourth: Wait on Ivan to show up and tell me what he needs routed for each song. The router tells the keyboard which module to trigger and which program changes are to be made. Ivan need only press one button for each song and the router programs the rest. Now all that's needed was Ivan's input.

I had a few hours to kill. Audio and lighting guys had arrived. There wasn't time — or need — to meet them. But I did want to hear war stories from Chuch and, you know…just hang out and fit in. I was barely twenty-seven years old and very green to this side of the stage. To tell the truth, I was a little star-struck even meeting the backline crew. The guys were standing around a table that had all things coffee. I slowly walked toward them trying to figure out what to say. Then Rogan says:

Nice hat.

He's talking about my big, puffy Aqua Net Eighties hair. It never occurred to me I could or should wear it any other way. I was immediately embarrassed beyond words, so just kept on to the table, poured a cup, and went back to keyboard world, proverbial tail tucked. Now every minute seemed like hours. I started to doubt myself but managed to talk me down from the ledge and waited patiently.

The band straggled in around five. They didn't come to the stage. Hung over from the night before, they headed straight for the liquor cabinet. A few drinks of hair of the dog later, Tony made introductions. There was a slight pause so I began technically explaining what I was going to do. After a moment, Ivan says:

Hold on. I don't know nothin' 'bout MIDI, man.

Do you have a song list? (He did.) Okay. What sounds do you need for each song? What I'll do is set up a one-button preset per song. The system will configure the sounds and do all the work.

Ivan seemed happy about that. We were making progress and went through each song like this: He'd tell me what he needed for the first song. First: I programmed the patchbay and assigned it to Preset 1. Second: Testing — Ivan presses Preset 1 and plays. The sound of Preset 1 came blaring from his wedge. Repeat First and Second steps with Preset 2. Ivan's amazed and thrilled at how easy the sounds change and asks if I can do that for all the songs. I laugh and say yes. Thirty minutes later, at the most, we're done.

I find Tony. Tell him Ivan's all set. Said if I could get my money, I'd get out of his hair. Tony reached into a moneybag and pays me. Then he says Stick around, Joey; keep an eye on Ivan tonight. Help him if he has any trouble. There will be more money in it. I like the way the rig sounds.

I can do that! And I did for the rest of the night.

Now the thing is, Keith's rehearsals are not like any other. They get there around 5:00 p.m. and do their choice of some drinking, some smoking, and/or some blow. Then around a couple of hours later, Keith meanders his way to the stage and everyone joins in. They make some noise for awhile. Checking to see if everything's working and sounding right. Then Keith calls a song and the band starts to play. They get through that song, maybe they do another...but mostly not. After a song or two, they meander off in the manner they meandered on and head straight for more hair of the dog.

Rehearsal drags into the night until it's called at 4:00 a.m. I was tired and ready to get home. On my way out of the building Tony caught me. Could I come back at noon and do the same thing I did tonight? Sure, no problem.

I was very excited about this new adventure but tried not to show it. Who knows, maybe I will even get to meet Keith tomorrow.

Tuesday, November 22, 1988

The first date of the tour was on Thanksgiving Day at the Fabulous Fox Theatre in Atlanta. Yet here it was, the Tuesday before, and the band had yet to run through the set in its entirety. The X-Pensive Winos consisted of Keith, Robert *Waddy* Wachtel on guitar, Steve Jordan on drums and bass, Charley Drayton on drums and bass, Bobby Keys on sax, and Sarah Dash singing background vocals.

Arriving at Lakewood around noon, there was a lot of activity on the set. Lighting guys were programming scenes for the show. Sound guys were testing monitors. Front of house was making sure everything was 4x4. I settled in keyboard world.

The band showed up at 1:00 p.m., disciplined and ready to work. They went straight to the stage and, with Steve Jordan acting as band leader, ran the entire set. Sometimes they'd stop and work on a part, but things kept moving.

They sounded great.

When the band took a break, Tony took me into the inner sanctum to meet them. They were as kind and courteous as can be and seemed genuinely glad to meet me. When I met Keith, he was a perfect English gentleman. He had a way of making a person feel comfortable. There's so much I wanted to say but all I can do was barely utter a Nice-to-meet-you-I'm-a-big-fan.

It's such a good feeling to meet someone you're a fan of and find out he's just a guy. A very cool guy, but just a guy.

Tuesday night rehearsal was a success. They were gelling. Kinks were worked out. They ran the show twice and the night seemed to fly by. Ivan didn't have any problems, so I felt confident. It's so cool to be a part of it all. At the end of the rehearsal once again Tony came to ask a question. Would I come back to the next rehearsal and watch over Ivan? That would be a big ol' Yes.

Wednesday, November 23, 1988

The day before opening night at the Fabulous Fox, I arrive at Lakewood at noon. The warehouse was bustling with more activity than the day before. The crew, preparing for the first show by getting ready for load-out after rehearsal, was packing extra gear not in use. The band showed up early. They weren't playing around today either. No waiting or socializing, they went straight to work. The setlist was a mixture of Keith's solo album Talk Is Cheap with a few Rolling Stones songs thrown in. They opened the show with Take It So Hard, the single from the record. Sarah Dash sang Time Is on My Side. Besides the material from Talk Is Cheap, Keith played Gimme Shelter, Little T&A, Before They Make Me Run, and Happy. The set flowed nicely and the band was really on. They ran straight through the show then took a break, ate, indulged, then took the stage and ran through the set again. I walked out front to hear it from there. There's a good vibe, everybody's hitting on all cylinders, and it sounded awesome. Rehearsal was over around 2:00 a.m. I say goodbye to everyone and was leaving when Tony stopped me and asked:

What are you doing for the next two months?

Thursday, November 24, 1988

I can't sleep. There's a lot of stuff flying around my brain, but the two prominent things are fear and excitement. Tony had asked me to be Ivan's Backline Tech for the tour. They were offering fifteen hundred per week. Of course I agreed. It's one of those times where I said Sure, I can do that but not really knowing if I can pull it off or not. That method of doing things has worked very well for me.

I didn't really have a suitcase big enough to pack all I needed for the tour. I later learned all I needed were black T-shirts, black jeans, and sneakers. Sandra, my mother-in-law, loaned me a suitcase. A quick trip to her house to pick it up and I was set. We were trying to make the transaction as covert as possible because Kim's dad didn't hold me in the highest regard. Making matters worse was the fact I wouldn't be there for Thanksgiving dinner. He ranted to Sandra: What kinda lowlife punks play a show on Thanksgiving?

I explained to Sandra that Keith was from England and they don't celebrate Thanksgiving there. She relayed that fact to Pepper, but it didn't make things better.

I climbed out of bed to get a diet cola. Kim was asleep but slept so soundly I could've dropped a tray full of plates from a Chinese restaurant and not woken her. I mulled around in the kitchen a bit looking for something to eat but nothing took my fancy. I went back to bed. We slept with the television on. It lit up the room with a ghostly glow. I watched Kim sleep. I'd be gone longer than ever before at that point in our relationship and was already missing her.

I sat on the edge of the bed and started thinking about what I'd gotten into. I knew my way around MIDI and keyboards but didn't know how to be a Backline Tech. I'd have to learn as I went. I didn't have to report to the Fabulous Fox Theatre until noon. I crawled back in bed, held Kim close, and drifted off to sleep.

Kim woke up early to get ready for Thanksgiving Day. She had her hands full. Our daughter Whitney was eighteen months old. I woke later hearing mommy-daughter noises in the living room. Went to say good morning to my two ladies.

Showering and dressing, I tried to remember if I had everything needed. Kim dressed and then dressed Whitney. We sat closely, enjoying coffee and spending the rest of the morning we had left before Kim drove me to the venue.

The plan was for Kim to drop me off at the Fox at noon so we had to leave our apartment a half hour earlier. Kim forgot the green bean casserole, so up I ran to get it. I came back down with it, still warm and covered with tinfoil. Whitney was laughing and making baby noises in the car seat.

Kim was looking sad. I was feeling anxious.

The anxiety went away once we started moving. Both lost in our own thoughts, we didn't say much on the way. I'd reach over and hold her hand for awhile. She brought my hand up to her mouth and kissed it. Whitney fell asleep. For a moment I felt safe. I'd remember this moment whenever stress from the road became high.

My heart beat like a hammer when she pulled up to the Fox and let me off at the front door. We kissed and hugged until a car horn blasted and knocked us out of our goodbye. She popped the trunk, I grabbed luggage and stuff, then leaned in and kissed her.

Told her I loved her.

Would call her every night.

She drove away slowly, turned right on Ponce, and was gone. Standing alone with luggage, I had no other information but be there at noon. Front doors were locked. I walked north on Peachtree Street to the right side of the building. There was nothing but a parking lot.

I turned and walked south on Peachtree toward Ponce and the left side of the building. Three identical tour buses were lined up front to back, perfectly parked on the sidewalk. Not knowing where I was going or what was going on, I tried the first bus door. Locked. Same result with the others. I saw a man next to a closed door on the side of the Fox wearing a yellow shirt with Security on the back in black, but I can't see that then because he was sitting in a chair leaned back against the wall emanating an air of authority. Clearly, though, he was the Pope O' Da Doorway.

Dragging luggage, I must have looked like a refugee.

So, uh, is this the door to the stage?

He slowly pointed to the door where Stage was stenciled in yellow and let me in without any credentials or identification. Still dragging luggage, in I went through the door and up a small set of stairs leading up to another door. I was getting tired of this, so me and luggage lunged up the steps and crashed through the door at the top of the stairs. I fell flat on my face. Opening my eyes I saw wood…a wooden floor. I sat up and realized I'd fallen into the wings stage right.

Tony Russell saw me almost immediately and, as if a man laying on the floor was normal, says Good, you're here. Need to get you a pass, itinerary, and a bus key. The backline is being loaded in soon. You been on the bus yet?

I had not. He knew I was green, so he took the time to take me to the bus closest to the stage door and opened a bay where I put the luggage. Tony unlocked the door and says Pick a bunk; if there's something in the bunk, someone already has it.

Happy to know the rules, I found one, front left bottom, threw the carry-on into it, and we went inside because the backline gear was being unloaded as we spoke and I had work to do.

Tony said not to worry; schedule and duties would be easy. Load-in at noon. Just set up Ivan's keyboards. Wire them up. Make sure everything is working. Fuck off until soundcheck around four.

I nod.

At soundcheck make sure Ivan can hear his keys and his vocals in his monitor.

I nod again.

Soundcheck's over by five. Go to Catering, eat dinner, and relax in the bus or the dressing room until thirty minutes before the show when you will go to the stage and check his setup and make sure everything is working again.

I nod a third time.

Watch him during the show. Get him what he needs. After the show, tear down the gear and tell the union guys where to put what in which cases. Oversee the union guys, load the backline gear into the trailer, then you're done.

I nod a fourth time. I can do this. Piece o' cake.

Backline techs are the most hated techs by the rest of the crew because they have it made. They're the last out of the bus and the first back on. They don't even have to get to the gig until noon and are done in less than an hour after the show. On the other hand, riggers have to be at the venue at six in the morning and the sound company loads in two hours after that.

Tony went off to do his million things he did every show day. I felt better but was still confused. While Tony told me just about everything, he didn't explain union protocol. I started to unlatch a case, but Chuch Magee says Don't do that; only union stagehands can touch cases; you have to tell them to open them and where to put the gear.

I didn't know where to set up Ivan's rig, so I just went with where it was during rehearsal. It turned out to be right. Chuch assigned two union guys to help me set up. It went like this:

Had them open the case and pull out the Hammond B3.

Told them where to put it.

They set it down.

Had them open the piano case.

Take it out.

Put it on top of the B3.

Had them open the Leslie 122 case and place it on the corner of the riser at stage left rear.

Then the Leslie 122 case is put offstage behind the backdrop.

The clavinet is placed on Ivan's right at a right angle.

Tell them to set the rack of sound modules to his left at a right angle just close enough to touch if he needs to.

Let the union guys go.

All that pointing sure was tiresome. I got to work. The cables were a little tangled from me packing them at rehearsal. I untangled them and started to wire things up. There's a D-550, an Emu sample player, an Akia MIDI router and a sub-mixer in the rack. Everything went into the mixer. From there we send a stereo mix to front of house. I connected the MIDI cable to the piano MIDI out, the controller. Then I plugged the cables into the piano and clavinet. A wah-wah pedal was inline with the clavinet. You can do very cool things with that.

Tony came by to check on me around 1:00 p.m. He says Ivan's rig needed moving so we just did it ourselves. Fuck the union. He said I was doing fine and gave me a laminate, bus key, itinerary, and one week of forty-dollar per diem. I looked at the money like a newbie.

Do we get this every week?!

As long as we're on the road.

He had me sign for the per diem then off he went like a flash. I opened the itinerary and looked over the 35 or so pages. On page two was a list of dates; other pages with contacts and duties; and each gig had a daily breakdown on a page by itself.

Damn. That looked like a good run to me. I was excited — and afraid I wouldn't meet expectations. It's my first time as a Backline Tech and I did not want to fail.

Ivan's keyboard rig was set and working perfectly. It sounded great through the wedges. The organ sounded good and loud in the mix. I made sure the vocal mic was in Ivan's mix, too.

Sometimes you have to focus on the little things. I asked Tony to order 9V batteries for the clavinet. Those would need changing daily since the instrument didn't have an adapter.

Two hours before soundcheck I was just hanging out by the backline. Chuch comes up and says it looked and sounded great. He suggested I get colored electrical tape to color-code the cables. He offered custom-length cables. He had a soldering iron in his work case and a roll of guitar cable. I'd measure today and we'd make them tomorrow.

Good things come to those who wait. The clock said 4:00 p.m. Time to soundcheck. The guys started wandering in. They looked like they partied the night before. Steve was holding his head and Ivan laid down on the drum riser. But Keith? He came onstage full of energy, strapped on his guitar, and began a twelve-bar Blues. He kept playing until everyone fell into the tune. Solos were played and even vocals. The song must've been a Howlin' Wolf tune or something like it.

Keith went into another song and the band followed. Ivan needed a couple of adjustments, but nothing major. He's a little confused about which patch went to what song, so I made a note to label it for the next show. I was starting to dig this job.

Keith started Take It So Hard, the band's opening number. It sounded great. Charley Drayton played drums. Steve Jordan and Charley switched off playing bass and drums. I liked Charley a little better on drums. Steve is awesome, but I like how Charley just beats the shit out of the skins.

It seemed like as soon as it started, soundcheck was over. Like mice running in different directions, the band guys dispersed. With nothing to do for hours, I went to Catering, ate grilled chicken and rice. Catering was good on this tour. I've been on the road a lot and I know good catering from bad. Back at the bus. Some of the crew was watching Bus Movie Number One: Blazing Saddles. I joined them.

Back in the day, there were no cellphones, satellites, or Internet. There's lots of downtime with this gig. I thought of Kim. I ached for her. I'd have to wait until I was in a hotel room to call her. These were the bad times when touring.

Sometimes touring is hard. It's a fact. Being away from family and friends. I miss them. I'm in a strange new environment, every day is the same, and the traveling is hard, too. Family, wife and kids, and friends bring a core to my life that I need: The consolation and the love that eases loneliness and pain.

Getting close to showtime. I left the bus and went back into the venue where the opening act had just finished. It's almost time for the show. I made way backstage and checked Ivan's gear. Everything's working fine. I was ready to put this bull in the barn.

Showtime.

The lights went down and the crowd roared. My adrenaline was pumping. The band took the stage in the dark. They didn't make any noise. Keith swaggered to center stage by the drum riser. Suddenly, the guitar cuts the dark and a spotlight is on Keith playing the intro riff from Take It So Hard. The band falls in and wow, what a groove. Just about everybody sang. The vocals were monumental. The band's energy was way more than rehearsal and soundcheck.

The songs seemed to fly by. Ivan needed a little more vocal in his wedge, so I run over and tell the monitor man. He had a couple of other issues, but everything went fabulous.

Sarah Dash sang Time Is on My Side. The crowd stood and cheered when Keith began Gimme Shelter. The show was coming to an end and the crowd jumped to its feet when Keith began the encore with Happy. They ended the show with a song from their record It Means A Lot and rocked the house. The crescendo built to a tension that had to be released. You can feel it come apart when they hit the last note.

All things must pass. The show was over. Time to work again. I unplugged and rolled up every cord and put them in the back of the rack ready for the union guys to put the gear in its cases. They came, they packed, they put the cases in line to be loaded. I watched the cases go into the semi's trailer and my day was over.

We had to drive to Memphis overnight, so me in my bunk let images of the day float through my mind. I felt like the first day as a Backline Tech was a good one. It will only get better. I thought of loved ones and drifted off to sleep.

Friday, November 25, 1988

New Daisy Theatre Nightclub, Memphis, Tennessee

I woke in a pitch-black bunk to a bus generator humming steadily, comforting, like safely being in the womb. I left the bunk, let eyes adjust, and went into the front lounge. The clock showed nine. The day sheet says the backline crew weren't needed onstage until noon. I was hungry, so I got off the bus and went into the club.

There's a lot of commotion going on with riggers hanging lights and front of house cabinets. I saw a sign with an arrow pointing to the left: Catering. Following the arrow, I ended up in a room something like a kitchen. A breakfast buffet was there with a chef making omelets while you watch. All that's needed was to pick out what I wanted in it.

There were mushrooms, onions, and green peppers. Tomatoes, spinach, potatoes, and avocado. Cheddar, Swiss, and goat cheeses. Bacon and perfectly cubed bits of ham. I chose Cheddar, mushrooms, onions, and ham. The chef made my omelet so well it looked effortless. He whisked three eggs and poured them into a hot pan, added my chosen ingredients, and let it cook for a bit after which he flipped the omelet by tossing it in the air and catching it uncooked side down. Thirty seconds more on the heat, then out it flips onto a plate. I thanked him for the show.

In the room were ten to twelve tables covered with checkered red and white tablecloths seating five or six people each, but except for me and the chef, the room was devoid of people. Orange juice in a red Solo cup next to my plate, I began to eat the wonderful breakfast. It's better than words can say and I ate it like I was starving. I cleared my dishes from the table, thanked the chef, and headed out to see if I could find somebody I knew. I ran into Tony Russell in the hall.

You had breakfast yet, Joey? Good; listen, just hang out on the bus until they need you.

I can do that. Went to the bus where backline crew were now up and watching a video. Someone made a pot of coffee and all were having it except for Rogan who was having PG Tips tea. I say good morning to all and all but Rogan say hello back.

Chuch says to take a load off because we weren't needed until noon. I sat on the couch next to him. We chatted for awhile, then he and the rest of the backline went to have breakfast. Was I coming? No, already had breakfast. They left and I continued watching the video.

When it was time, we did setup and waited for the band. They come and do soundcheck then were off to the hotel. Our dinner was in Catering with several of the backline guys, Tony Russell, and Tripp Khalaf, front of house engineer.

Tripp was a big guy with a loud husky voice he used to deliver opinions on the show to politics to everything under the sun, and liked to share those opinions with everybody. He was not a bad guy, just loud and scary sometimes.

Clair Brothers Audio had just introduced one of the first full-range concert speakers and were very secretive about it. One time during the tour a speaker blew in one of the cabinets. So that nobody (not even the other people on the tour) could see inside while it's being repaired, the sound technician was draped under a big black piece of cloth.

The show was special for Keith because it was in a nightclub that held a maximum of only two thousand. But to Keith, he felt intimate and close to the audience there. One can feel the energy the crowd gave back that night. The band finished, did an encore, and then we did tear-down. After the show most of the backline guys just chilled out on the bus which was stocked with many different kinds of alcohol: Rebel Yell, Stolichnaya Vodka in the freezer, Scotch, gin, peppermint schnapps, and a cooler full of beer.

I poured a stiff Rebel Yell and mixed it with diet cola. Alan Rogan told me to fix him a Scotch, neat. I started to get up and do it but Chuch stopped me with a You don't have to do that, kid.

I sat back down and enjoyed a drink with Chuch and Artie. The bus started rolling an hour after midnight. It's getting too crowded in the front lounge with all the light and sound people milling about. I finished my drink and go to my bunk, lay down, pull the curtain completely shut. The air conditioning was cold as fuck, but with covers up over my head I drifted off to sleep, wrapped up and warm.

Saturday, November 26, 1988

Hyatt Regency, Washington, D.C.

The bus stopping woke me two hours after noon. We had the day off so, luggage in hand, I went to the Hyatt's front desk and asked for my reserved room. The girl found it relatively quickly and handed me a key. I get to the room. So far, so good.

I step into the foyer. The room is huge. There's a sitting room with a couch and two chairs, phone, and a TV. Bedroom with huge bed. Phone and TV in there, too. The bathroom, off to the left if you're laying in bed, was done all up in marble with a bathtub and a separate shower. You can see everything from the shower because it's made of glass. Glass and marble, everywhere.

On the back of the bathroom door is a robe that looked so cozy I just had to put it on right then. It's very soft and comfortable.

Back in the sitting room was a room service menu. Regular cheeseburger and fries popped out of the menu and hit me like a brick. Sometimes nothing else will do when I'm hungry. So, I call room service and ordered one along with two diet colas.

Room service arrived and the waiter wheeled it in. The food hit the spot. I really didn't feel like getting out and seeing the sights, so I stayed in the hotel room. A Jack and cola from the mini bar. Then another. I laid in the huge bed and watched TV all night. I ordered a wake-up call for ten the next morning and finally dozed off around 2:00 a.m.

Sunday, November 27, 1988

Constitution Hall, Washington, D.C.

I woke to a ringing phone. This is your ten o'clock wake-up call, a pleasant voice said. I showered and dressed, ordered a large pot of coffee, drank most of it. Took the elevator to the front desk, settled incidentals, checked out, and waited in the lobby for the runner with the rest of the backline crew.

Arriving at the venue, we went straight to Catering. There's a breakfast buffet like before but no omelet-making chef. After breakfast it's time for us to hit the stage. Setup and testing all went as smoothly as it had for the other shows. It was getting faster to set up, leaving even more time to kill before soundcheck. Sometimes I played with the B3 and piano to help Tripp get his line level out front and Dave get his signal to set the monitors.

Here's something which stood out that day.

We were having power problems and asked Constitution Hall's electrician to help troubleshoot. I swear this guy wasn't using any protective gear at all. No gloves or rubber-ended screwdriver. Nothing. He used his bare hands to test 240V. I'm not talking 120V coming out of your wall. I'm talking the feed supplying the breaker box. And here he is checking connections with his bare hands. I've never seen anything like it.

But other than this sideshow, the day went the way things go on show day. Soundcheck at four. Dinner in Catering. Waiting to begin. Then the show rushes by at the speed of light. Tear down. Load out. Enjoy a couple of drinks after the show. Go to your bunk.

Drift off to sleep when the bus starts moving.

Monday, November 28, 1988

The Mayflower Hotel, New York City

We arrive in New York mid-morning; took the day off. This was only the second time I'd been to New York City and so was excited and anxious. There's a lot of noise coming from under the bus, so I investigate. The cacophony was from all the crew getting their luggage.

Alan Rogan says You're the rookie; I'm the Rock Star Backline Tech. You have to tend to my luggage. Tag number ten.

I find and place it on the luggage cart then retrieved my luggage (tag number sixteen) and placed it on the luggage cart, too. I go inside and check in where Rogan shouts from a chair in the lobby Hey, boy, where's my luggage?

I cocked my head toward the luggage cart and say The bellboys will deliver bags to rooms by luggage tag number.

Chuch heard Alan yell at me and says Joey, you do not have to carry his luggage; he's just taking the piss out of you.

Oh. Okay. Thanks, Chuch.

Sometimes I'm a little slow on the uptake. Anyway, I don't know if Chuch talked to Rogan, but the bullshit stopped. Don't mistake what I'm saying. Rogan was still a surly, rude, and obnoxious Brit, just wasn't aimed at me so much.

The hotel was old. My room had a Fifties vibe. Huge living area. Ceiling probably twenty feet high. The bedroom was smaller, which made it feel comfortable. The bathroom was standard, but the tub was huge. And twenty-four-hour room service, too. The hotel kitchen passed the Club Sandwich Test with very high marks. Now I can move up to spaghetti. I took a hot bath in that huge bathtub. It felt so refreshing.

It was the right thing to do at the time.

Tuesday, November 29, 1988

The Beacon Theatre, New York City

Got up early to explore. Tried to blend in but most New Yorkers can tell a visitor in their midst. Walked across Central Park West and checked out Central Park. There were lots of runners and people walking. The park was full. I didn't get to see all of it but what I saw was cool.

Next, I checked out The Dakota where John Lennon was murdered then followed West 72nd to Broadway and had a Gray's Papaya hot dog, best in the world. Then I wandered back to the lobby of The Mayflower Hotel for lobby call. Then load-in. Set up.

Soundcheck. Catering. Waiting. Showtime! Break down. Load out.
Drift to sleep while the bus rocks on.

Wednesday, November 30, 1988

Warwick Hotel Rittenhouse Square, Philadelphia, Pennsylvania

Philly's a short drive from New York City and we arrive at the
hotel around 3:00 a.m. There were problems with our reservations.
Well, isn't this just in the Christmas spirit? Tripp asked me why. I
told him getting refused at the inn was very much as Christmas as it
gets. He laughed. Eventually things were straightened out and we
got our rooms in the swanky hotel. Because the trip from New York
was so short I'd stayed up drinking Jack Daniel's with Chuch and
Artie. I was feeling pretty drunk but mostly sleepy and went out like
a light.

We had the day off but when I woke I didn't feel like
sightseeing. I called room service and ordered scrambled eggs with
cheese, toast, and sausage. But most importantly I ordered a large
pot of coffee. I attacked the food. It's good for my hangover. I drink
the whole pot of coffee. I really didn't get out of bed all day. It felt
good to have no responsibility for a day.

We were playing two shows in Philadelphia so I'd have this
hotel room for a couple of nights. There would be no bus rides for
awhile which was a good thing.

Thursday, December 1, 1988

Tower Theatre, Philadelphia, Pennsylvania

Jumped out of bed at half past nine. Ordered breakfast and a large pot of black coffee. Jumped in the shower. Snagged the terrycloth robe off its hook in the closet and threw it on. It's uber comfortable. A knock at the door, room service arrived. I down a cup of coffee. It was good. Took tops off plates and scarfed down breakfast.

More coffee, blow dry my hair, dress, and have fifteen minutes before lobby call. I drink another cup, grab a diet cola from the mini bar, and head to the lobby. Chuch and Artie are already there. We're just waiting on the surly HRH. He arrives ten minutes later.

Tower Theatre was built in 1927 and starting in 1970 became popular as a music venue. Our buses and tractor trailers are parked beside The El (elevated train) giving the neighborhood a very Chicago vibe. We head to Catering, but I hang back and go to the stage. I stood in the middle and looked out at the seats. I said to myself Someday I'm going to play a theater like this.

I was not wrong.

The guys arrived from Catering and we unloaded the truck. It wasn't even an hour after noon and I was finished. I went to a dressing room, laid on a couch, and fell asleep. Napping quite nicely, I woke when I heard Check one-two, two, two, check one-two.

That meant Dave had rang out the monitors and was ready for levels. I ran down the stairs and onto the stage. By now I pretty much knew how Ivan wanted his wedges to sound. Dave had me play piano until it was loud enough. Then the B3. We checked the D-550 and the sample player in the rack. Did the same thing for front of house.

Took fifteen minutes total, therefore had a lot of time to kill. So I found a payphone and called my wife. I missed Kim very much. Call finished, I went to the bus and relaxed until soundcheck.

I wandered inside around 4:00 p.m. waiting for the band to arrive. They showed up fashionably late. Everybody grabbed their instruments and Ivan went to his keyboard rig. We exchange pleasantries and he starts playing. Everybody's checking their gear. Then they played Don't Take It So Hard. Ivan had me turn up the piano through his wedges. They finished that song and then played Make No Mistake which had a really cool horn part in it Ivan played, doing an excellent job duplicating the part the Memphis Horns had played on the original record.

The Memphis Horns were a two-man American horn section. Their many appearances on productions of Stax Records made them famous. The duo was Wayne Jackson (trumpet) and Andrew Love (tenor sax). An offshoot of the Mar-Keys, they worked together for over thirty years. They contributed their sound to eighty-three gold- and platinum-award-winning songs and over a hundred high-charting records like Otis Redding's Sitting On The Dock of the Bay, Al Green's Let's Stay Together, and Elvis Presley's Suspicious Minds.

And then as quick as soundcheck started it was over. Everyone's happy. I went to Catering for steak and baked potatoes and vegetables and a huge salad bar, all quite good. Off to the bus to chill and watch TV. Time drags until showtime, which is when the party starts. During a show, senses sharpen and you're ready for anything. Time flies and before you know it the band is doing an encore.

First-show jitters long gone, tonight the band was especially on and seemed to enjoy themselves. When the band finished, they were rushed to a couple of passenger vans and swept off into the night. All the backline crew had to do was power down everything since we were playing tomorrow night in the same venue. We caught a passenger van back to the hotel. I needed to tell my wife how much I missed her so I went to the room and called. Then I watched TV until I fell asleep.

Thursday, December 2, 1988

Tower Theatre, Philadelphia

I slept late because we didn't have to be at the venue until 2:00 p.m. Breakfast came, and I drank the whole pot of coffee. Got a case of the caffeine jitters.

At the venue all equipment got turned on and, thank goodness, everything was working. Although our equipment was ready to go, we still had to wait for Dave to ring out the monitors and get levels, didn't take long. And now we wait for the band.

They arrived around 4:00 p.m. and were moving kinda slow. Since we didn't have to overnight it on the bus, the band had partied like the Rock Stars they were. Ivan laid down on his riser and moaned. Steve Jordan sat at the drum kit where his mic swiveled and poked him in the eye. Everyone was moaning. Except for Keith. He's energetic and happy and took no mercy on the band, which was moving too slowly for him and he's trying to hurry up the process. He called Take It So Hard and started it with his riff. The parade of pain the band was in was tough to watch. And they had background vocals, too. It was obvious they were hurting bad.

Keith continued to call out songs. The band struggled through four songs. It was the longest soundcheck on tour to date, but he finally let them off the hook and they caught the passenger van back to the hotel.

When they came back to the venue that night they seemed to feel better. Maybe a little hair of whatever dog they favored? They started the show hitting on all cylinders. Even the mistakes sounded good. Turned out to be the best show of the tour so far.

We overnighted to Boston.

Friday, December 3, 1988

Ritz-Carlton Hotel, Boston, Massachusetts

Day off. Time to do laundry. Per diem arrived; had already saved over five hundred dollars. I didn't want to pay the hotel to clean my clothes, but I didn't want to do the washing either. I put the clothes in a laundry bag I'd brought and called the concierge to ask if there was a Wash and Fold nearby. There was. I say thank you very much, carried my clothes down through the lobby, and go in search. Sure enough, one street over and two blocks down, there it was. Clothes would be ready after 4:00 p.m. Me and my ticket walked back to the hotel together. It's noon and I'm kind of hungry but had grown tired of room service. Touring can be hard sometimes, even while living in the lap of luxury and having everything at your disposal.

Only two weeks left in the tour. It was going by fast. The hardest times were when there was no show to prep for. That's when I missed Kim the most and I'd call her on those days off to tell her I was homesick. She'd be supportive and remind me how much time was left before I could come home.

I went to the lobby, sat at the bar, and ordered a good, old-fashioned cheeseburger with fries and a diet cola. It hit the spot.

The tour continued to roll. Most of the time I saw only the hotel, gig, and bus, over and over. The last part of the tour was in California. We played the Henry J. Kaiser Arena in Oakland where Tony Russell introduced me to impresario Bill Graham. That was a real thrill. I also got to meet the keyboard player for The Grateful Dead, Brent Mydland, at the venue. He was very cool. We talked about music and equipment for an hour. He would die two years later. Damn.

Next we commuted to Los Angeles to play the Universal Amphitheater in a star-studded event. Everybody that's somebody was there. Too many celebrities to name.

The next show was at the historic Hollywood Palladium where the show was filmed and recorded. It was exciting but with the film crew and extra sound crew for recording, the stage was a bit cramped. During that show I developed a healthy hate for cameramen. They'd step on cables, unplugging them, or step on snakes, breaking them. They'd literally run you over like you weren't even there. All in the name of getting the shot.

Backstage, I met Slim Jim Phantom, drummer for Stray Cats. He says I looked familiar. I told him I get that a lot.

The show at the Palladium on Sunset was rockin' and the band was on fire. You can get a DVD or a CD of the show: Keith Richards and The X-Pensive Winos Live at the Palladium. Check it out. You know, I believe it's also on YouTube now.

I went back to The Hyatt House and got some sleep. We were taking the redeye to Newark, New Jersey, the next night. I woke up and walked down Sunset to the Red Dot for an everything bagel. Back to the hotel where I watched TV all day. At nine we gathered in the lobby and a runner took us to the airport. We arrived at Newark at half past six the next morning.

The final show of the tour was at the Brendan Byrne Arena (now called Meadowlands Arena) in East Rutherford, New Jersey. It's Keith's birthday and they're planning a hell of a show. Johnny Johnson, Chuck Berry's piano player, was to sit in with the band. The Replacements were opening the show. I actually had to kick Bob Stinson off the stage for not having the right pass. He's just there taking pictures like it was no big deal. Still, The Replacements did a great set in their drunken glory.

Then the Winos went on and absolutely killed it. That show was one of the best, if not *the* best, of the tour. I felt proud to be working with one of my heroes. Such a pleasure and an honor. I learned a lot, too. Keith never phoned it in. He's on and enjoying himself every night. I also learned a lot of new things from watching Ivan — especially when not to play.

Tony Russell and Chuch Magee were a godsend for taking me under their wings. They knew I was a musician having to backline tech for a paycheck and they respected that.

I flew home the next day and took a cab home to surprise Kim. When I walked in she gave me a big hug and kiss. I picked up Whitney and kissed her on the forehead. I held her awhile before putting her down.

It was a great tour but damn it was good to be home.

1952: Joey's Mom and Dad in Pikeville, Kentucky.

MY FIRST DISAPPOINTMENT

Our family drove the hundred and forty miles across Kentucky from Pikeville to Lexington a few times each year and every time I begged Dad to stop at the Snake Pit. Ten miles out, signs promising the greatest things in the world began popping up. When I'd see them I'd get excited at the promise of the most mysterious, exciting, and scary things possible — live, dangerous snakes. There were pictures of rattlesnakes, striped snakes, and even cobras. The closer we got, the more signs we'd see. Each promising more adventure and fun.

With sighting of the first sign, I'd begin a campaign to get Dad to stop: Beg, scream, cry, hold my breath, and stomp on the backseat. To no avail. I even tried the old I have to go to the bathroom ploy but he said it cost too much money or the people who ran the Snake Pit were nothing but charlatans. He'd have a good reason for not stopping every time. I might have stayed mad, but in five minutes I'd be on to something else and be happy again.

Then one magical day when I was four I started my Snake Pit pleading. To my joy and amazement Dad says Okay, we'll stop, I need something to drink anyway.

Thrilled, I can hardly contain myself and thanked him fifty times until we arrived. But first:

Beside the pit was a gift shop/convenience store. Dad says we had to go in there to get tickets and he had to get a drink and relieve himself anyway. Mom concurred, saying there were probably pretty things and toys in the gift shop. At the word toys my eyes got big and I about wet myself. Dad went in and did his business and I pulled Mom by the hand thinking we can get inside sooner. Opening the door, a blast of artic air came blowing through our hair. It's the middle of summer and this was about the coldest inside place I'd been in.

Rubber snakes and creepy spiders, fireworks, candy, and ice cream hypnotized me. I wanted it all. Then I spotted a rubber snake, green, about two feet long with red eyes and its forked red tongue sticking out. I called to her because she'd be easier to manipulate. Mom! I have to have this now! We bartered like only a determined four-year-old and a tired mother can. I was so happy.

1964 L-R: Jeannie Davis, Lisa Biliter, Joey (3), Frosty Davis, and Charles, Joey's brother

In the meantime, Dad did his bathroom thing, and bought tickets, a Fresca, and pretzels. I was upset because we'd have to wait until he finished eating to see the snakes. Struggling to get him outside, I was pulling on his hand like God reaching out to Adam in Michelangelo's most famous ceiling painting job.

The tour was self-guided, so we went unescorted. Anticipation became stronger with each step. The pits in the distance seemed like a mirage with the sun dancing off the round, four-feet-tall stone walls with a chicken wire dome over them. I thought there just had to be a lot of dangerous snakes in there to have a stone wall and chicken wire.

We arrive.

It's the most anticipation I'd ever felt in my short life.

It was better than my birthday, Christmas, and snow all at the same time.

Dad picked me up to see over the wall.

A rattlesnake and copperhead were as exotic as they got; most were a bunch of plain, ordinary, and lazy black and brown snakes. Every now and then one moved slightly but overall they slept.

Where were the cobras and black mambas and multicolored striped snakes writhing away?

Dad, Dad, Dad! Can we feed 'em? Poke 'em? Get 'em to move?

Nope, said Dad, a stoic man who didn't have time for nonsense, but I was getting mad...and feeling an emotion I'd never felt. I felt empty. Like there was a big hole where my stomach was. I wanted to cry but not because I was sad or physically hurt. It's like what Johnny Rotten of the Sex Pistols said with a snarl to a crowd in Dallas:

Don't you feel cheated?

Yes, I did. This was the first time I felt so empty and hollow. I didn't cry or pitch a fit. In fact, I didn't know how to act. When Dad said it was time to go, I somberly followed him back up the path to the car. Didn't say a word for the rest of the trip but inside I was deep in thought:

I always got caught and punished when I lied. How can people lie and get away with it? Why can't the police arrest them?

It took a few years to figure out what I was feeling. Getting jacked up so high, full of hope, having the rug pulled out from under. It's happened many times after but I think this one hurt my little-boy virgin soul the most. From then on, whenever we drove to Florida for vacations and saw enticing signs for alligator farms, I'd remember the Snake Pit and keep my mouth shut. As I've gotten older, I still get sad, feel empty and hollow, but I don't do anything about it and just move on. I don't get angry much anymore, either.

LOVE LETTER TO DAD

Dear Dad,

I regret not being a better son. I regret the time you had to bail me out of jail in Paintsville, Kentucky, when I was 16. I regret not traveling back to Eastern Kentucky enough to see you and the rest of the family. But you supported my decision to be a musician. You taught me to think and be independent and taught me right from wrong.

When you let loose and laugh, it makes me feel as if everything just might just be okay. I never heard a racist remark from you. You taught me all people are equal and deserved respect. You're a quiet man with a big heart and I love you, Dad. I'm happy you found love again after Mother passed away. I know she makes you happy and keeps you young.

I am forever grateful.

Much love, your son
Joey

Dad served his country as a Marine in the Korean War. An All-State halfback in high school. He worked hard his whole life. He still rides his motorcycle every day. He works out almost every day.

To Joey Huffman with thanks, Bill Clinton

THE WHITE HOUSE

Call me the Forrest Gump of Rock & Roll. I've had many surreal and unbelievable experiences, but none compared with this. On September 21, 1993, Soul Asylum was invited by President Bill Clinton to play at a ceremony on the White House lawn commemorating his signing the National Service Act into law.

Soul Asylum was the first band invited to perform at the White House under the Clinton administration, so it was quite an honor and something I will not forget.

We flew into our nation's capital the day before the command performance. We arrived at the hotel, checked in and got settled, then gathered at the bar for a celebratory drink. As well as the band, we had the band's manager Danny Heaps, the band's road manager Bill Sullivan, Winona Ryder, the entourage, and the band's wives.

The band, Danny, and Bill Sullivan were scheduled to catch town cars to take us to the White House and survey the gig site, do a soundcheck, and get the deluxe tour. In our way of thinking, if we're going to the White House, what better way to arrive there than to arrive drunk, right? After all, we're known for our outrageous and destructive behavior. Why let decorum stand in the way of a good adventure?

The cars arrived and we settled in for the fifteen-minute ride to the home of the most powerful man in the world, chattering like schoolgirls about what we thought it'd be like and how much history surrounded the White House. We truly felt honored and humbled by the gravity of the situation. A private tour of the White House. How cool was that?

Upon arrival, we proceed to a checkpoint to show passports and make sure our credentials were in order. Frankly, I'm surprised I was able to pass a background check what with my checkered past. But seeing I'd not written any threatening letters to the president and was not a felon, I was escorted straight inside. Clearing checkpoint without a snag, we proceeded up a walkway to an entrance on the side of the building. Once inside we were met by our liaison/minder/guide: White House Communications Director Mr. George Stephanopoulos. He's there to answer our questions, show us around, get us acclimated, and school us on proper etiquette.

George was quite charming and only thirty-two. He had a sense of humor and was a fan of the band. As excited to meet us as we were to meet him. The tour started after a bit of small talk and shaking hands.

The interior of the White House was overwhelming. We walked down a hall with the original unfinished painting of George Washington hanging in it. We saw:

Portraits of all the presidents to date.

Silverware purchased by Jackie Kennedy.

Rooms full of furniture purchased by Nancy Reagan.

China from the Lincoln era.

There was so much in the same tour everyone takes when they pay to see the White House. Then we went off the grid. George took us to the West Wing where Marine guards protected a short hallway. Once down that, we're in the West Wing Colonnade. It's there we ran into Fawn Hall. The day before our tour she had achieved notoriety after being accused of sneaking incriminating documents hidden in her panties to keep her boss Oliver North from being indicted.

But the true story about this came out on a Saturday Night Live Weekend Update segment — back when SNL truly knew how to use a skewer. According to SNL, Fawn was in the clear since Oliver North was wearing her underwear at the time.

As fate would have it, Fawn's mother was President Clinton's personal secretary. Her desk was right outside the Oval Office and just off the Cabinet Room. Fawn had a job at the White House doing what I don't know, but there she was. Mr. Stephanopoulos made introductions. Fawn seemed thrilled to have us there. Usually we felt like redheaded stepchildren, but now we're being treated like kings. It felt nice. We exchanged pleasantries and then she was off and the tour continued. We inquired about Vice President Al Gore and were told he was out of the country on a diplomatic assignment. George (it's hard to call him Mr. Stephanopoulos because he seemed like one of us) then asked if we'd like to see Gore's office.

Uhhh…yeah! Who wouldn't?

Down a hall and up some stairs and suddenly we're in the office of the Vice President. George told us to look around, not to be afraid to touch things or sit at his desk. George seemed to get a kick out of the situation. We asked if we could take anything as a souvenir. Hilarious, he said by way of permission. We grab pens, stationery, pencils, and basically anything not nailed down. We rifled the VP's office while the White House Communications Director stood by howling in laughter.

After plundering Gore's office, we headed back down for a visit to the press briefing room. I'd seen it on TV many times, but it looked smaller in person. Pretending to make speeches, we took turns standing at the podium with the presidential seal behind us.

Yes Helen, do you have a question?

It was too much fun and we were like kids in a candy store. Ten minutes for that fun, then we proceed toward the Cabinet Room. As we made way, a young lady comes running up the steps adjacent to the hallway yelling She's coming, she's coming, Dragon Lady's coming.

George says Quick, in here! and we duck into a side room to hide. What is going on, George? He explained Dragon Lady is code for First Lady Hillary Rodham Clinton and that it was most always better to steer clear of her. I thought I understood his reaction. She seemed like a scary lady at the time. Frankly, she still does.

It turned out to be a false alarm so we came out of hiding and proceeded to the Cabinet Room. The room was impressive with a long table and lots of chairs situated around it. It's mind-boggling to think of the history just in that room alone.

Kennedy getting briefed on the Cuban Missile Crisis.

Vietnam.

The Iran hostages.

The Cold War.

The list goes on and on and we marveled at the Cabinet Room for ten minutes then were ushered into the outer room of the Oval Office. We meet the President's personal secretary and George asks Is he in?

We were thrilled to visit the White House, ecstatic to get to see the West Wing, but never in our wildest dreams did we think we'd meet the President. But that's the way things happen in the world of politics and Rock & Roll. So when the secretary said he was in, we were ushered through the door of the Oval Office.

Standing in front of his desk facing us, warm smile on his face, was the President of the United States of America, Mr. William Jefferson Clinton, or Bill as he is most often called. We were speechless.

He says Hello, welcome to the White House. How did you enjoy your tour?

Someone mustered the courage to say Very nice, Mr. President.

We're excited to have you playing here on such a historic occasion.

Danny Heaps says Thank you, Mr. President.

Dave Pirner asks Will you break out your sax and jam with us tomorrow?

President Clinton says Oh no, you guys pretend like you're the band and I'll pretend like I'm the president.

Everybody had a good laugh. Then George told Bill about us rifling Al Gore's office. The President thought that was hysterical. Everybody laughed more then made small talk for a few minutes. I really wish I could recall exactly what was said. Mostly talk about the show and how we'd be playing under a big tent on the White House lawn. A large contingent of Congressmen/women and Senators from both sides of the aisle would be present as well as some of the first young people volunteering for AmeriCorps.

When anyone meets the President at the White House is a photo op. This occasion was no exception. The official photographer entered the Oval Office and we formed a line in order to shake President Clinton's hand and have our picture taken. This was early in his first term and he didn't seem so beat up and tired. He looked young and healthy and exuded energy and charisma.

When it was my turn to shake Clinton's hand, he asked my name and said how nice it was to meet me. He made me feel like the only person in the world. Time seemed to stand still. When I shook his hand, Dave commented out loud that I'd voted for Bush. In the picture you can see the smirk on his face and everybody laughing. But it didn't bother the President. He was a class act in every way and made me feel so secure I wasn't even embarrassed by Dave's big ol' jokey remark.

Then we said Goodbye until tomorrow to the President, and George led us to the tent on the White House lawn where the stage awaited soundcheck.

The White House has its own official Hammond B3. I was very impressed by this. The organ was immaculate. I've never played a nicer one. Not one scratch on it. I can even see myself in the shine. Not only that, it sounded fantastic. There was a guy whose only job was to take care of that organ. Shaking his hand was almost like I had played a holy relic.

We rehearsed Don't Stop by Fleetwood Mac because that's the song the President was to walk out to instead of Hail To The Chief. The Rock & Roll President indeed. Everybody seemed to be a little concerned about the volume but it came down from the top to let the band play as loud as they wanted. We had *carte blanche*, felt good about the gig, and were touched by the welcome. During soundcheck, an uptight Wolf Blitzer commented to a news reporter outside the tent It's not your father's White House anymore.

We checked out and drove back to the hotel where we had a nice dinner and retired to our respective rooms to rest up for the big show. Showtime was 8:30 a.m., so we needed our rest.

DAY TWO

The alarm went off at six. I jumped out of bed, showered, dressed, and met the seven o'clock lobby call where we loaded up into the town cars. Arriving, we piled out, went to checkpoint, and were escorted to the stage in the tent on the White House lawn.

There were rows of wooden chairs for the Congressmen and Senators and a special platform for the AmeriCorps volunteers. Of course, even that early there was an open bar. The stage was at the far end of the tent and our gear was ready to go. We jumped onstage and did a last-minute check before the crowd started coming in.

Everything worked perfectly. The White House spared no expense and supplied us with the best gear we could ask for.

Man, we sounded good and we were loud.

Around 8:00 a.m., dignitaries, legislators, White House staff, and special guests wandered in. I recognized Ted Kennedy and remembered thinking I should probably belly-up to the bar before he drank it dry. Barney Frank from New York was there and many Senators and Congressmen I recognized but couldn't call their names. I was getting nervous. I felt as out of place as a guy at a formal wedding dressed in ripped jeans and T-shirt.

Showtime rolled around and everybody took their seats. It's a pleasant day with a hint of fall in the air. At 8:35 we get our cue and start playing our short set before Clinton made his appearance. We played Black Gold, Runaway Train, Somebody To Shove, and a few others. The highlight of the morning was seeing Senator Strom Thurmond from the great State of South Carolina with fingers in his ears. It felt good to piss that asshole off. If he didn't dig it, then we were doing something right.

After our last song, we got the cue and started playing Don't Stop by Fleetwood Mac. President Clinton walked across the lawn surrounded by the very first class of the AmeriCorps volunteers and made his entrance into the tent. The volunteers took their place on their platform and the President went to a desk where the AmeriCorps bill was waiting to be signed into law. We ended the song when President Clinton arrived at the desk. He took a seat surrounded by aides and advisors. Clinton made a short speech and then the signing began. He used the same pen that President Kennedy used to sign the Peace Corps into law. In five minutes AmeriCorps was law. It made me proud to be an American and witness the democratic process. The President thanked his guests, the press, and especially us. We started playing Don't Stop and the president made his exit.

After the crowd cleared, President Clinton posed for another photo op with our party on the White House lawn. He thanked us again, left, and we went back to the hotel.

We had flights later that day, so we retired to the bar and proceeded to get hammered. This was one of the most incredible adventures of my life and I will never forget the majesty, pageantry, courtesy, and kindness we were shown. I remember thinking Wolf Blitzer was right:

It wasn't my father's White House anymore.

There Was a Woman Named Star

She's petite with long, blonde, curly hair. I like her button nose and big blue eyes. She's definitely attractive and seductive.

I meet her when my band Hijinx is playing Nitetown Club in Destin, Florida, in 1982. I notice her immediately sitting at a table up front near the stage.

Star's very well dressed. Black pumps, worn jeans, and a Stevie Nicks kind of long lace top. Makeup, but not too much. And bangles and necklaces and earrings and rings. Silver and gold dance all over her head and body. Oh. My.

I go to the bar and order a kamikaze with a wine cooler back, walk slowly toward her table in a manner designed to make her see me heading her way — she does — and sat at a table next to her.

A big smile graces her face. She grabs my hand and says Hi, my name's Star.

I smile, too. Hi, my name is Joey.

I know. I saw your picture at Franco's in Pensacola and asked around about you.

Well, I hope you only heard good things.

We laugh.

I've heard some very interesting things about you, Mr. Huffman.

As we talk, she comes and stands close, casually makes contact. She's very affectionate and gentle. Usually I need my space but didn't with Star. Besides, I'm curious about her.

What have you heard about me?

I'll let you know in good time. So, where are you staying; are you a local or a tourist?

I live in Pensacola, but I spend a lot of time in Destin.

Why are you so interested in me; are you here to whack me; are you writing a story on me; or are you just chasing a loser?

No, I'm here of my own volition and have selfish reasons. Cool.

Don't know what the word volition means, but I can tell she's teasing. I finish the drinks and excuse myself to get more before we play our next set. Thought about her on the way to the bar. I immediately like her.

Beautiful and smart. Mysterious and deep. Talks like she knows me. Easy to talk to, also. Which I find out all night between sets as we tell each other our life stories. Last set finishes, I go to her table. It's last call, so I offer her a drink, but she declines.

The lights come up and it's closing time. She has to get home and doesn't want to take me with her that night. I pout while she drives away. But she promises to be back next Tuesday.

We load the bus and make way to our next venue. Star's already there when I arrive. After taking care of my gear, I order a dirty vodka martini. Naturally, I make way to her table, drink in hand, and offer to buy her one. Again she declines with a No, thanks. She's almost falling asleep on the way home the other night and didn't want that to happen on this night.

That's the responsible thing to do. I don't have to drive, so that doesn't stop me from drinking like a frat boy. We talk music, fashion, politics, creativity, and art. She can't stress enough that I should be reading books as much as possible. She herself is well-read and well-traveled. She peppers me with questions.

Joey, if you could travel anywhere you wanted, where would you go?

Easy. Have to be England; that's where more than half of my records are from; my influences are Ian McLagan and Nicky Hopkins.

What do you think would happen if you went there?

I hope I could absorb a bit of their mojo. Who's your favorite artist?

Joan Jett!

circa Star

I like Joan Jett, too.

You know, you look like her; I've seen her live and you definitely favor her.

Joan Jett. As if. Channeling my thirteen-year-old self, I laugh so hard I almost piss my pants. Her face turns red. I embarrassed her. One of the pitfalls of getting to know each other, right? Then she surprises me.

I'm a lesbian, she says.

But that kind of slips through the cracks of my brain. Goes in one ear and out the other. Star shows up every night that week and I talk to her every night between sets. But now it's Sunday. We finish the last set and the lights are turned up. I walk her to her candy-red 1982 Mustang convertible, open the door and she slips in. I close the door and she rolls down the window with a question:

When will I see you again?

Tuesday night at Franco's in Pensacola.

I kiss her on the lips; she kisses me on the forehead. With a heavy heart I watch her drive off. Back inside, I tear down my equipment and help load the truck. On the bus I lay down but can't stop thinking about Star.

Star.

Star.

Star.

The next day, when I'm alone, my mind drifts to Star. She's definitely interesting. Getting to know her last week had been fun. Not always fast on the uptake, it finally sunk in my brain: Whoa! Wait! She's a lesbian? Then why's she still hanging out with me? Just enjoying the conversation as much as I did? Or something else? Things wind down for the day and I'm getting sleepy, so I put my guitar in its case, brush my teeth, and go to bed. Laying there, my mind wanders again to Star. I hope she shows up tomorrow. But what does she want from me? What does she want to ask but is reticent about? Am I falling for her? I fell asleep with a brain full of unanswered questions.

Star Asks a Question

Just as bus call came, I remember my guitar and it and me take a somber ride to this week's venue. Nerves get to jangling before I go on. [That would always happen to me with Hank and…well, every time with any other artist or group I've toured with.] It's this fight-or-flight feeling. Brain screams No! But my heart's saying When you get up on that riser and hit the first note, everything is going to be okay.

There she is. Sitting at the main-floor bar having a Bloody Mary. I walk up. Tell the bartender I'll have a dirty vodka martini. Then I hug Star like I haven't seen her in weeks. A short kiss and I sit down next to her. She grabs my arm and hugs it like she's afraid I'll leave her forever.

We arrived at about eight and are supposed to start the show at nine. Star wants to go up to the second floor to get more privacy. I pay the downstairs bartender for both tabs and leave a tip. Upstairs is empty except for another bartender. We find a table where we can see the stage. Does she want another drink? She does and I order a single Bloody Mary and one dirty Absolut martini. As I wait, I stand with my back to the bar so I can see her. I drink her in. She sees me looking and I turn away, embarrassed.

I sit beside her and take her hand in mine. She stirs her fresh drink and takes a ladylike sip. It's obvious something's on Star's mind. She has something to say but can't find the words. All the time we had spent together the last week talking and listening. Me crushing on her and her seeming to have feelings for me, too. But this thing she wants to ask goes deeper than all that and she's having a hard time asking.

She's distant and quiet this night, which isn't like her. Is she alright? She smiles and assures me she is. So we quietly hold hands. I feel a wave of peace run through my body that makes all seem right with the world.

Then it's time to go to work.

After the set, I go back upstairs to where Star's sitting in the same place. She gives a tiny round of applause. The kind you give when you don't want to be loud. I smile, sit next to her, ask how we sounded. We sound wonderful, she says, and leans over to grasp my hands. She says You're a very talented man, playing your keyboards and guitar and you make it seem effortless.

Don't say that; you're embarrassing me.

Oh, Joey…and modest as well.

Seriously, it's hard to take compliments.

Well, you need to; stay modest and humble; don't ever lose that part of you.

We sit in silence for a few minutes because, while she wants to say something, she can't quite pull the trigger. The tension is palpable. So, I think I'll give her a little nudge. I kiss her forehead, put my arm around her shoulder, and murmur words of assurance:

Star, I know there's something you want to say. Just say it. I promise I will not be angry. Just tell me. I've been seeing you for awhile. I have a huge crush on you. Do you not feel the same way about me?

A tear runs down her cheek.

Oh, Joey, I've fallen for you, too. Been hanging with you to see if…

And here it came. The Big Ask.

…to see if you'd be a good father for my baby.

She says all the right things: I think you'd be a good father. You're gifted, talented, intelligent, funny, vulnerable, and kind. All the traits I want my baby to have. I want to have a baby with you.

Naturally I'm taken aback. A man must think carefully before answering such a question. But she continues before I can say anything.

I didn't want to love you, but it happened. I didn't want to like you, but how could I not? I came to meet you hoping you weren't an asshole. You're humble, a good listener, and perfect. And you're only nineteen years old!

She stands and wipes a tear and looks up as if to ask the Universe: How can I ask him to be the father of my child?

I thought she was going to leave, so I grab her wrist and gently pull her back. She lands on my lap, arms around me. Time stands still. I kiss her passionately for about a minute. She kisses back. We kiss and gaze into each other's eyes for awhile. I feel so safe with Star. I speak first to break the silence...and to answer her question.

Star, I'm falling in love with you. I want you. But I need time to think this through. A baby is a big responsibility. I'm only nineteen! I don't know if I'm ready to be a daddy. I have to think about it.

Star breaks in: That's the thing, Joey. I'm not asking you to be a daddy. I don't want any money from you. You wouldn't have to see our child unless you wanted to.

But, I'd want to see my child.

I sit, hold her hand, deep in thought, trying to get an answer for Star. I'm thinking about being a daddy and how she can make enough money on her own to raise our kid. What does she do for a living, anyway? I'll have to contribute money. And what if she changes her mind? I don't know. I just don't know! This is weighing heavy on my mind and heart.

Star assures me I don't have to decide right this second. She says We can just have some fun. Let's do something after the show. I think you'll really enjoy it, but if you're uncomfortable, we can leave.

I whisper in her ear: I'll follow you anywhere, Star.

After the show we get in her Mustang and are out of there.

The Seduction Continues

Around 2:00 a.m. we arrive at an after-hours bar called The Footloose. It's crowded for a late-night-Tuesday-slash-early-Wednesday-morning. Star finds a parking spot. We walk in, she holding my arm as if I was her chaperone. I pay the cover charge. We look around for a table but don't find one. There are a couple of stools open, so we swoop down and claim them. The room's electric.

A bartender came up. Hey, Star. What'll you have tonight?

Hey, Curtis. A round of kamikazes. This is my new friend Joey.

Curtis says Hey, Joey. Damn, girl. Are you robbing the cradle tonight or what?

Fuck you, Curtis! she says, kidding him.

The joint's hopping. People dance on the dance floor and beside their tables waiting to be asked to dance. Vintage Disco mixes with current dance music, loud and thumping. There's a DJ rig with nobody operating; must be playing mixtapes.

Men dance with men and women with women. Some dance with themselves. There's a drag queen. Star introduces me and I talk to Lola for awhile. She's from New Jersey. Came to Pensacola on vacation and never left. She's wild. Talks in that Jersey accent like she has it all figured out. I've never been in a gay bar before, but I was open to the experience and love it.

Star says Let's dance!

Musicians don't dance.

Star grabs my hand, says This one does.

So, out I go. I'm shy and think everybody's looking at me. But nobody judges anyone here. I do my best and make my way through a couple of songs. Then they play Easy written by Lionel Richie and performed by The Commodores. That's one of my favorite songs. I can slow dance my ass off and have the first of such a dance with Star.

I put my arms around her waist and hold her tight. She puts her arms around my neck and snuggles into me. I rub my nose on hers and we smile at each other. We're in our own little world, swishing and swaying to a beat only we feel. It's the most intimate time I'd spent with her thus far.

Star orders more kamikazes from Curtis and they arrive. She makes a toast: May we kiss who we want and want who we kiss.

We shoot our drinks back. Another dead soldier. More drinks arrive and we shoot them back, too. I'm getting gloriously drunk. I can't tell how high Star is.

Whoa. Last call!

We have one more drink. Is she okay to drive? She is not. We make it out to the car and drive off.

I want to see where you sleep, Joey; let's go to your house.

I try to talk her out of it. But she's as stubborn as she is radiant. So off to the band house we go. Only takes ten minutes to get there. We jump out of her car and hold each other up so we don't fall and stagger to the door, which we promptly fall through all tangled up and giggling.

The lights are off. Everyone's sleeping. It's pitch black. We're trying to be quiet but that just makes it worse. Star keeps giggling and being silly and I can't get her to stop. We fall onto my bed and start making out with some heavy petting. I'd earlier decided not to have sex with her until I made up my mind about the baby. She seemed cool with that. We did more heavy petting. I start rubbing her back and she seems to like that. It feels good to be next to her in an intimate setting. I love to cuddle her. I love the way she smells. I put my nose in her hair and breathe in her pheromones. We hold each other and drift off to sleep.

I wake up first but stay quiet. Watch her sleep. She's a vision. She opens her eyes and catches me looking at her.

Not now, wanna sleep, she mumbles, turning the other way.

I lay back down and try to sleep but my mind's on the baby. The romantic side of me wants to have a baby with Star and live happily ever after. But the pragmatic side's saying it doesn't make sense. I'm not old enough to care for a baby. A baby changes everything. Am I willing to give up on my dreams? I don't know. I think I'm in love with Star but what if that goes sour? Will the agreement change? I fall into a fitful sleep.

Star wakes and dresses. I wake when she gets out of bed and says I'm going home. I'll see you tonight, sweetie.

Okay, drive safe.

I want to tell her I love her, but she couldn't have been able to hear me anyway because she was gone. I drift into a deep sleep. Later that evening, dinner over and dressing done, it was time to take the bus to the club. And there she was. Waiting for me. I came into her arms and gave her a wet kiss and a heartfelt hug. I sat next to her. Our knees were touching.

What time did you get here?

About seven forty-five.

I missed you today.

I missed you too, darlin', and she smiles.

How was your day?

Oh, it was okay.

Are you tired of hanging out with me yet?

No, baby, you shine when you're up onstage. I love seeing you in your element. And I love talking with you. I'm learning so much about you. Don't worry. I'm not going anywhere.

Okay. Just checking. Should I wonder where all this money is coming from?

Don't worry about it. It's cool.

Time to turn on equipment and tune up, so I gave Star a kiss and went on my way. She was so patient. She'd seen our show nine times and just soaked it in. And she talked to me during breaks though I was afraid she'd get tired of that, but that's just me, I'm a worrier. Talking to Star made the evening go by quick. It seemed we just get started and then it's over.

I ask What do you want tonight? We can go somewhere and have a few drinks.

She says No, baby. Tonight you're all mine. I'm going to take you to my home.

We left the club and went to her car. I helped her get the top down and secured. In the low sixties, it was a nice night for it. The wind in my hair felt good.

Star's Apartment

We walked up a flight of stairs to apartment 201, first door on the right. Star fumbled trying to get to the house key on the ring. Finally found it and opened the door.

We walked through a small foyer straight into the living room where a dark purple Persian rug was on the floor. There's a purple velvet couch with a bunch of red and purple velvet pillows strewn about it and a wrought iron rectangle coffee table with a beveled glass top and fleur-de-lis coasters. Against the wall from the couch was a velvet purple chair. Next to the purple chair was a purple credenza with five drawers on the left and five on the right with shelving between them; a deck of tarot cards lay on it. A breakfast nook had a table and four chairs and sliding glass doors on the back wall. Candles were everywhere.

I moved a few pillows and sat on the couch. It was very comfortable. Star put her bag on the coffee table and put on some music. Just the local AOR [album-oriented rock] radio station. She went to her bedroom and slipped into a robe. Then she went in the kitchen and I heard the sound of glasses clinking.

Joey, have you ever had Grand Marnier? No, what is it? It's an orange-flavored liqueur sipped from a snifter; makes a nice change from drinking vodka all the time…besides, I think it's kind of sexy. Okay, I'll try some.

Star came out of the kitchen with a tray holding a bottle of Grand Marnier and two snifters. She put it on the coffee table, then walked around lighting candles. Lights went off. Vanilla incense was lit. Now there was a very nice romantic vibe.

It was a new bottle of Grand Marnier, so she opened it with the knife side of a wine opener to cut through wax all the way around the neck of the bottle, and popped the cork. She sat close on the couch. Poured an ounce of Grand Marnier into each snifter. Picking up her snifter, she rolled the glass around. I see the liquid had good legs. I picked up my snifter and did the same, smelling the scent of the bitter orange.

Let's make a toast, Joey. I'm following your lead, Star; how about a toast to us? That's a wonderful toast! To us!

We held snifters to our lips. I drank mine like a shot. It tasted really good and had a bite.

No, no, Joey; you're supposed to sip it, not drink it like a shot.

She was laughing so hard. Now it was my turn to be embarrassed. She poured another round into my snifter. This time I sipped slowly and enjoyed the experience.

Star had taken her pumps off. Her nails were also painted purple. Obviously, purple must be her favorite color. She changed position until she was stretched out, legs dangling off the arm of the couch, head in my lap. I stroked her hair and took another sip of Grand Marnier. I looked around. Star had turned an ordinary living room into an intimate space.

She got up and changed the music to Gino Vannelli's Brother to Brother album. Good choice. She took the pillows off the couch and we laid down. We spooned with her in front. We fit together nicely. The music was relaxing. I liked smelling her hair. Tonight it smelled of lavender.

She says…

Well, it's very personal what she said, but I replied That's very flattering; if you keep believing in me, I might get the big head.

She wouldn't say how old she was but would only say Ancient Chinese Secret. But I thought around thirty-five. I was pretty sure Star wasn't her given name and asked what it was.

She laughs It's my real name. My mom and dad were hippies. My last name is [redacted for privacy] if that helps. Satisfied now?

She reached over to the coffee table for her snifter and gave me mine. I took a couple of sips and gave it back to her. She set both back on the tray. Star turned around to face me. She says I think I love you, Joey Huffman.

I think I love you too, Star, I whisper.

She starts kissing me very softly. It escalates into full make-out kissing. Then heavy petting. Clothes came off and her robe drops to the floor when she stands. Her silhouette by candlelight was a vision. Naked, we kiss, slowly, which turned into heavy petting really quickly. Then it happened. We made love.

It was Electric.

It was Emotional.

It was Absorbing.

It was the best sex I'd ever had in my very short life.

We lay on the couch after, covered in sweat, breathing heavy, basking in the glow. When she gets her breath back, she suggests we move this party to the bedroom. I agree. I pick up the tray with the Grand Marnier and go to the bedroom where there's a king-size bed with a purple comforter. I set the tray on a table.

Star's busy blowing out candles in the living room. I don't know which side's hers, and position myself in the middle. She crawls into the bed on the left side and snuggles up.

I want more and after some caressing we make love again. I was breathing so heavy I could almost not say Star I love you. Heart rates return to normal and we fall asleep in each other's arms.

I wake up around noon to the aroma of bacon cooking and coffee brewing. As if by magic, Star appears wearing a silk robe tied at the waist and says Good morning. Are you hungry?

Good morning to you, too. Something smells awfully good. I think I can eat something.

Coffee?

Yeah, I could have some.

How do you like it?

Black.

How do you like your eggs?

Scrambled with cheese. Do you have a robe or something I can put on to walk around in? I don't want to put my clothes on from last night.

Yeah, I think I have something for you.

Thank you.

She walks into her closet and comes out with a blue, not purple, terrycloth robe, throws it on the bed with a smile and a There you go, Joey.

I get out of bed, put it on, and it fits. I go out to find Star. Probably in the kitchen. Following my nose, find her scrambling eggs, come up behind, put my arms around her waist. I'm kissing the back of her neck and she says Stop it, you fool, I'm trying to cook breakfast.

The kitchen's all in white except for the silver refrigerator. Star says sit at the breakfast nook. So, I do. She comes out of the kitchen with a plate full of scrambled eggs with cheese, slices of bacon, and whole wheat toast. She sets it in front of me and goes back for jam and butter and a glass of orange juice.

Are you going to eat too?

Yes, Joey, I'm getting mine right now. Oh, I forgot your coffee.

She went goes for the coffee and brings it back. Then gets her plate and finally sits. I wait for her before I start eating. Food is a good idea. I'd had nothing to eat since Dave's spaghetti last night. It's a very good breakfast.

Thanks for the breakfast. It was really good.

You're welcome, Joey. Did you have enough to eat?

Yes, and it was very good. How about you?

Mine was good. I just want to take care of you.

She clears the dishes and brings a coffee refill. I thank her and off she scampers to the kitchen again. It's 2:00 p.m. and I need to get to the band house and get clothes. Star's in her room getting dressed.

What do you want to do today?

Do you want to pull down the top of your car and ride out to the beach? I don't care where we go. I only want to be with you.

The beach sounds like fun. I like to drive there and hang out.

I have to go by the band house and change clothes first.

Not a problem.

Oh, and I have to be back at the band house by six so I can get ready for the show tonight.

Okay. You ready?

I change into last night's outfit, put the robe on the bed. Star changes into a paisley sundress; it looks great on her. I think she has a bikini on under it. She grabbed a pair of sunglasses.

Ready?

Ready.

The day is sunny, but the weather's not too hot. Seems like a good day to take a drive. Arriving at the band house, I quickly change into khaki shorts and a T-shirt with the sides cut out. Pushed tube socks down around my ankles and put on sneakers to finish dressing. Comb my hair, brush my teeth, and get my wallet. I go out to the car where she's waiting and hop in, head to the beach. The drive over has a picturesque view of Pensacola Bay from a huge bridge. The wind blows through our hair. When we arrive at the beach, we find a place to park, walk on the beach, talk, get our feet wet. We go to the bar at the dock and order drinks.

There are things I have to work out personally and things concerning us.

She says I understand.

We leave the beach so I can go to the band house and take a shower and dress for the gig. We make good time what with no traffic to speak of.

What time should I expect you tonight?

Same time as usual.

Okay, see you there.

She drives off and I go in to get ready for the show. We make it to the club. There are a few more people than earlier in the week. I see Star at her favorite stool, walk over, give her a hug and kiss. I need a drink. I'm feeling a little anxious. I drink half the martini in one swallow. Tell the bartender I'll have another, then take another mouthful of the martini and ask Star how she's feeling and she says she's a little tired.

Well, we both should be tired. After last night we should be dead.

I know, I haven't been much of a caregiver lately.

Don't blame yourself. I wouldn't change a thing about last night.

You're a sweet man.

Yeah, keep that to yourself.

More drinks. More shivers. Time to turn on my gear and tune my guitar. Takes ten minutes. I come down from the stage and Star and I talk a little less than before. The silences are comfortable. You don't have to talk all the time to have a healthy relationship.

Star continues to come to the club all week. She's always at the bar first and always upstairs at our table. We always end up at her apartment after the show and talk and have passionate sex at dawn. One night I'm undressing her only to find a surprise awaiting. She's wearing black thigh-high stockings with a seam running up the back and matching panties and bra. It's the first time I've ever seen someone wearing them in person. She says Do you like them? and I can't answer at first but finally manage a heartfelt Sexy.

The End of Star

There are a lot of firsts with Star. My first fine-dining experience where she has to buy me a white dress shirt and tie to wear under my suit and show me which silverware to use and when. She teaches me how to order and which recent years are good for wine and orders an excellent Cabernet. She seems to get satisfaction in teaching me new things. Maybe this is the mother in her that she's so desperate to bring out. I have it bad for her; never felt this way about anybody before this.

After the band finishes our engagement in Pensacola, we play Thunder's Tavern in Pascagoula, Mississippi. Star visits there as well. We continue to see each other regularly for six months. On weeks off I stay at her apartment.

I haven't seen her in three weeks and am looking forward to the visit. She's going to call when she checks into the hotel in Dothan, Alabama. The phone rings and I pick it up. It's her. With her first Hi, I can tell something's wrong. There's something she needs to say but can't do it over the phone. She arrives ten minutes later and I eagerly run out and get into the passenger side of her Mustang. It's raining. The windshield wipers keep time to an imaginary song in a cheerless silence. Her eyes are red and swollen from crying. When asked what's wrong, she pauses for what seems like forever. Then finally an answer.

I went to see my OB/GYN last week because I was worried why it was taking so long for us to get pregnant. The doctor did some tests and…

She begins crying again. I hug her, stroke her hair. Between sobs she manages to say the words that are killing her and all her hopes and dreams.

I can't have children.

She cries harder and goes limp in my arms. I'm at a loss. What can I say to that? I hug her tighter. Wait for her to speak. She pulls herself together and explains.

The doctor said premature ovarian failure. My ovaries stopped producing eggs.

There's nothing that can be done?

They'll run more tests but the doctor doesn't seem very hopeful.

I'm so sorry for her but don't know what to say.

Star sobs and says There's nothing to say; oh, Joey, I feel so helpless.

This news shakes me to the core. It's such a hopeless feeling knowing there's something wrong and I can't fix it and it's out of my control and there's absolutely nothing to be done. But you know what? I tell her I'll always be there for you to lean on. I still love you with or without a baby.

I love you, too.

We drive to her room at the Holiday Inn, lay on the bed where I hold her, and we fall asleep. When we wake she says she's driving back to Pensacola. She doesn't want to come see me play. She probably feels like being alone where she can deal with this news. Back at the hotel, I hug her and tell her again I love her and she says I feel the same.

Then she drives off.

I watch until she's out of sight. After that day we talk on the phone a few times but I never see her again. Maybe I remind her of her condition and the crashing down of all of the hopes and dreams we share.

The thing is the perspective of time has helped me see Star had her agenda and that agenda was all about what she needed. Her body clock was ticking, and she wanted a baby. She chose me because I looked like Joan Jett and, after checking me out and finding I was a decent guy, actively pursued me as her baby's father. But when she found out she was infertile the situation changed and she disappeared from my life forever. Her leaving hurt the worst of anything I'd ever felt before that time. It took time to recover. To this day it still stings a little when I think about it, but you know what?

Life went on. And Life's been good. I met a good woman. I became a daddy. Twice over! I love my children and am so very proud of them.

Star, I hope you went on to have a wonderful and fulfilling life.

HIJINX

1980. I was just seventeen. My band Hijinx was playing Nitetown Club in Destin, Florida. It's a Tuesday night, so not very crowded, with about fifty people in a venue that held fifteen hundred. Then the lights came up and it was closing time.

We overnighted it so I spent the whole night on the bus drinking an entire bottle of Crown Royal. I howled at the moon for awhile then passed out. Woke around noon to a sun beating down like a sledgehammer. Must've been 110 degrees inside. I was slightly disoriented and had a raging hangover. Four ibuprofen and a shot of whiskey for my sins: I'd go in search of that cure when I could finally stand.

Eventually got off the bus. Compared to it, the outside temperature seemed air-conditioned. I went into the main house. Took ibuprofen with a diet cola chaser but couldn't find any whiskey.

The band house was a rundown 2/1 with kitchen, common area, and dining room. It included an adjacent building with two more rooms. A big room with four mattresses on the floor and a small room with one bed and nothing else. I took the smaller because it was next to the bathroom and was pitch black and cold. No windows in the building, no sunlight could pierce its veil, no way to tell the time.

I woke. Where am I? Oh, yeah...right.

This process of not knowing then remembering happens regularly and takes anywhere from ten to thirty seconds. I've never thought to ask anyone if it ever happens to them. Would be interesting to find out. The ibuprofen had taken effect and my head had stopped hurting, but I was still wearing what I wore onstage the night before. I changed to a T-shirt and shorts. No shoes.

Hungry. Went to the house. Made a turkey and Swiss sandwich, adding a diet cola. Found a comfy place to sit and eat. The TV was on from the night before. The sandwich tasted like the most wonderful sandwich ever made. Ric woke and skulked around in the kitchen. It's clear the band went to the bottle club after the gig last night because no one was awake. Good, I'm not the only one debilitated from last night. I took four more ibuprofen, again washing them down with diet cola.

Eventually I took a shower and did my hair. Dressed in black spandex pants and a shirt with a Japanese character topped by a red scarf. Put on Capezios and headed back to the house.

I waited around watching TV until time to go. We liked to get there about an hour before showtime, relax, have a drink. We loaded the bus and made way to Nitetown. There's a contest of some sort so the crowd had doubled from last night.

We played Tuesday through Sunday at Nitetown. Mostly Monday was a day off. But now it was Sunday and time to pack our gear.

We overnighted to Pensacola, arriving at the band house at five-thirty in the morning. I was still awake. Monday morning meant one thing: Laundry day. After gathering and sorting dirty clothes, I fell asleep around seven and woke around noon with a startle response. That's where I wake up alarmingly fast, often yelling and not knowing where I am. All that drama over, I rolled out of bed onto my pile of dirty laundry. Stuffing it all into the pillowcases from the band house, I brushed my hair, put on deodorant, and jumped on the bus to ride to the Wash and Fold.

The whole band was on the bus. That made me happy. There was Ric, guitar. Bill, or Bubba as he was called then, bass. Milo, also known as Mike, drums. And me, keyboards and guitar. We all sang.

I loved laundry day. It's one of the few times we'd be together as a band except for onstage and some meals. We loved to play together. They were my brothers — my family. I liked to be around them. We didn't have a home to go to and played dives every week of the year. We were gypsies carrying only what we needed: Our instruments, pots and pans for cooking, and lots of love to share everywhere we went.

Laundry day was an adventure every time. This one time, Bubba bought a three-pack of white Hanes wifebeaters and Rit dyes in blue, red, and yellow. He called it a science project and we wore these onstage. They looked good.

But today, while the clothes were washing, a few of us went to lunch at the sandwich shop around the corner. I had The Yardstick By Which All Other Food Is Measured. It wasn't bad.

We got on the bus with still-warm laundry on our laps. It makes me feel good to have fresh, clean clothes.

Next stop: Big Star grocery to get enough food for the week at the band house. Our bus driver and spotlight operator, Dave, was also our cook; he learned that in the Army. Dave was in charge of the grocery money. I always argue with Dave over how much stuff I can get. At least I didn't stomp my feet and cry and throw myself about, but like a kid begging Daddy, it'd be Can I get this and that? We'd get to the checkout and they'd scan a big bag of plain M&M's Bubba or I snuck in while Dave was comparing meat or something. He wouldn't find them until checkout, then he'd have such a meltdown and lecture us on the importance of not breaking the budget:

We only make so much so put it back!

Please, oh, please, can I have just one copy of The World News to catch up on Bat Boy?

Alright, but that's all…and I mean it this time!

Dave didn't talk much about the Army. All he'd say was he'd been stationed in Seoul, South Korea, and got out with an Honorable Discharge at the rank of sergeant. We never could quite figure him out. He'd yell Korean phrases at us when he was drunk and always mumbled under his breath to Asian women. Usually nothing happened. Maybe he thought all Asian women spoke Korean. Who's to know?

But this one time he must've said something vulgar while passing an Asian woman because she stopped and yelled I beg your pardon?!?

The Korean woman and Dave started arguing. It was very animated and intense. Dave spoke mostly in English peppered with Korean and she did the opposite. He had insulted her by saying the worst thing one can say to a Korean. At least I figured that's what he did. I'd heard it often from Dave and it loosely translated to some version of a yo-mama insult. Anyway, I guess he spoke good-enough Korean because this Korean lady was all up in his face. The altercation took maybe five minutes, but it seemed to last forever. He was walking away still shouting and she was doing the same in the other direction.

When I got bored, I'd study what he was saying in Korean. No more than a few phrases. But when he got into arguments with Koreans, they seemed to know more than the few lines he knew.

So, we finished grocery shopping and headed back to the band house, unloading groceries and putting them up. Dave was shouting out orders like a drill sergeant. Heaven help the grunt who fucked up the Unpacking of the Groceries Official Procedure.

Some band houses didn't have a kitchen let alone pots and pans. So we carried a full set with us as well as utensils making us a self-contained unit and cooked at the band house. That's pretty much a synopsis for the first part of Laundry and Groceries Day. We were usually done with chores around 3:00 p.m. and had from then until load-in at noon on Tuesday as free time.

I played a game on the My Arcade GameStation for awhile. Got bored. I'd brought my Gibson SG from home and went to get it off the bus. Earlier, I heard Bubba playing around with a song idea in the other room. I went in to see how it was going. Maybe he wanted me to play on it?

We recorded a little more on our Tascam portable four-track recorder we used for song ideas. We had a 57 and 58; that's the extent of our mic collection. And a Rockman for distorted guitar tones. We all wrote songs, but Bubba wrote the most. If it sounded like something the band would do, we'd work it up for rehearsal.

I played with Bubba on his song. It was good. I came up with a riff right away and we kept grooving and recording parts. Bubba on his bass. My guitar and an extra Mini Moog. We made pretty good demos on that Tascam.

Things were winding down for the day and I was getting sleepy, so put my guitar in its case, brushed my teeth, and went to bed.

The runner picked us up around noon for the ride to the Pensacola venue. We'd come back to the band house on the bus after soundcheck and shower and do stuff then. Soundcheck was successful if not mind-numbingly boring. The room sounded good with a warm sound onstage. We worked up a few songs. Tommy Tutone's 867-5309, which we mastered pretty fast. Photograph by Def Leppard took a little more effort. We'd debut them tonight. I was on guitar for both.

We went back to the band house where Dave proceeded to the kitchen to finish cooking supper, another culinary masterpiece. I watched TV, then scored the bathroom to shave and shower. I washed myself off good and shampooed, rinsed, and put on and rinsed out conditioner. Dried off and combed my hair. Then just waited around a bit until time to do my hair up. I used a blow dryer, twisting and turning the hair. When finally dry, it was time for the Aqua Net.

First: Using hands or a towel, fluff the hair.

Second: Aqua Net it in place.

Sometimes I did what we euphemistically called a Rooster Bath.

One: Open a tall-neck Budweiser.

Two: Empty contents all over your head.

Three: Take a towel and keep teasing the hair up and out.

Budweiser is far better than Aqua Net once it dries.

Dressed in leopard-skin spandex pants and white dress shirt rolled up to the elbows topped with a skinny black leather tie and a pair of white Capezios, I looked in the mirror and was satisfied. One more thing before I'd be completely stage-ready. Sharpening an eyeliner, I spread it on the inside eyelid, top and bottom. This particular enhancement is why I'd get indignant when people stared askance when we went out to eat after a show.

Hey! It's called Show Biz, people!

Just as bus call comes, I remember my guitar and it and me take a somber ride to this week's venue, nerves jangling.

Franco's was a three-level nightclub that looked like it used to be one of those Big Daddy's that were all over Florida in the late Seventies. There's a guy in the foyer carding patrons and another taking money and stamping hands. The main room bar runs front to back on the right of the dance floor. Big and long, but it had to be because it was the only one downstairs. Barstools along its entire length. Waitress stations at both ends. Pool tables in the back beside the stage. Dance floor covers most of the downstairs area with vari-colored floor lights blinking under dancers. Second and third floors, crowded by tables and chairs, had bars at the right. The dance floor can be seen from those balconies.

The first drink of the night always gives what I call the shivers. The shivers happen when I take a big gulp of a strong drink and make a sour face. There's a two-second delay as the alcohol hits the bloodstream, rewarding with a full body shiver lasting two to three seconds. Big swig of martini delivered, I froze up for a few seconds to enjoy the warm intense tingling.

Time to go to work.

The rest of the guys were onstage so I jogged downstairs and up to the stage. Ric was tuning and Bubba was just looking bored. Milo was ready to go. I pressed the preset on my Prophet 5 for Working for the Weekend. Milo counted it off and we were underway.

The next day, Dave came in beating a stock pot with a wooden spoon and shouts Wake up! Wake up! Its five o'clock. Dinner time. Your favorite. Spaghetti. Dinner time.

Blah-blah-blah, he kept repeating the same thing until we all got our food. Dave cooked a lot of good things but on spaghetti night everyone attended. It was the best spaghetti I ever had up to that point. He used beer in the sauce. My own spaghetti sauce is based on Dave's, but I use wine because it gives the sauce a sweeter taste. I grabbed a plate and stood in line. When it was my turn, I loaded the plate with pasta and covered it with sauce and grated Parmesan cheese.

With eight people jockeying for seats, finding a place was difficult. I sat on the porch steps. Bubba joined me. Me and him usually chased waitresses in the clubs we played. Bubba once declared If she totes a tray, I love her. He's silent for a couple of minutes then he says

Haven't seen much of you the last couple of weeks. (FYI: This was during Star.)

Bubba, it's complicated. I'll tell you about it when there's time.

Well, we miss you, buddy.

We continued eating. It went down quickly. I went for seconds; this time just sauce on the plate to sop up with garlic bread. I certainly couldn't eat like that now but when I was that young my waist was a lady's size five and I loved wearing girlfriends' clothes.

I'd bought a woman's suit a month before. It was the Eighties, so you get the picture. The gray pinstripe suit had baggy pants and a matching jacket. Made of a cotton blend it helped keep me cool onstage and helped me look cool, too. I pulled it out and put it on over a wifebeater. Capezios, eyeliner, and a splash of Bubba's cologne. Now I looked and smelled good and was ready with fifteen minutes to spare.

Seven-thirty. Bus to the club.

1982: With Ric Seymour of Hijinx

There were a few more people than earlier in the week. I drank half a martini in one swallow. Told the bartender I'd have another. More drinks. More shivers. Time to turn on my gear and tune my guitar. Took ten minutes.

After the band finished our engagement in Pensacola, we played Thunder's Tavern in Pascagoula, Mississippi.

Being with Hijinx was my college education. I was with them for four years, from 1980 to 1984, when I was twenty-one. I learned how to pick up girls. That was fun. Most importantly, though, I learned how to jam. Even if I didn't know a song, they'd play it and I'd hang on for dear life until I figured it out. Jamming felt like I was banging my head against the wall. But then all of a sudden the music all made sense and it felt like flowers blooming in my mind. All was revealed. There was knowledge where there had been none.

But as much as I loved those guys and playing with them, I felt there was something more in the big city, so I moved to Atlanta to play with Ean Evans. We put together a band. But I went on to a funk band with a record deal and he went on to play bass with Lynyrd Skynyrd. He was with them for about nine years until he died of cancer in 2009.

The first night in Atlanta I also met Kim, who would later become my wife.

1986: Kim and Joey marry

THE YARDSTICK BY WHICH ALL OTHER FOOD IS MEASURED

I've been around the world more than once. An American sometimes has trouble finding something familiar to eat. Yes, there are the fast-food places we all are drawn to so we can say that it tastes the same as it does back home — or doesn't. This is not a story about the so-called persona of the ugly American. If that is what you're looking for, this story is not for you. Instead, this method is about how to eat real food in a foreign country.

You can order from room service and get something familiar, or you can opt to go out for dinner, find everything is different, get angry and confused, and go back to your hotel room hungry. Well, let me introduce you to a method I've created that is tried and true and really works. You must follow the method exactly as written or you will get hosed. First, let's get something straight. The Club Sandwich is The Yardstick By Which All Other Food Is Measured. Got that?

Step Number One: Call room service and order a Club Sandwich and fries.

Step Number Two: Patiently wait until it arrives.

Step Number Three: Tip the waiter an extra 10% even though an 18% gratuity is included on the bill.

Step Number Four: Take the lid off the entrée.

Step Number Five-A: Inspect the contents. There should be three pieces of mayo'ed bread between which are stacked turkey, ham, bacon, lettuce, and tomato. If they leave the ham off or you don't eat pork, that's okay, just take the pork off the sandwich. The sandwich should be cut into quarters with toothpicks impaling each quarter, holding the sandwich together.

Step Number Five-B: Important! Take the toothpick out of the section you will eat before you take a bite. Does it taste good? Good...move on to presentation.

Step Number Six: How do the fries look? Did you get a tiny bottle or a little container of catsup that you can dip the fries in? Did you get a little bottle of mustard, too?

Step Number Seven: Does your plate contain anything unusual? For example, in Germany my plate was garnished with headcheese. That is unacceptable — unless you like it. Otherwise, send it back and ask for another without. Just looking at that stuff is creepy. If you don't know what headcheese is, it looks like leftover parts in a meatpacking plant that are swept up off of the floor and combined together to make a nauseating cold cut. You see eyelids, snout cuts, and...Oh, God, I can't describe anymore of it than that. If you can still eat the Club Sandwich after seeing that, then go to —

Step Number Eight for your next meal: Take another step with the menu. I suggest pasta with the red sauce. It is hard to fuck up but amazingly different from hotel to hotel. If you get noodles with catsup poured over the top, you may have to go The American Embassy — a/k/a McDonald's.

I stayed in a hotel in Barcelona that had twenty-four-hour room service. In the daytime the service was excellent. But after midnight I don't think the guy answering the phone spoke English. No matter what I ordered, spaghetti was what I got. It's as if he was told if anybody speaking English calls, send them the pasta. This happened to me three nights in a row so I called the valet to have him place my order.

Don't laugh.

This is my life.

This kind of stuff happens on a regular basis. You got to roll with it or you'll go nuts.

If the spaghetti is good it's safe to order anything you prefer. The steak will probably be good depending on the sides. Salads will come with normal vegetables and dressing. Although I'm talking about room service, this method can be used at restaurants and for Catering, too. Just remember the golden rule:

The Club Sandwich:
The Yardstick By Which All Other Food Is Measured.

Speaking of food…

DUMPSTER DIVING

In 1985, I was playing with the band Bareback. We had a couple of after-show drinks at the bar. The bartender says we'd have to drive to Jackson to find an open anything where we could get food. So, we paid our tab, tipped the bartender, and stumbled out the door.

We drove around looking for a restaurant or fast-food place, but can't find anything open close by. By this time Scott King, bass player and good friend, and I were halfway through a bottle of Crown Royal and desperately in need of some kind of sustenance. It is always better to have food in your system when you're drinking whiskey. Scott and I were soaking it up like a sponge with nothing to buffer it.

We pulled into a convenience store. I noticed an employee throwing something into the dumpster but thought nothing more about it and went in to join the rest of the band. The convenience store was a drag. There was no fried chicken, pizza, hotdogs, or any food of that nature. They wouldn't have hot food until tomorrow. One can buy chips or candy. There were microwavable burgers and sandwiches, but those are hard to get next to. I bought a bag of Doritos and something to drink.

Scott and I headed out and joined the band at the van. Then curiosity gets the best of me: What had I seen the employee throwing away? I told Scott about it and he says he's always up for a good dumpster dive and off we went. Scott boosted me up to look in. It was pretty empty but on the bottom there seemed to be some kind of food in separate closed boxes. It was worth investigating. So Scott boosts me over the top and I land with an awkward thump…but we struck gold in the form of boxes filled with chicken and French fries. I picked up one box. Damn, still warm. They had only just now thrown them out and it was our good luck to find them.

There must have been twenty-five boxes at least. Up and over I threw Scott as many as I deemed necessary for everybody in the band and crew to have one. I had to figure my way out of the dumpster and found a sliding door on the side. It was only five feet to manage so it wasn't too hard to get out. We took the boxes over to the guys.

No way! Nobody was going to eat dumpster food. They were thoroughly repulsed. And after all my hard work! I was insulted. Well, more for us. Scott and I chowed down on some pretty good dumpster chicken and fries and washed it all down with more Crown Royal.

Later, the rest of the band were complaining about being hungry. But even then, they weren't desperate enough to eat dumpster food. Scott and I were full, drunk, and content. We played cards all night and had a great time.

So that's my dumpster diving story.

Not proud of it, but I've eaten worse and paid a lot more for it.

JAZZ BAND

This is a story of thirteen-year-old-Joey antics. By that age I played drums in the high school band, some guitar, and had been playing piano for a few years (even if I did ditch lessons and spend the money elsewhere without telling Mama).

Thirteen. What a weird age. Thrust from childhood into the crazy, upside-down world halfway between childhood and adulthood. Girls are discovered and you're usually doing something that shows you're insecure and, last but not least, there's the acne. You're hyperaware of yourself and what you do. Mind racing and God forbid you talk to a girl and say something stupid.

That was me. But music was my main interest. The first semester of eighth grade our band director, Eddie Prichard, was forming a high school jazz band. I didn't know what that was, but wanted in. I casually stopped him in the hall.

Heard about the jazz band; need a guitar player?

No, but I do need a bass player; can you play bass?

Yes!

Good; rehearsal starts in two weeks.

Excitement was quickly replaced by panic. What did I know about playing bass? It's like the first four strings of a regular guitar except lower. I thought it'd be the easiest thing to figure out. But where was I going to find a bass and an amp? What's the best thing to do in a situation like this? I'll tell ya —

Lie. Lie. Lie.

And thus I proceeded to do just that when the family was having a lovely meal. Everyone's relaxed and I wait until a lull in the conversation to drop the bomb by shouting very loudly Lie Numero Uno: I have to play bass in the high school jazz band. Mom and Dad, shocked: *What?!?* Lie Numero Dos: Mr. Prichard says I have to be in the high school jazz band and Lie Numero Tres: I have to buy a bass and an amp!

Mom and Dad ponder this for what seemed like an eternity, then start with a litany of questions. Are you sure that's what he said? How much is a bass? Can you play the bass? What is a jazz band?

Question after question, I fobbed off, bent half-truths into truth, and outright lied some more because I wanted this and I wanted it bad. They thought about it for a bit and discussed it. When I was turning in for the evening, they say We are behind you, Joey, and will get you that bass and amp. I thank them and try to sleep but can't because all I could do was picture rocking on an arena stage with the spotlight shining on the next Rock & Roll legend to take the world by storm:

ME!

Thus the dreams of this thirteen-year-old boy saw me into Sandman Land.

A couple of days later, Dad and I drive to Lexington, Kentucky, to Carl's Music and, of course, I start looking behind the counter at the expensive basses. I knew nothing about them except that Fender and Gibson made the best at the time. Now, if I were a practical little guy I'd have asked questions like What would be proper for a beginner playing in a high school jazz band? and await the salesman's professional opinion.

But it was too late. I'd already seen it hanging behind the counter. At this moment I'd like to clarify another motivation: As a thirteen-year-old in 1976, I was officially The Biggest KISS Fan In The World.

KISS had been my very first concert.

I had every record KISS released.

And, most importantly, Gene Simmons played a Gibson Ripper onstage.

It was immediately recognized by its rounded headstock at the tuning pegs but I'd never seen one in person. After seeing it in black, I just had to have it. Everybody says Joey, this one might be too much bass for you, maybe you should look at the Fender P-Bass.

But I wasn't hearing any of that. That simply would not do. So, they took it down and handed it over. It was like holding an ancient holy relic. I knew the premise of playing bass was mostly one note at a time. So I played around on it. I didn't know what a bass was supposed to sound like, but I knew what one was supposed to look like.

Alas, the Ripper was too expensive, but I had a backup plan. I saw another Gibson: The Grabber. With a natural finish, round headstock, and one pickup that slid back and forth to change the tone, it too was a large-scale bass. Most importantly, Gibson was prominently on the headstock. Second importantly: This one was in my father's financial ballpark.

They further suggested a Peavey TNT transistor 15-inch bass, so Dad bought the two. I was so happy having a KISS-style bass and daydreamed about above-the-fold *Appalachian News-Express* headlines in 48-point Arial Bold typeface. [See next page.]

However, back to reality. At thirteen I was only five-feet-four and that became a dilemma because I can barely reach the bottom fret which meant I had to move the bass to my right to press it. When I put the bass perpendicular to the floor it was taller than me. Everybody got a kick out of that.

I went on to play in the high school jazz band, figuring things out as I went. At first I couldn't sight-read so I'd learn the songs at home and play from memory at the next rehearsal. Eventually, I learned to sight-read bass clef really well. There's a huge shortage of bass players in town, so I played with the college jazz band, too.

I've continued to play bass even after switching to keyboard. It's a little-known fact that I play the bass just as well as I play keyboard. I still love to play bass in the studio and at home.

Hey, the next time anyone needs a bass player, give me a call.

N EWS-EXPRESS
A P P A L A C H I A N

THE CONSCIENCE OF EASTERN KENTUCKY

Pikeville, KY   Delivery 38 Cents

JOEY AND HIS GIBSON BASS ROCK RUPP ARENA IN EPIC OPENING FOR KISS!

by Jeremy Jenkins, Entertainment Reporter

Making us proud is our very own hometown boy. Yes, Joey Huffman thoroughly rocked the Rupp Arena last night when he and his bass, a GIBSON by the way, opened for the rock band KISS. This reporter has it on good authority that after Huffman and his GIBSON BASS produced an epic opening that left the audience gasping in delight, KISS almost canceled the show because Joey Huffman and his band were sooooo awesome.

[Pictured below: Richard Ratliff, drums, Joey Huffman with his GIBSON BASS, and Mark Clark on guitar.]

CLIVE DAVIS

This is a tale of embarrassment and guilt. It's 1986 and Clive Davis has come to Atlanta to see Native, a band I was a member of. We later changed the band name to Witness. Showcasing for him at the East Point Theatre, we were very nervous and excited. I mean, the culmination of playing gigs, writing songs, doing covers, sweat equity, and everything else is The Coveted Record Deal.

Clive finally shows up, one fashionable hour late. We took the stage and played from our souls while our manager, Charlie Brusco, was sitting out front with Clive convincing him how great we were. To make this short I'll leave out the details about the show and negotiations, but Charlie comes back to the dressing room and says Clive said Yes.

We were now Arista recording artists. Time to celebrate.

Clive invites us back to his suite at The Ritz-Carlton in Buckhead where he was going to fill our heads with dreams and desires of being Rock Stars. The band and Charlie met in the lobby of the hotel and rode the elevator up to Clive's suite. I was stoked. I mean, this was the guy who signed Janis Joplin, Bruce Springsteen, Santana, Aerosmith, Pink Floyd, Billy Joel, and a cast of other artists and bands too numerous to mention that went on to worldwide fame.

Charlie knocks on the door. Clive answers in his robe and invites us in. I was star-struck. I'd never been in a hotel this nice. His suite is huge. We sat in a circle around him on comfortable couches.

The first phase of his career, Clive Davis had been General Counsel of Columbia Records and was appointed Vice President and General Manager in 1966. In 1967 he was named President of the company. Then in the early Seventies, he and Columbia Pictures formed Arista. This is the guy who'd go on to sign Whitney Houston. Clive was a legend in the music business.

So there he was, sitting in a power position in the room and starts telling us what our future held. We listen, hanging eagerly on his every word. While Clive was talking I noticed a deli tray with meat and vegetables sitting on a table. I hadn't eaten anything before the showcase and was a little hungry and so reached over and took a piece of broccoli from the plate, dipped it in ranch dressing, and threw it in my mouth. Clive stopped talking, gave me a very strange look, then started talking again.

Heads full of dreams, hearts beating fast, we hung out for about an hour before we left. We walk out of the door and it slammed behind us the way doors always seem to do in hotels. When we're in the hall Charlie whispered at me like a mother scolding an unruly child in a restaurant:

What the hell did you do that for?

I was surprised and taken aback. I didn't think I'd done anything abnormal or rude.

What'd I do?

Charlie delivered the bad news very firmly.

You ate out of Clive's dinner plate.

I was embarrassed as hell. I felt guilty because I may have lost the deal for the band. Then I thought to myself Hey, that's what Aerosmith would do. It's a very Rock & Roll thing to do. I just looked at Charlie and say I thought it was a deli tray. One second goes by, a second that seemed like an eternity. But after that beat, we laughed. I'd never live that down while the band was together. Something bad would happen and they'd collectively say: Well, at least it's not as bad as the time Joey ate off Clive's dinner plate.

1986: L to R: Allen Stroo, Joey, Debbie Davis, Eddie Boyd, and Eddie Moody.

Waiting In the Can

Most of our first Arista album, the self-titled Witness that included the single Do It Till We Drop, had been recorded in 1986-87 at Fantasy Studios in Berkeley, California, with Kevin Elson behind the console producing. Debbie Davis and I wrote two songs with Neal Schon from Journey. Witness was between guitar players at the time, so we had a revolving door of guitarists on the record. There was Neal Schon, Brad Gillis from Night Ranger, and Danny Chauncey and Jeff Carlisi from .38 Special. Witness, the album, was my first LP and I was stoked.

It sat in the can until release in 1988.

ROCK STARS!

1988: The year had its ups and downs. Great highs followed by depressing lows then new highs again. The Witness record was released in February with great anticipation and expectations.

Do It Till We Drop made the AOR charts. Every week we'd see which stations added the single. At first, we're getting eight or nine adds a week and then it sort of tapers off. We had a good run at it. We opened a few dates with Skynyrd when it had to be called Lynyrd Skynyrd Tribute. They had a new pass for every show; I still have the laminates somewhere; I ought to dig them up. Anyway, the highlight of opening for Skynyrd was playing to a sold-out crowd of 52,000+ at the now-demolished Atlanta-Fulton County Stadium.

Witness went on to do an East Coast run to support our first album. It was the first time I'd been to New York City, so that was cool. We visited Arista Records, our label. Posters of the band were haphazardly hanging on the wall. I've always been of the opinion those posters were hastily hung when they heard we were coming to visit. Kind of like a high-class hooker who changes out pictures of her regular johns to boost the ego of the one she's expecting.

We met with Clive Davis who still insisted we were going to be ROCK STARS! We played the notorious Cat Club that night. We were excited to play NYC. We soundchecked and ate. At showtime only record company employees were in the crowd. It was the harbinger of things to come.

We finished our East Coast run playing to small crowds until September. Then the bottom dropped out. No tour buses. No tour support. No nothing. Arista pulled the plug on everything. Just for the record I have to say this about Arista Records:

They were inept at promoting a rock band, period. Just ask Michelle Malone and Drag The River. I played with them in '89-'91.

Clive Davis signed us, too. It felt like Groundhog Day all the way down to only record company employees at the Cat Club.

But that's another story.

After the Witness record stiffed, I was beyond disappointed. Getting a record deal is what every musician aspires to. It is the culmination of all the hard years playing in cover bands, writing songs, staying at one Motel 6 after another, practicing till fingers hurt, and everything else music-related. Getting dropped is like having the rug pulled out from under you and you land hard on your ass on broken glass. I moped around and played with a cover band for awhile. Then in November, the week of Thanksgiving, Debbie Davis called.

1990: MICHELLE MALONE TOUR

Debbie was working as a runner for the Keith Richards rehearsal at a warehouse on the lot at Lakewood Amphitheatre. They were asking if she knew anybody who can program keyboards and she gave them my number. I was a huge Keith Richards fan and probably would've done the job for free just to meet him.

ISAAC HAYES

With the 1988 Witness tour DOA and not getting the option of a new album, and the Keith Richards tour over, I needed something to do. I was playing in a local cover band when I got the call to play with Isaac Hayes in 1989. I thought cool, he wrote Soul Man and Shaft.

I agreed to do the gig being too stupid to know that playing in a soul band might be different than playing in a rock band. I watched Isaac's show tapes and started working on his material. I quickly realized I was in way over my head. This music had a lot of fancy chord changes. I had to revert to music theory and apply it to Isaac's music to work out his chord changes. It was challenging but I made it work. There were three or four distinct keyboard parts on the tape. Not knowing which I was to play, I worked them all up, vigilantly programming synth, strings, and horn sounds, working eighteen hours a day for a week before our first rehearsal.

The day of the first rehearsal arrives and off I go. As I'm setting up, a man walks up with a bunch of musical charts, something that would've saved a lot of time if I'd had them when I was working out the chord changes. At the time I could read charts but couldn't read them by sight the first time through. I do better having a day to memorize.

I also discovered my only part in the band was to play electric piano and certain synth lines because there was another keyboard player and Isaac also played piano at center stage. We ran down several songs, which I faked my way through. I keep waiting to play Shaft because I had many string and flute parts worked up. When we finally got to Shaft I found out all the orchestration was pre-recorded to tape. The band played along with the tape. The drummer received a click track through a set of headphones. Oh, man, was I disappointed. I started playing the flute part along with the tape and Isaac turned around and says We've got that. In other words: Don't improvise…just play your part.

Okay, all I had to do was play a two-chord piano part and act like I was playing the orchestral parts. At the end of the song where the majority of orchestration occurs, Isaac stands up and faces the keyboard riser pretending to direct the orchestra in a very animated manner, like a cross between an orchestral conductor and Elvis doing karate moves. Isaac was a big man. Watching him conduct was entertainingly amusing to me.

I was starting to think maybe I'd made a bad career move. Hayes didn't do anything he wrote for Sam and Dave, songs like I Thank You; Hold On, I'm Comin'; Soul Man; or When Something Is Wrong With My Baby. He played a twenty-minute version of By The Time I Get To Phoenix and a thirty-minute — longest thirty minutes of my life! — medley of some of his popular soul songs. But this was the first step in my sideman career and being out of my element was good for me musically.

Bottom line: All art doesn't feed all souls and a paying gig is a paying gig. Daddy had kids, so Daddy did what Daddy needed to do. So I just accepted my position and off to Europe I went with Isaac Hayes.

When we arrived at Gatwick Airport north of London, we found out Isaac's people had not acquired my work permit. They tell me to act like I wasn't with them at passport control and customs. The customs agent seemed to know I was with the band and interrogated me relentlessly: Who are you visiting? Where are you staying? How much money's in your wallet?

Fortuitously, I had addresses and phone numbers from some of the crew from the Keith Richards tour. Finally he relented, stamped my passport, and sent me on my way. It was very stressful.

We played the Dominion Theatre in the West End of London for my first gig. We take the stage and it's going pretty good. I'm feeling good about my parts. Then we came to the part of the show where Isaac introduces his aggregation. He starts on the opposite side of the stage from me and introduces the band members one by one. When he gets to the keyboard riser he explains to the audience this is where the strings, horns, electric piano, and orchestration are emanating from. He says Ladies and gentlemen, on the keyboards…Joey…ummm, Joey…uhhh…he turns and shouts over the music to me

Hey, Joey, what's your last name?

I felt the smallest I've ever felt in my life. I was so embarrassed it took half the tour to recover. But recover I did and can laugh about it now. I played with Isaac off and on for six months. When I arrived back stateside, I started playing with that cover band again. I was just having fun playing music. I didn't care whose music it was. I probably could've been content to play clubs around Atlanta but like it has so many times, fate lent a hand.

ATLANTA COCA-COLA MUSIC AWARDS

Early 1991. I'm with The HellHounds having the time of my life playing in a band with so much swagger. The band consisted of me, Rick Richards, Rick Price, and the late, great, amazing Randy DeLay on the drum kit. We were playing frat parties, regional clubs and, of course, every Sunday night at The Cavern.

One day Rick Price calls with good news. The Coca-Cola Atlanta Music Awards had nominated The HellHounds as Outstanding Local Rock Band. He gave the date and time and said to wear Sunday-go-to-meeting clothes because it was a semi-formal event.

We'd soon find out you can dress them up but you can't take them out. Our friend Yogi had a limo and offered to drive us to the event, gratis. The plan was for us to meet Yogi at The Cavern and depart from there. The awards show at the Fabulous Fox in Atlanta turned out to be a bigger deal than we thought:

It was televised.

Dozens of limousines waited in line to drop talent on the red carpet. I heard lots of young female screaming and was depressingly sure it wasn't for us. We ask Yogi to pull around the building to the backstage door and pushed our way out of the limo. In the distance we hear the crowd going crazy. TLC was on the red carpet. It was like Beatlemania all over again.

All we wanted was to get inside and find a fucking drink. We lurked in the shadows. After trying a few doors we finally found one unlocked and go inside.

Randy, being our go-to guy, walks inside the backstage door. We follow. A guard is there but was confused and let us walk on in. Inside were stairs that exited into the front of house. We slipped right in and walked up the aisle like we owned the place.

The lobby was too crowded and, again, all we wanted was a drink or two but there was a major schmooze-fest happening making it hard to navigate. Then we spotted an open bar at the far end of the packed lobby. We pushed and pulled our way through the crowd, occasionally stopping to say hello to someone we knew.

Finally, we made it to the bar. Everybody's drinking doubles except for Randy, who chose water. A couple of doubles got us tipsy, then it was time to walk downstairs to find our seats...or rather, try to find them.

We gave the tickets to a young guy who appeared to be an usher. He drew his flashlight like a light saber and showed us to our seats. All of us know how long awards shows can seem. But we had a program that listed the order of presentations. Being of good cheer and having to be in our seats in thirty minutes, everybody but Randy decided more drinks were in order. We stumble-bumble over people in our row to get to the aisle and headed back to the bar.

Drinks ordered, the chatting started. Charlie Brusco was there, so I talked to him for awhile. There were no video monitors in the bar or lobby to follow the show. We were pretty toasty but all was well until Rick Price checked his watch and hollered with alarm: We're ten minutes late! No problem, these shows run behind. We finished our drinks and headed toward our seats again.

Fumbling through the dark, every few rows someone was saying congratulations. We say Fuck that, we know that gag. We are men of the world, we've seen that one a hundred times before.

Finally seated, we got comfortable. At first our toasty brains didn't realize something was askew. Then as subtle as a flying brick we realized we'd won the award. And much to our chagrin, we look up at the stage and what did we see?

Randy DeLay. And doing a fine job accepting our major award. It's probably for the best. We were pretty toasty. Ushered backstage, stunned we'd actually won, we reunited with Randy. Drivin N Cryin were the ones who presented the award to us. The two bands were getting rounded up for a photo op when I saw my friend Rick

Diamond shooting the event. It was good to see a familiar face. We posed like drunk Rock Stars and the pics were done. Next question: Is there any liquor backstage? The simple answer was no. But we knew where we could find enough.

We made way to the limo and found whiskey, then Yogi drove us to the after-party. Total strangers made it crowded but worst of all they'd run out of liquor. So Yogi drove us back to The Cavern where we had our own party that lasted all night. I passed out on the pool table.

A loud clap of thunder jolted me awake around noon and I saw other people passed out around the room. I vaguely remembered what happened. There is nothing worse than driving home with the sun up. It's like the walk of shame but with your car. I had a hangover and knew Kim was going to be pissed.

But, man, was it ever worth it.

2006: DRIVIN N CRYIN

HELLHOUNDS

L-R⟩ ⟶
Rick Richards,
Randy Delay,
Rick Price,
Joey Huffman

COCA-COLA
AWARDS SHOW:
DRESSED IN OUR
SUNDAY BEST

1991

SINKHOLE DE MAYO

The ride up from Atlanta to Nashville was uneventful. The bus was already at the Kroger parking lot when I pulled up. I boarded and stowed my bag. Bandmates got there and stowed their stuff, too. Everybody showed up relatively on time. We're leaving earlier than usual so I fought back the inclination of drinking too early in the day. We say hi and give each other hugs. We get along great. We were like family.

Jimmy and Nathan always went to Kroger and stocked up on bus food. They got two kinds of beer, sodas, hummus, pita bread, three kinds of chips, almond milk, cookies, cereal, yogurt, peanut butter, jelly, toaster pastries, mixed nuts, bread, sandwich meat and cheese, beef jerky, breakfast bars and — every now and then — a bottle of wine.

I ran into Kroger for SlimFast and Powerade.

The bus was a Prevost. When parked, one side of the bus can slide out about eight feet. It had all the comforts of home. Wi-Fi, which worked most of the time, allowed Internet access on long rides and connection with a phone. The thing was huge with two lounges and twelve bunks with privacy curtains. Top bunks were designated as junk bunks where we stowed guitars we wanted to play on the bus, and other random shit.

Bunks also had DVD players with small fold-down screens. Never once used mine. Don't know anyone that has.

I've been asked many times how I manage to sleep in those little bunks. Ever get claustrophobic, Joey? Never had a problem. Wrapped in a blanket with curtain pulled feels like a cocoon. All I hear is the comforting, steady deep rumble of the diesel generator and sleep like a baby.

Fredericksburg, Virginia, is an eleven-hour drive from Nashville. ETA: 4:00 a.m. The special thing about this trip was we had a day off before the show and get our own rooms — beds to sleep in and some privacy.

Since we're leaving so early, we're going to pull over at eight to eat dinner somewhere. As the bus pulled away, Tony, Ricky, and Mike were in the back lounge, no doubt playing guitars. Michelle Poe, Derrek, Jimmy, and I were up in the front lounge bitching that Hank isn't doing more shows. Jimmy was doing business on his iPhone.

Later, Tony asks if I want to do a shot of whiskey with him. He'd brought a bottle of Maker's Mark from home. I acquiesced so we went to the front lounge and poured two shots each into two red Solo cups. The whiskey felt good when it hit, moving warmth from stomach to extremities. The first shot is always the best.

Time to eat. Everybody was getting ready to get off the bus, stretching. I wasn't hungry so I just had a SlimFast. To stretch my legs, I walked to Subway with Mike and Tony. Mike is one of the best steel guitar players ever and I respect him very much. We became good friends during my tenure. Tony was an awesome guitar player. He can play any Classic Rock or Country song request — and do it right. He played with such feel. We became close over my time with the band. He was my partner in crime and had each other's back.

Back on the bus, the scents of Subway sandwiches mixed with Chick-fil-A spices. Within thirty minutes everybody was finished and the bus was rolling out. Tony tried to find something to watch on the satellite but got bored. Michelle got into her pajamas and read in her bunk. Jimmy went to bed and Mike and Ricky headed to the back lounge. Derrek sat at the table working on his MacBook.

Tony says It's just you and me. Wanna drink some whiskey?

Damn straight!

Tony poured shots. I got a diet cola for chaser. Cheers!

Then Tony poured two more. We cannonballed those. Tony poured another, then Derrek showed interest in having a shot with us. Tony poured Derrek a stiff shot and we downed them in unison.

Derrek is a phenomenal drummer. He's played with everybody and does lots of recording sessions. And though I hadn't known him for that long (he joined the band the year before) I considered him a good friend. Funny and laid back yet a monster onstage. I consider myself lucky to play with him.

Tony poured another round of sipping shots as he called these. I, in a glowing buzz, and Tony talked music, with Derrek putting in his two cents every once in a while until he went to bed. We sipped whiskey and talked until midnight when I called it a night. Tony asked if I wanted to do one more. That'd be an affirmative. Only a quarter of the bottle was left. He poured one each. We threw the shots down our throats; I chased with diet cola and took four preemptive ibuprofens to keep from being too hung over in the morning.

Walking back to my bunk, I was a little tipsy and kept bumping from side to side in the hall. I got to my bunk and did what I called the Stop, Drop, and Roll method of entering. Because I drank too much, I didn't take my meds and fell straight to sleep.

The bus rolled up to the Hilton Garden Inn right on time. Still inebriated, I struggled with luggage but finally made it to the room. I woke mid-morning, still face down, having trouble remembering where I was, but it came after a few seconds. Time for a SlimFast breakfast so off to the bus I went to get it.

Back in the lobby, the concierge says the food at the Mexican restaurant was excellent. Five stars. So that pretty much dictated what I was doing for dinner.

I threw extra SlimFasts in the room fridge, scooped up my MacBook Pro and external Thunderbolt drive, set them on the desk, wired it all up, and turned it on. It only took fifteen seconds to boot since I replaced the internal drive with an SSD hard drive. I typed in my password and the screen came alive.

Quick call to the front desk got the hotel's Wi-Fi password and I logged on to check and answer emails and Facebook messages. I can blow an entire afternoon searching for gear. An eBay and Reverb search for deals on vintage studio equipment, mics, and amps lasted until 3:00 p.m. Time then to make business calls, call home to check in and…done!

Time to call Izzy, a backline tech on the tour. Now, Izzy and I immediately connected when we met. Though he's a lot younger, he has an old soul. We have the same taste in music and the same sense of humor. He's a talented songwriter, guitar player, bass player, and owns his own vintage guitar business. He only comes on tour with Hank to get a vacation.

Izzy picked up the phone and says Whazzup?

I say Fuck off!

Back and forth we insult each other. It's just this fun thing that we do. I told him the concierge says Nuevo Laredo Cantina is five stars and a plan's made for dinner. Some Forensic Files and one good nap later, I logged onto Facebook for some mindless browsing and twenty minutes flew right by until it was time to meet Izzy in the lobby.

The cantina's lighting was dim, giving it an intimate vibe. It was decorated in a tasteful Mexican motif. A mariachi band entertained patrons at their tables.

After ordering drinks, I excused myself to go to the restroom, then sneaked around to find our server. Told her it was Izzy's birthday. Can they do something special for him? Why yes, they can. I walked back to the booth and innocently scrutinized the massive menu. Izzy didn't know what he was going to order either. I ordered the Number 38 Combo and Izzy the Fajitas.

We sat in silence for a moment when Izzy said he was going to tell them it was my birthday. I said he didn't have the balls to do it. He said he did. Then he said maybe he'd do it next time. It was all I could do to keep a straight face. This was going to be so funny since

I'd already told them it was Izzy's birthday. Was he ever going to be pissed off.

At that moment Izzy sees Michelle Poe, our bass player, at the door. He waves her over. She hadn't heard from anybody and decided to come here to see if she saw someone she knew. We invited her to sit with us.

Michelle joined the band the same time I did. She's an excellent musician, singer, and songwriter. She and her partner had a band called Burns & Poe. Michelle felt like my younger sister. I'd get protective over her if things got weird. I enjoy playing with her and am happy to call her Friend.

We told the server Michelle was joining us. The server came right back with Michelle's margarita and a menu. While Michelle decided on food, Izzy and I chatted and tried to outdrink each other. I said she and I must look like a couple taking their son out for dinner. Michelle didn't think that was funny.

Number 38 Combo, Fajitas, and Michelle's salad arrived. The food was excellent and smelled of exotic spices and meat. The portions were so big. We barely talked and occasionally made yummy sounds. Still, we needed to-go boxes there was so much.

We were relaxing and digesting when the mariachi band approached asking for the birthday boy. I pointed and said Birthday boy's name is Izzy, and somebody puts a purple sombrero on him and says he had to wear it. Tradition! they said and played Happy Birthday. Izzy turned red and looked like he's going to kill me. Everybody's looking at our booth trying to figure out what was going on because Michelle and I were laughing way too hard.

The band finished their version of *Feliz Cumpleaños* and began serenading him in Spanish with a traditional Mexican folk song which seemed to go on forever. Izzy gave a little smile. Payback's a motherfucker, he mouthed. I keep laughing.

When the band finally finished that song, the musician wondered if we wanted a song for the pretty lady? Nah, don't waste your time, we're divorced and she's a fucking bitch. Michelle screamed *Joey!* really loud and punched me hard in the arm. Ow! I grabbed my arm where she hit me and rubbed it. See what I mean, I told the band.

The band didn't know what to do and silently stared. Izzy was laughing now, too. Michelle finally did the diplomatic thing and put them out of their misery: Thank you, you did a wonderful job, thank you very much.

They backed up slowly, turned, and walked off in a hurry.

Michelle said I was being mean. I apologized and she calmed down. Izzy knew I'd one-upped him and raised his glass to toast me. We clinked glasses and killed what was left.

Our server came up and asked us if everything was alright. It was and we asked for to-go boxes. Izzy and I were drinking yet another double and I was starting to feel it.

When our server came back with the to-go boxes I asked for the check. It's the least I can do having embarrassed them. We put our leftovers in the boxes, Michelle thanked me for the dinner saying it had been an interesting evening to say the least, and left. Izzy says You motherfucker, but he had a smile on his face.

Izzy and I stayed and drank until last call. We were pretty drunk. I paid the drinks tab. Had to catch our balance when we stood and slurred Izzy, what a night to be gloriously drunk! He concurred. We staggered out of the cantina to the hotel, holding each other up. Inside the lobby we said goodbye. Phrases like I love you, man and That was awesome were heard in the lobby. When the elevator doors opened, we fell inside. I made it to my bed and fell face first on it. Passed right out. Didn't even turn out the lights.

2013: The Hank Williams Band

Keith Richards Chronicles 2

1992

Dates, Venues, Cities, Countries

11/27	K.B. Hallen, Copenhagen, Denmark
11/29	Sporthalle, Cologne, Germany
12/02	Marquee Club, London, England
12/04	Rotterdam Ahoy, Netherlands
12/07	Zénith Paris, France
12/9-10	Sala Zeleste, Barcelona, Spain
12/13-14	Aqualung, Madrid, Spain
12/17-18	Town & Country Club, London, England

KEITH RICHARDS CHRONICLES — 2 OF 4

My friend Kiera called one day at the end of October 1992, very excited: My boyfriend is looking for a piano player that plays like Nicky Hopkins. I told him about you. He wants to fly you to New York. You'd be perfect! I gave him your number and he's going to call you.

Later that day Pierre de Beauport calls and we talk and hit it off. He'd pay for my ticket, and I'd stay in his apartment. The plane landed at LaGuardia, where he met me at the gate.

Pierre had a nice home studio with a Neve broadcasting console. And he'd rented a Kurzweil PC88 from SIR. I decompressed for a couple of hours, then started to jam. His tunes were good and precisely in my wheelhouse. We played for a couple of hours and then got something to eat at Papaya King on the corner of 86th Street and 3rd Avenue. They make the best hotdogs in New York.

Pierre was Keith Richards' guitar tech. I told him I did Keith's first tour in 1988. What a coincidence. He said The X-Pensive Winos were releasing a new record and rehearsing at The Black Box and we'd go to rehearsal at nine-ish-ish, that is to say Rock & Roll Time.

The first person I see is Tony Russell, still tour manager. He gave me a hug, asked where I'd been, and said they've had been trying to get in touch. Hired on the spot, I was about to go on another exciting adventure. Tony took me to see Keith. He remembered me and, cigarette dangling from mouth, gave me a hug, too. Tony told him about the rehire. Wonderful, he says in that raspy voice.

Tony took me to Ivan's keyboard rig. It was all thrown together. I say You should rent my equipment. I was familiar with it and had a lot of rack sound modules that could create any sound. I got the organ from Keyboard Specialist. I knew Paul, the owner, and knew he'd hook me up.

I greeted everyone; they were happy to see me. The rehearsal followed their normal routine. Ron Wood stopped by and when I gave him some compliments, he shyly and humbly said Thanks. The rehearsal went good but I can tell that Ivan was uncomfortable. He didn't have the right sounds for the songs.

The first thing to do was fly home and tell my wife I had another gig but this time I'd be gone for four months. Knowing we needed the money, she accepted it calmly and was even happy. I packed equipment and overnighted it to New York by Rock-It Cargo. I'd be back to NYC in a couple of days. I needed more time with family: Kim, Whitney, and by now little Jojo. I hated leaving them.

Back in New York my racks full of gear were waiting. I got a song list and talked to Steve Jordan about what sounds we needed on which songs. This gave me something to do for the next couple of days. Plus, I had a copy of the new record for reference. I put together a proper rig for Ivan, getting the right sounds for him at the right time. I spent a lot of time listening to the album and tweaking the sounds. In two days it was up and operational.

We rehearsed and tweaked more at The Black Box for five days. On November 23rd, we and the equipment traveled to Copenhagen, Denmark, setting up at K.B. Hallen, the venue of the first show of the European tour.

Rehearsals went smooth; the band had a fire lit under them. Three days went by like that. On November 26, 1992, Keith had Catering prepare a Thanksgiving dinner for us. That was very sweet of him. It was a big affair and we enjoyed it very much. It added a little home to a faraway place. Not that Copenhagen was like a foreign land. It's very cosmopolitan, like New York City but without the grime. Plus, Danes love Americans and love to party.

The band and crew had a lot of nervous energy the night of the first show. But on the first downbeat everything felt normal. There were a couple of equipment glitches but the band played great. After the show the band and crew assembled in the hotel bar for a few drinks. The mood was jovial.

The method of transportation on this leg of the tour was commercial airlines. We'd fly to the next city the day after a show and spend off days there. We almost always had two to three days off between shows.

Mostly at first, I hung out with Pierre but very soon became friends with the rest of the crew: Anthony Aquilato, drum tech, and David Rule, the other guitar and bass tech. They were a great bunch of guys. To this day I consider them all friends.

I also was becoming close with Chris Wade-Evans, monitor mixer, and Benji Lefevre, front of house engineer who was Led Zeppelin's sound man back in the day. He had a rich history in the business. I felt like I belonged because I had mates to hang out with in hotel bars after every show. We were a close-knit group.

The tour was a blast. Playing the Marquee Club was special, too. The Stones used to play there regularly in the early days. So did Jimi Hendrix, The Who, The Kinks, and a lot of others. It was the place to play in the 1960s.

While we're loading in, we had to cross the street. I went to step off the curb but Pierre grabs me by the shoulder and yanks me back just in time. You see, I'd forgotten we were in London and that traffic came from the opposite direction than in the U.S. I'd looked the wrong way before stepping off the curb where a red double-decker bus was roaring by. Pierre saved my life and that is no exaggeration.

Mick Jagger was at that show and sat in the balcony, but he left when Keith started Gimme Shelter. Perhaps he'd heard that one before?

After the first show in Barcelona, we were invited to a bar that had a shrine built in honor of Jack Daniel's. That night I drank a lot of absinthes, the real stuff, not the weak shit you get in the U.S. Before going to the hotel, to those buying me absinthe, I promised them entry into the show the next night and caught a cab to the hotel.

I passed out at four. Three and a half hours later the phone rang and I yelled What are you doing calling me at 7:30 in the morning? But it wasn't morning, it was 7:30 at night. Shit! I missed lobby call.

I panic and bolt out of the room. Had the concierge call a cab and arrived at the venue around eight. Most everyone was in Catering. I walk in fully expecting a reprimand. But I didn't get in trouble. Instead, they say my punishment is to buy everyone a forty-dollar glass of Port in the hotel bar after the show. I was relieved, but I could kiss my per diem goodbye.

By the time we got to London again we're ready for a break. We only had two shows left to do at The Town & Country Club before we returned to New York. The stage was small, but we made it work. The band played well and Keith, as always, was spot on. We left Gatwick and headed stateside.

When I'm in New York, The Mayflower Hotel is always home. I stayed there so much I started to learn names of the staff. For a couple of days I handled equipment issues then flew home on the 22nd for a nice but short Christmas. It was good to be home for a little while. I got to have some quality alone-time with Kim and see the joy Whitney and Jojo experienced when they saw what Santa brought them.

I stuck around until the 27th then flew to Chicago to film a segment for the VH-1 series Center Stage on December 28 at the studios of WTTW-TV. It was a typical television situation: Run through songs over and over to block camera angles. Being there from eight in the morning until midnight made it a long and exhausting day, but the band had a lot of patience with the process and the performance was great.

We flew back to New York the next day. Keith had a longtime friend called Freddie Sessler, now deceased, who supplied the best drugs available. Upon meeting Keith, Freddie gave him a gift of one ounce of Merck prescription cocaine in a sealed bottle. So it was only natural that when we got back to the States the tour was offered service from Freddie: One gram of almost pure cocaine, hermetically sealed in a plastic package, for fifty dollars. There was no shortage in that supply chain. This kept us from going out to the streets and taking the chance of being rousted.

With three days off until the next show on New Year's Eve at The Academy in New York City featuring special guests Robert Cray and members of Pearl Jam, I scored some blow and used it on my days off. There was nothing better to do. I got high and made felony phone calls and crashed and ordered room service. I'd meet colleagues at the bar in the evening and drink to balance out the effect of the cocaine. I often hung out with Benji and Chris. Tony Russell showed up, too. We had a riot in that bar.

Keith Richards Chronicles 3

1993
Dates, Venues,
Cities, Countries

01/17 Paramount Theater, Seattle, Washington
01/19 The Orpheum, Vancouver, Canada
01/21 Civic Center, San Francisco, California
01/23 Universal Amphitheatre, Los Angeles
01/24 Bally's Events Center, Las Vegas, Nevada
01/26 Golden Hall, San Diego, California
01/28 America West Arena, Phoenix, Arizona
01/31 Denver Auditorium Theater, Colorado
02/02 The Legendary Roy Wilkins Auditorium, St. Paul, Minneapolis
02/04 Aragon Ballroom, Chicago, Illinois
02/06 Massey Hall, Toronto, Canada
02/08 Fox Theatre, Detroit, Michigan
02/10 Constitution Hall, Washington, D.C.
02/13-14 Orpheum Theatre, Boston, Massachusetts
02/16-17 Tower Theatre, Philadelphia, Pennsylvania
02/19-20, 22-24 Beacon Theatre, New York, New York

KEITH RICHARDS CHRONICLES — 3 OF 4

The New Year's Eve show came and went. We were now going to set up camp at SIR on 52nd Street and rehearse for the American leg of the tour. We loaded into SIR straight from the show at The Academy and were looking at a few needed days off before rehearsals. Kim and I were fussing about something and, not wanting to go home to that, I stayed in New York. More likely, though — and sad to say — the cocaine was whispering in my ear Don't go home, stay with me, we'll have a great time.

The crew reported to SIR for rehearsals on January 5th. We methodically unpacked the backline and set it up. Sound and Lighting had started the day before us and set up the monitors, front of house, and lights.

Kim flew up from Atlanta to spend a few days. She came to rehearsal one day and was sitting on a couch next to Keith and a couple of other band members smoking a joint. Later she asked where Keith was. I tell her she'd just sat with him on the couch while they got high. She blushed. She didn't know.

Kim had a good time in New York during her three-day stay. It was her first time there. She went sightseeing, mostly by herself. We saw each other when we could, but it was hard: SIR at noon until four in the morning because we never knew when the band would show up and had to be ready when they did.

Ten days and rehearsals went well. We were ready to fly to Seattle to start the tour. Gear was packed and put on trucks immediately heading to Seattle. It would be a real bummer if we arrived in Seattle and there was no equipment.

January 15th: The crew flew to Seattle where the band hit the stage and played a furious set. Keith had a new opener for the

American leg of the tour I'd never heard of. Soul Asylum was from Minneapolis and had a unique sound. I stood at the side of the stage and listened to the entire set. They were good.

The merchandise guy on the tour was Jim Sullivan; everyone called him Sully. Jim worked for Brockum Merchandising. He introduced himself saying we had mutual acquaintances. He'd worked with The Georgia Satellites for their first three records. Outgoing and energetic, Sully was from Rhode Island, had a heavy New England accent, and knew practically everybody. He can tell stories for days. I liked him immediately and we became good friends.

January 21st: Soul Asylum had to miss a date on the tour to go play the Presidential Inaugural Ball. Izzy Stradlin opened the San Francisco show. My good friend Rick Richards was playing guitar with him. I had him ask Izzy if I could sit in with the band on that show. That was okay with Izzy.

So, the night before the show I took a taxi from the hotel to SIR San Francisco to rehearse with Izzy's band. It went pretty good but I lived with the record for the next twenty-four hours. The night of the show I took off my black backline tech shirt and put on a blue button-down shirt, untucked. We took the stage at eight and rocked for forty-five minutes. It's easy to play with the band because I used the same keyboards I'd set up for Ivan. They were already dialed in. It felt good to play with a band again.

After Izzy's set, I changed shirts and did my Keith gig. Then it was pack up and load. The tour was chugging along. Everything was great. The band, the crew…

The red wine and drugs…

Whew.

On overnight bus rides, Benji, Chris, and I used to commandeer the back lounge and drink so much Merlot our lips and tongues stained purple. There's an endless supply of wine and blow, but we always had a day off after a bus ride so knew we'd have time to recover.

Tony pulled me aside for a chat: I was not to feel obligated to keep up with those two; people have died from trying. That warning went in one ear and out the other.

Every day the tour was getting shorter and would soon be a memory. In Philadelphia, Sully quietly had a talk with me. He'd been talking me up to Soul Asylum. They'd been looking for a B3 player to do Saturday Night Live with them, so they wanted me to come to their next soundcheck and play on Runaway Train and Black Gold. I'd heard them play these songs all tour and pretty much knew the chord changes. Sully gave me a CD of their new record and I went to the bus and listened to it.

I hung around at Soul Asylum's soundcheck and waited to play with them. I hadn't even officially met them and here I was, playing with them. Everything went well. They finished soundcheck and Dave Pirner spoke to Sully: They wanted me to play with them on those songs tonight. I say that's cool but sooner rather than later they're going to have to talk to me.

I played with Soul Asylum every night for the rest of the tour. It gave me a boost like better things were on the horizon. Their manager, Danny Heaps, asked if I wanted to play Saturday Night Live with them. I named a price and they agreed. I asked Sully what his cut was and he says nothing. All I had to do was wear a Brockum baseball jersey live on TV. He even slipped me five hundred to do it.

The tour ended with a bang: Five nights in NYC at the Beacon Theatre. It's an exciting time. By this time Soul Asylum was actually talking to me. We'd hang out in the bar at The Mayflower and close it down. It didn't seem like the tour was ending so much as we were moving on to new things.

I had to stay a day after the last show and sort through equipment and classify it, store things where they belonged, and ship them where they needed to go. That was boring but I was excited by the future so the time seemed to fly by.

Going to see my wife and kids soon! I can't wait. I was so excited. I flew to Atlanta, grabbed a cab home, and surprised Kim.

We got the kids together and went out for Mexican. We finished dinner, went home, put the kids to bed, and fell asleep on the couch watching TV.

The next day Izzy was playing The Center Stage in Atlanta. I was invited to come down and play the set with them. I called Kenny Cresswell and had him deliver my B3 and piano to the venue. I don't remember why Kim didn't come to the show. I think it was a weekend and she had to work.

But I had this funny feeling and got to wondering. So, before I went to the venue I threw my suitcase in the car. The show was sold out and it was a great show. Right after it ended, I got called into the production office and, just as I suspected, got offered a job. Izzy asked how much I needed to finish the tour with them. I threw out a figure after taxes and everyone thought it fair. My only issue was that I needed time off to play Saturday Night Live with Soul Asylum. Izzy agreed. I didn't even go back home. I just jumped on the tour bus after the show and rode overnight to Memphis.

I'd only been home one day and was already going on tour again. Kim was pissed.

She'd barely seen me in four months and was at home alone with the kids and needing a break. But my career was starting to happen. I chose it over my family. One dreams of being a Rock Star with a capital R and S and will do anything it takes to make it happen. It may not have been fair, but it was real.

The X-pensive Winos Tour fast-tracked my career. They had two opening acts and I ended up playing with both. It was definitely my time...but hindsight is 20/20. You can look back and connect the dots and see why things happened the way they did. One phone call from a friend turned into my moment in the sun.

SOUL ASYLUM AND SATURDAY NIGHT LIVE

How all of this applies to the band is that there's going to be an excessive amount of waiting around. This will eventually lead to drinking. Performing with Soul Asylum on Saturday Night Live in 1993 was also one of the highlights of my career. NBC protocol and schedule for the show was as follows:

- Arrive at NBC.
- Go through the lobby to the elevators where there's a security checkpoint.
- Get searched.
- Get assigned an NBC page to be your minder for the day.
- Tuesday and Wednesday: Blocking camera angles, skit rehearsal, and musical guest run-through.
- Thursday: Day off.
- Friday: Practice run-through of the show and trim sketches that aren't working.
- Saturday: Fine-tune the show. Another show run-through.
- Saturday, around 7:30 p.m.: Let audience in.
- Saturday, 8:00 p.m.: Tape a dress rehearsal with an audience to act as a safety in case something goes wrong when you go live. It's on a tape delay so if someone says fuck on-air they switch to the safety and everything is okay.
- After run-through: Turn the audience and go live at 11:30 p.m.

- Remember: Don't fuck up. There are only ten million people watching.

Tuesday: They like to have you on the stage in the spot you're going to be standing for what seems like hours. Nothing seems to be happening but they're adjusting lights and blocking camera angles. You can't play your instrument because it impedes the crew's ability to hear each other. After this comes soundcheck. Check all lines. Make sure they're working for someone you can't see because the control room is on another floor. Eventually you get to play your songs.

And play them…

And play them…

Aaaand…playyyyy…theeeeeeemmmmm…

Then you do it with a cue like the host is introducing you. Finally, you're free to hang out. Don't wander too far from your designated area or minders will be forced to come get you. Apparently one must stay with the herd. Minders are like border collies herding the straying back into formation. There is a TV in every room to see what's happening on set. Sometimes it's just carpenters building. Sometimes it's a cast member rehearsing. Sometimes it's just nothing. They keep you around from noon until nine or ten o'clock. Then they search for you again and make sure you get off the elevator and leave. Limo back to the hotel and boom!, free to do as you please.

Wednesday: Carbon copy of Tuesday except you get to play a little more. Dinner is deli delivery…turkey sandwich…yum.

Thursday: Much-needed day off.

Friday: Show starts to resemble what you'd see in the live broadcast. We did three run-throughs around two hours in length. They still need to cut thirty minutes from the show. They went about with more fine-tuning and we sat around a lot. Yeah, Baby! I met Mike Myers. That was kind of cool. Miranda Richardson was the host that week. I didn't see a lot of her. Some of the skits were pretty funny.

I'm beginning to realize that I'm playing SNL and getting nervous.

Saturday – Day of the Show: We bring clothes for dress rehearsal. We do one dress rehearsal as if it was the live show. In the show the band played twice. The show's pace seems better. We have to go to makeup for the Safety Run. They are letting in the first audience. We're a little nervous. Our first song is twenty minutes into the show. We watch the show on the monitor in our dressing room. Miranda comes out and does her monologue. We watch a few skits and then it's time for us. We go to the stage in the time it takes to run the commercials. The light comes on to signify we're back live. Miranda introduces us and we break into Somebody To Shove.

Once I got up, thinking only of my parts and doing them, then it wasn't so scary. Before I knew it, it's over and we're back in our dressing room feeling good. High-fives all around. Now we wait until the next song. We're looser and at ease now we have one under our belts. Time flies by and it's back out to do Black Gold.

We nail it.

We now wait for the audience to turn and 11:30 p.m. to arrive. Not as nervous as before. Time's flying by. We go back to makeup and get touched up. I'm back in the dressing room ready to play. Then the show starts: This time for real. We hear the band kick out the theme song and Don Pardo introducing Miranda. She does her monologue. The crowd is with her. They seem to be into it more than the earlier audience.

Time flies and time to play!

We rush to the stage and take our places.

We're back live…

Ladies and Gentlemen…

Soul Asylum!

We're on! Live in front of 10 million people. What a rush! The crowd is into us. Song is over. We're herded back to the dressing room tooooooooo…

…Wait again.

But hey, by now we're old pros at this. Weekend Update. Another two or three skits and we rush to the stage to take our places.

We're back live...

Ladies and Gentlemen, once again...

Soul Asylum!

We break into Black Gold. I almost felt high. We fly through that song and it's back to the dressing room to party. While they roll credits the only thing left to do is stand on the stage like Rock Stars — which we nailed, too.

All in all it was a fantastic experience. Off to a club closed for the private party where a good time was had but the band pretty much hung together at our own table. We went to an Irish pub after that. Danny Murphy said I did a good job. Then he asked what I was doing this summer. I say Playing with you. We laughed. He explained they had a few shows to do without a keyboard player but they were doing the Alternative Nation tour with the Spin Doctors starting in June and that's when they wanted me to start. I was ecstatic. I learned a lesson in the way life works from my experience of the past year.

For instance: I thought Rick Richards going to play with Izzy was bad luck for me.

For instance: I had to be a tech again after playing in three bands.

For instance: I thought I was taking a step back but was actually taking two forward.

For instance: When God closes one door on you, He opens another. You just have to have faith and believe in the power of positive thinking. I'm living proof of that adage. But it isn't always easy. I will tell you about that later.

1994: JOEY, MICK JAGGER, BILLY PITTS, PHIL HADAWAY AT CASINO STUDIOS

SPRING BREAK

This is a slice of my life being a father, husband, musician — and drug addict. This story is circa 1994. My family had a trip planned for Spring Break that year.

I was conflicted. The dad in me wanted to participate but the addict wanted none of it. I mulled it over and justified not going to the point where I considered myself not only right but doing my duty to stay home and defile myself.

Sure, I told myself, I'd write, record, practice, and do business. But that's only fooling myself — okay, call it what it was: Lying — into doing a very selfish thing. I was going to do Flaking Out 101 and pick a fight with my wife right before we're supposed to leave for the airport. It doesn't matter what the argument was to be about as long as it could be used to say I'm not traveling with you, bitch, and I hope you never come back.

Oh, yes, I had a plan.

The night before we're to depart for the beach I was playing bass at a record company showcase with a band I'd produced. I was doing methamphetamine and drinking shots of Jim Beam, feeling no pain very fast.

The show came off without a hitch. The band and I were confident we sounded great. While we're busy patting ourselves on our collective backs, a record company A&R man slips up and says he loved the show. I thought, good. Maybe this band will get signed and I'll produce their record and get rich and famous.

We sat down to talk. He started talking bullshit about how he liked the band but he had to hear more songs. He didn't hear a single, he said, and a single translates to the band having to do more demos...but the record company wasn't going to pay for it.

We chatted at the table for a bit more, then the subject of strip clubs came up. I tried to talk more business but the conversation kept coming back around to strippers. They had heard about Atlanta having some of the finest strip clubs in the world, which was true — well, at least at the time.

I started to see the rest of my night was going to be babysitting these record company assholes from Texas at a strip club. I chose Tattletales because it was close and one of the more tasteful strip clubs in town. We grabbed a cab and set off on our great adventure.

We arrived at Tattletales. They head directly to the stage and take a prime viewing position. They were more than eager to stick dollar bills into garter belts and thongs. I hung back at the bar with my back to the stage. I didn't want to be part of the entertainment so I just drank more Jim Beam. Every now and then a dancer offered a lap dance, but I decline.

I was thinking about how staying out all night before the family vacation would really piss Kim off and she'd say How dare you come home in the morning drunk, high, and too impaired to drive? This plan was coming together easier than I thought. I couldn't have written it any better.

After about an hour one of the record execs asks if I can score some blow. I'd check it out, I say, and ask the bartender who directs me to a Latino guy in the kitchen.

I bought a gram for eighty dollars. They can always get more if they wanted it. I gave the packet to the record guy and we all went to the bathroom together — nothing conspicuous about that! — and huddle inside a stall passing the bundle of blow around and doing bumps with a car key. When everyone was finished, we look in the mirror for VCR — Visual Cocaine Residue. Once presentable, we made way back out to the main room. They go to the stage, I to the bar.

We carried on like that for a few hours. Then as dawn was breaking we called it quits and staggered out of Tattletales like a bunch of hobos. Somebody called us a cab to take the record guys to their hotel and twenty minutes later drop me at my car.

Too impaired to drive, I proceeded to do just that. Got home, ready to face the music of my own making. Which is what I did, reasoning that I deserved a week alone to do what I wanted without having to answer to anyone. Which is quite ironic because I didn't answer to anyone anyway. Talk about illogical logic fueled by delusional thinking. Still, I'd have the house to myself and nothing to interrupt the rendezvous drugs and I were going to enjoy.

So, I got home around seven that morning and let the argument proceed. Kim and I were battling it out the minute I walked through the door — just as I'd planned.

I was indignant. Said there was no way I was going anywhere with her.

She says she's had enough! Says she didn't want to be around me at all.

Now all I need do was to drive my family to the airport and I'd be free. FREE! Free-free-FREE!

Kim screamed the entire way to the airport giving me a headache and a very foul mood. I'm not saying I didn't deserve it; just stating the facts as they happened. I finally drop them off at departures and drive off into the sunrise. To calm down, I turn on 99X. Remember when they weren't corporately programmed? Those were good ol' days.

Anyway, I hear a few songs and then this particular song comes pouring out of the radio. I really liked it. It had B3 organ on the track and it rocked. I started listening more closely. I was grooving along and really into the organ part when it occurred to me that there was something peculiar with it. Hey, that's what I would play. I started getting worked up. Then there was a riff that's one of my signature licks. Now I got angry. This guy is ripping me off. The song unfolded and it seemed like this upstart kid had studied me. By the end of the song I was furious.

Then the DJ announced it was the Vigilantes of Love with their new single Struggleville. I was shocked. That was me playing the organ on the track. I'd recorded it over nine months prior and had utterly forgotten about it. I felt like such an asshole. I was embarrassed for myself.

It's time to cut back on the dope and whiskey, I thought — at least, for a moment this delusional, self-absorbed, asshole musician did think that. But you see, I didn't expect the guilt factor and that ruined my so-called vacation. To this day I still feel guilty about what I did to Kim and the kids.

SOUTH AMERICA

On a lovely spring-like day in early March of 1994, I was frustrated. I always got frustrated when I put off packing for a tour until the last minute. This time we'd be away from home for two months, so packing was most intense as I tried to get it all to fit in one suitcase and a carry-on.

I'd been washing clothes all morning and trying not to forget anything. I only needed to pack one pair of shoes — my running shoes; mostly I'd wear Doc Martens. Had to make sure I didn't forget my shaving kit, shampoo, and conditioner.

An early-evening flight to Miami and I'd meet up with the band to catch a flight to São Paulo, Brazil, then a connection to our final destination — Buenos Aries, Argentina, where Soul Asylum was kicking off the first leg of our tour opening for INXS.

The town car from Rock & Roll Express was to be at my doorstep at 3:00 p.m. Panicking because I hadn't even showered, the open suitcase still had piles of clothes scattered around it. Somehow, I was going to fit all that in.

Shower done, toiletries went on the bed next to the suitcase, and I dressed. Earlier that morning I bought two eight-packs of socks from Target. I mostly packed flannel shirts, black T-shirts, and two pairs of jeans.

Passport and plane ticket? Check. Phone card and a couple of credit cards? Check. Carry-on bag with stuff and magazines, book A Son of the Circus by John Irving, CD case and player, Xanax bars and Phentermine pills? Check and check and check and check again and I was officially packed.

It's 2:30. I had thirty minutes to just sit on the couch and relax with Kim. But you know what? I couldn't wait to get to the airport, check in, and hit a bar.

Too soon the Rock & Roll Express town car rolled up and it was time to leave my wife and kids. I hugged and kissed them as the driver loaded luggage. Then off to the car waving goodbye on the way. The driver opened the door for this Accidental Rock Star and in that guy went.

Half hour later I checked in, cleared security, and found my gate. The plane wouldn't start boarding for at least an hour. Finally, I can go to the nearest bar, order a double Absolut and cranberry, empty it, and two minutes later order another double. And another…and one more for the skyroad. Headed to the gate, where they start loading just as I get there. I was a Medallion member, so boarded at my leisure.

The two-hour flight was uneventful. It took thirty minutes to make the trek to the International gates where I'd hang out and wait for the band. Finally saw tour manager Bill Sullivan and waved him over. We hugged and exchanged hellos. One by one the rest of the band and crew showed up: Dave Pirner, Danny Murphy, Karl Mueller, Grant Young, a/k/a the band, and crew Dave Bruster, Eric Pierson, and Brendan.

The first order of business after Bill got a headcount was to find another bar. With a four-hour layover, we had ample time to get hammered and obnoxious. Time flew by as we drank and got caught up. Bill Sullivan announces it's time to board so, tabs paid, we wandered to the gate where, flying business class, we got to board almost right away. (International business class is like domestic first class.) The aircraft was a 747. Business class was upstairs where they used to have discos during the Seventies. It's nice to be separated in our own little cabin.

Now airborne, the drink service started. I was already toasty and didn't want another, so just ordered a diet cola. Bill, in the seat next to me, ordered a beer.

The flight from Miami to São Paulo was seven hours. I dug a Xanax bar out and chased it with diet cola. Planning to get sleep while I could, I didn't even make it to dinner service. I was out like a light, only waking on final approach. The flight attendants came through collecting trash and making sure seats were in the upright position. The seatbelt sign was on. I had to use the lavatory, but was strapped in until we landed when a restroom was my first call. We had a five-hour layover. Landing at 1:00 a.m. meant bars and restaurants were all closed. So was money exchange. All we can do is find our gate, lay on the floor, and try to sleep. I took another Xanax and slept.

Bill woke me at 4:30 a.m. just as the airport was coming to life. Gate attendants set up desks. I heard a vacuum cleaner in the distance. We had boarding passes, so no need to check in. Attendants began boarding an hour later. Our seats were at the very front. Danny (Murph), in the aisle seat, was next to me. I had the view. All of us were eagerly anticipating coffee and breakfast. It seemed like it took forever to get airborne, but soon the seatbelt sign went off and we were free to walk through the cabin. Breakfast service was starting as well.

In business class the breakfast menu was as follows: An omelet with cheese, bacon or sausage, toast, orange juice, and coffee, which is what I had. Or if one preferred, one could get the continental breakfast of coffee and bread, butter, and jam.

After eating, I went on walkabout to the lavatory. Back at my seat, I dug out the Phentermine, shook a capsule into my hand, and took it with orange juice. Being the libertine that Murph was, he was not going to let me speed alone. He asked for one and I gave it to him with a Have a nice ride. Forty-five minutes later I'm feeling the Phentermine. Murph says he's feeling pretty good, too. A little over two hours later we're making descent into Buenos Aries and through customs without incident.

Outside in the main terminal, the promoter was there to meet us. Introductions made, we boarded a bus, and off to the Sheraton in downtown Buenos Aires we went. After checking in, I find my room and face-planted onto the bed where it took me five minutes to get going. We were free until noon the next day, so I went to find a place to jog, see the moneychangers, and sightsee.

First, I felt like I had to get in a good workout. I looked out of the window but didn't see a jogging trail. Saw a sidewalk and figured that's as good a trail as any. Dressed in workout clothes, I headed out, then ran until that sidewalk came to an end, made a U-turn then a right and ran until I noticed what I thought were apartment buildings. I continued to follow the sidewalk that went straight on to an incredibly stout gate. I keep going. Suddenly, soldiers poured out of the guardhouse, every one of them pointing an AK-47 straight at me, and screaming —

Alto! Alto!

I don't care what language you speak, pointed guns and soldiers screaming Stop! Stop! can be understood by everybody. Around I turn on a dime and take off. Lucky for me they liked that and never fired or made chase. I stopped around the corner then took off for the hotel like a rabbit on legs still shaking by the time I was waiting for the shower to get hot. Finally calmed, I dressed in ripped jeans, a black T-shirt, socks, and Doc Martens when the phone rang. Bill Sullivan had my laminate and per diem. I was to come get them. Grabbed wallet, passport, and room key and went to Bill's room.

Did Bill want to go out later and see the sights? He would, but must make phone calls first. Said to call him later. I took the elevator to the lobby and went to the front desk to exchange money. The line was short. While waiting, I saw Dave and Karl at the bar.

It's my turn to exchange U.S. dollars into Argentinian pesos. The clerk asked for my room number and passport, then wrote my name and passport number on the transaction form. I handed her a hundred. She put it in a cash drawer, had me sign the transaction form, and handed over 11,291.50 ARS in varying paper denominations and change.

Putting away the money, I thanked her and headed for the bar where a seat was open beside Dave. I ordered a double Absolut and cranberry and we shot the shit for a bit. They were thinking about going out, finding a place to eat lunch, and exploring the city.

Soon the concierge was asking what kind of cuisine we were looking for. Karl told him local. He knew a good place not too far away, gave us directions, and out the sliding doors we went. This part of the city was known as the Almagro Barrio, the best neighborhood for the arts and music. Bars, clubs, cutting-edge arts venues, cultural centers, theaters, and restaurants went up and down the cobblestoned street as far as I can see.

We were looking for a café called Las Violetas about a quarter mile up the street on the right. We soon found it and got seated at an outside table. The waiter immediately came with menus and soon reappeared with Absolut and cranberry times three. We asked what the natives ate. Empanadas, pastries filled with beef or ham and cheese, he says. We ordered some of each.

The day's lovely. Slight breeze. Mild temps. Buenos Aries is south of the equator which meant that, unlike Atlanta now transitioning from Winter to Spring, Buenos Aries was transitioning from Summer to Fall. The food arrived and smelled and looked awesome. We had some of everything and it tasted great — was satisfying, not too heavy. We ate all of it, ordered another round of drinks, and sat on the patio basking in the glow. Then off for a walk, just taking in everything.

After World War II, and sympathetic to the Nazi cause, a lot of war criminals and other Germans sought refuge in Argentina. It's a historical fact. One thing I noticed was an inordinate number of blonde-haired, blue-eyed people. Don't get me wrong: I'm not calling those people Nazis. It's just that genetics has nothing to do with politics and there they were, German ancestry on full display.

* * * * *

I woke with a start. The clock said 11:00 p.m. Looked like I missed dinner. Lobby call was not until tomorrow afternoon so, determined to be well rested for tomorrow's gig, I took a Xanax bar. Waking at 8:00 a.m., breakfast got ordered. The combination of the coffee and the two Phentermine had me feeling very motivated and there it was only 9:30 a.m. I put on workout clothes and went down to the hotel fitness center. An hour later, I'd jogged five miles on a treadmill, changing speeds and inclines throughout, and felt invigorated.

Anxious and excited about the tour, I was ready to go to the venue: Vélez Sarsfield Stadium, where promoters expected one hundred thousand at the show. This was going to be more people than I'd ever played for. I needed to call my wife and check in.

I dialed the 1-800 number that connected to the long-distance server for cheaper flat rates and thus avoided paying international call rates. Kim answered and we talked for about thirty minutes. I told her about the flight and the café we ate at and that everybody was doing well. She sent them her love. I love you we say and hang up. I'd only been gone two days and missed her greatly already.

I got A Son of the Circus out of my carry-on, laid down, and began to read. Time goes by pretty quick when reading a good book and next thing I knew it was 1:30 p.m. We had been scheduled for soundcheck at 4:00 p.m. The passenger van was leaving two hours before that so we'd have Catering if we wanted to. We also had to check out the rented gear and dial it in and, if anything was not working properly, have it replaced until satisfied.

I marked my place in the book and down I went to the bar. Absolut hit my bloodstream and there came a nice shiver. The band and crew showed up in the lobby one by one. Dave joined me at the bar and had the usual, too.

It's a good day to have a drink, he says to no one in particular.

Came time and Bill herded us toward the passenger van taking us to the venue fifteen minutes away where we are taken backstage. The promoter's assistant, Marta, showed us to the dressing room. Like ducklings not wanting to get lost in the big wide world, we followed her closely because the backstage was absolutely huge.

So was the dressing room. The contract's rider had already been filled: Deli tray, vegetable plate with dip, fruit tray, bread, condiments, water and soft drinks, and — most importantly — plenty of Absolut and cranberry juice.

Most of the guys followed Marta to Catering. But I stayed in the dressing room and had a turkey and Swiss cheese sandwich and a drink. I was feeling pretty good, ready to play. It had been three months since we'd played together. It was time.

Bill stuck his head through the door: Joey, you want to go to the stage and check out the Hammond B3 and piano the backline company provided?

It was a good ten-minute walk to the stage and I followed Bill closely. Dave Bruster, the guitar tech, was there. I gave him a big hug. Dave's from Nashville and was the only other person from the South in the organization. Everybody liked to give us shit about being Southerners.

Dave walked me over to my keyboard rig. I can hear the B3 right away because it was hooked up to a Leslie 122 somewhere offstage. Piano wasn't in my wedge yet. The B3 had colored lights underneath the keys making them glow red and blue. The monitor engineer, from Brooklyn, was Brendan. Dave got Brendan's attention and had him unmute my piano in my wedges. It sounded good. And it had weighted keys to simulate the action of a real piano. I was happy.

The rest of the band made it to the stage, checked amps and drum kit. Everything was up to our standards. We started soundcheck. First, monitors got rang out. Then a line check for front of house. Only then were we ready to play a couple of songs and they sounded good onstage. Little adjustments were made and then we played another. After that, our sound man said he's good. We were happy with the monitors. Soundcheck was over and we went to the dressing room. We weren't going back to the hotel. Scheduled to go on at 8:00 p.m., we'd play one hour.

In the dressing room we started our pre-show routine: Lots of vodka and cranberry juice, banter, and a battle of wits. I was sitting on a couch with the usual in a red Solo cup. It's about two hours before we go on when, out of nowhere, Michael Hutchence, co-founder of INXS, walks into our dressing room. Everything about him screams Total Rock Star. Knee-high white fur boots, white spandex pants, a vest without a shirt, and clinging to each arm were model-quality women.

Looking at him on this day — he was thirty-four and smiling and robust and assured — one would never have thought this guy would kill himself in three years. I'd be shocked and saddened like many around the world upon hearing that terrible news. But for now, we were in South America having a great time being Rock Stars and he says with a smile:

Hello, I'm Michael Hutchence. How are we doing today, mates?

We introduce ourselves one at a time. He was very cordial and friendly and said he was looking forward to seeing our show. He was a fan of the band, he assured us. We chatted for a few minutes and then he says it was nice to meet us and walked out, women still clinging.

Pirner says Wow, that's interesting.

Showtime was closing in fast. We walked to the stage and stood in the wings. The crowd was massive, but we're sedated enough not to let that panic us and we took the stage precisely on time. Bill Sullivan introduced the band and we started with Without a Trace. What a great show. It was so good to be playing together again. The crowd sang all the lyrics to Runaway Train. The crowd was good to us. We finished the set and walked offstage feeling good about ourselves. Back at the dressing room we finished the vodka. We were a disaster looking for trouble.

We didn't stay to see the INXS show that night. We hopped in the passenger van and headed back to the hotel. When you play South America it's like taking a factory tour for blow. Bruster scored an eight ball of cocaine from a local crew guy for only twenty-five dollars American. He pulled it out in the van and we all looked at it sparkling like a diamond. The local crew guy said it was uncut, almost pure.

Soul Asylum had a euphemism for doing blow. When you wanted a bump, you'd ask the guy holding Can you ruin my day?

When you had some to share, you'd ask Do you want me to ruin your day?

We watched Bruster do a couple of bumps. He sat there with his head laid back and after thirty seconds proclaimed Wow, this is some good shit.

So I say Hey, Bruster, can you ruin my day?

It would be my honor, sir, upon which the eight ball was passed. I took a guitar pick and scooped up cocaine from the baggie and snorted, repeating the ritual for the other nostril.

The thing about almost pure cocaine is it doesn't give you that jittery feeling blow in the States does. You feel euphoric...and numb. Heart doesn't race, and you don't want to do a bump every ten minutes. Helps keep you awake but is not invasive. You can drink like a fish while doing it, but the hangover was only from the alcohol.

After I was done, Bruster passed the dope around and ruined everybody's day. It was an exciting night. But I was ready to go back to the hotel. I was jet-lagged and partied-out. We'd be in South America for ten more days and would have plenty of opportunity to party with INXS. Besides, we were flying to São Paulo the next day to set up camp at the Maksoud Plaza Hotel. Dave and Dan were going to do press and we were going to play a club show on our own before meeting back up with INXS on March 10 in Rio de Janeiro.

We arrived at the hotel. I went straight to my room and arranged a wake-up call for the morning. Then I laid down and fell asleep with my clothes on. I didn't even need a Xanax.

Hello, this is your wake-up call.

I stretch and get up. Finally ready to go, and with time to kill, I flip through the channels trying to find something interesting to watch. I stopped when I found Bonanza dubbed in Spanish. It was a hoot. It's funny what you notice when you don't understand the language. The first thing I noticed was the size of Little Joe's ears. Those things were huge...like cab doors. Then I noticed the way Hoss reacted to Little Joe. When he was talking, Hoss was very animated. It's freaky.

Me and my luggage made the trip to the lobby. Some of the gang were already there; some were dragging ass. Bill managed to get us rounded up and headed toward the passenger van to the airport. Passport control decided not to hassle us and just waved us through. We cleared security and found our gate. Then we searched for the nearest bar. We were so transparent: We drank until it was time to board...like all good Rock & Rollers do.

The flight to São Paulo was only two and a half hours — time enough for a Bloody Mary. It seemed one moment we're taxiing down the runway and the next we're on our final descent. Always afraid of being strip-searched or detained, I was agitated, nervous, and fidgety going through passport control. But the agent just glanced at my passport, asked a couple of questions, stamped it, and let me pass. Customs was next. I was lucky, didn't get singled out, passed through unscathed. Not that I was smuggling anything nefarious, but still nervous.

We were met by the same promoter who greeted us in Buenos Aries. He had transportation take us to the Maksoud Plaza Hotel about an hour away. By now the sun had set and the ride was comfortable.

Ten miles out of São Paulo we saw a *favela*. A *favela* typically comes into being when squatters occupy vacant land at the edge of a city and construct shanties of salvaged or stolen materials. *Favela* housing generally begins with makeshift structures fashioned from wood scraps and daub. Over time, more durable materials such as brick, cinder blocks, and sheet metal are incorporated. The lack of infrastructure gives rise to improvised and jerry-rigged plumbing and electrical wiring. Often water must be ported great distances. Rudimentary methods of waste disposal pose health hazards. As a result of the crowding, unsanitary conditions, poor nutrition, pollution, and disease are rampant in the poorer *favelas*. Infant mortality rates are high.

This *favela* was sprawling and continued for the ten miles into the city. It's a sad state of affairs. There's a lot of poverty in Brazil.

We roll up to the hotel and gathered in the lobby. Bill checked us in and we found a bar, lounged in chairs, smoked cigarettes, and drank. We made jokes at each other's expense and talked shit. We had the collective mentality of a sarcastic teenager. No one was off-limits. It got vicious at times, but it was all in good fun.

Bill joined us at the table with room keys and passed them out. We weren't ready to go to our rooms yet, so he ordered a drink and we hung out for about an hour when, one by one, we drifted off to our rooms where I call Bruster's room and ask:

Do you want to ruin my day again?

I'd be happy to ruin your day again, he answers.

Well, alright then. I'm on my way.

I headed off to his room where he'd already laid out four lines on the table. Handing me a hundred-dollar bill, I snorted two lines, one up each nostril. I got quite the rush from this almost pure cocaine. Bruster did the other two.

Now, you are probably wondering if using a hundred-dollar bill is a Rock & Roll thing. That somehow we use these big bills because we're Rock Stars. No. There is a very practical reason why hundreds, occasionally fifties and maybe once in awhile a new twenty are used. It's very simple:

They aren't wrinkled and they roll up nice and tight making the snort efficient because you can push it farther up your nose.

Anyway, we had tomorrow off so we hung out all night doing blow and chatting early into the morning. Around dawn I went to my room and got Bruster a Xanax and took one myself. We'd be crashing soon. I say my goodbyes to Dave and go back to my room where I undressed, lay down, thought about the events of the day, and waited for the Xanax to kick in.

I awoke with a start seven hours later. Room service delivered breakfast. I ate it then got dressed for a workout. After what happened in Buenos Aires, I was going to give the treadmill a try. The hotel had an awesome workout facility. It felt good to sweat out the toxins from the previous day. Apparently, I was sweating quite a lot because one of the guys that worked there came up and handed me a towel. Workout and shower over, my mind was on getting out of the hotel and walking around a bit.

Rolling terrain prevails within the city of São Paulo except in its northern area where the Serra da Cantareira mountain range, full of walking trails, reaches a higher elevation. It's also where the famous Brazilian band Mamonas Assassinas died in a plane crash. It reminded me of San Francisco except the city was not on a bay. São Paulo is the fourth-largest city in the world and is spread over a vast area. I left the hotel and went looking for shops, restaurants, and bars. After an hour and not finding anything that interesting on my own, I'd ask the concierge for hints and tips.

Back at the hotel, I called Bill who says the record company's going to take us out to dinner at seven and to meet in the lobby at 6:45 p.m.. Three hours to kill. Turned on the TV. There's a lot of English-language content because the hotel had cable. I settled on CNN International and drifted off into a nap. Waking at 5:00 p.m. and feeling restless, I headed down to the bar and found Dave, Grant, and Murph having a drink in comfy chairs. I ordered a double Absolut and cranberry.

The currency of Brazil at the time was the *cruzado* and it was losing value at an astonishing rate. The promoter told us to pay for everything on credit cards because the value of the *cruzado* would be half of what it was when we first got here and we'd get a hefty discount by charging everything.

We changed money at the front desk and noticed almost immediately that the pictures on the bills resembled famous Rock Stars and actors. There was a Freddie Mercury, an Elton John, a Wilford Brimley, and a Mickey Rourke. We'd be paying for drinks and say things like Trade me three Eltons for a Freddie or I need two Wilfords. I'll give you five Mickeys. That's how we identified the money.

Seven o'clock arrived. The record company treated us to a Brazilian steak house. It was good but I can get steak in the States.

Record company reps seemed nervous around us. Probably because we drank and cursed like sailors. We were loud and obnoxious. We were on top of the world and wanted everybody to know it. We were doing what we thought Rock Stars were supposed to do.

One of the record company reps hooked us up with a cocaine dealer so we all bought an eight ball at only twenty American dollars each. Now everybody was holding and we could all ruin our own day. We went back to Bill's room, did some bumps, then went down to the bar and closed it down.

I had the next two days off so I stayed up all night with Bruster. The rest of the band had press to do in the morning, but they didn't seem to care. We were pretty much extremely drunk, but the cocaine leveled us out. Just before dawn it was time to start winding down. If we wanted another drink, we had to get it from the mini bar.

I went to my room and took a Xanax bar, though it really didn't seem that I needed one, and drifted off to sleep. I woke up the next day and immediately popped four ibuprofen. It's March 6 and the band had interviews to do. I killed time for the next three days exercising, drinking, doing blow, watching TV, and ordering room service. The days seemed to creep by. I finished my book and needed to find another.

On March 8 the band had a gig booked at a popular local club called The Columbia Bar. The venue held about five hundred people and we'd already sold it out.

* * * * *

We're ready for you guys now, Brendan says with his head poking through the dressing room door at the venue. We hit the stage, do soundcheck playing Somebody To Shove so Dave can check his Telecaster running through a fifty-watt Marshall amp. Through another half then a whole song, adjustments were made, and we were satisfied. It was a good-sounding room. Tonight was going to be fun playing in front of five hundred loud, excited, and sweaty Brazilians. It's very intimate show playing in front of a club audience.

We took the passenger van back to the hotel and went our separate ways. I heard Bill shout LOBBY CALL NINE. Curtain call was an hour after that.

Time to go. We all had our own sack of blow. So at the venue, most everybody started re-upping in the privacy of the dressing room. I mixed Dave, Murph, and myself the usual and we enjoyed the pre-show cocktail.

Soon it was showtime, so I mixed another drink to take onstage. Dave and Murph followed suit. Brendan came into the dressing room saying We're ready when you are.

The lights go down. We can hear the crowd roaring. We hit the stage and played a two-hour show. Everything went great. It was good to be alive. We hung around the dressing room for about forty-five minutes drinking vodka and doing blow until we left to go back to the hotel.

The band had a press conference the next day, but didn't seem too worried about it and closed down the hotel bar at 4:00 a.m. Some of us went up to Bruster's room to continue the party there. Two hours later everybody went to their respective rooms. I took a Xanax bar and watched TV until I drifted off to sleep.

On March 9 the band had a press conference in the hotel lobby/bar. It started an hour before noon and lasted all day. Dave got irritated when some reporters asked him about his relationship with Winona Ryder and he ignored the questions. I don't know how he had any patience at all after staying up so late. Every hour different journalists replaced the previous batch but all asking Dave and the band the same questions all damn day long. I don't see how they did it. It had to be stressful and mind-numbingly boring.

The press conference was over at 5:00 p.m. Three hours later we were scheduled to go to Rádio Transamérica's studio to record an unplugged session to be broadcast on that network the following Friday. The passenger van picked us up and took us to the studio.

We met the DJ's and the crew. Nobody seemed to know exactly what was going on. Dan and Dave pulled out acoustic guitars and started getting tones. There was an upright piano — in tune. They threw a mic on it. Karl and Grant hung out in the shadows. They set up a vocal mic for Dave and got tones. Dan, Dave, and I were ready to roll tape by 9:30 p.m.

I had no idea what we were going to play. We started with songs from Grave Dancers Union. Then we did Closer to The Stars and Stranger. We did Rhinestone Cowboy and Key to the Highway. We played new songs that were going to be on the next album and finally ended with a fun little jam session.

Two hours later the music was over but the band still had to answer a few questions listeners had sent in. That took about an hour. We thanked everybody, gave them our regards, and headed back to the hotel for another night living as a libertine.

March 10 we took a short morning flight to Rio de Janeiro to meet back up with INXS where we'd play the Estádio do Maracanã, an outside venue that held over one hundred thousand people.

And it was sold out.

The band met in the hotel lobby and headed for the venue. We were ushered to our dressing room where I mixed the usual.

Are you seeing a pattern start to develop?

Hotel, venue, and party.

This was our life. We never went sightseeing. We never hung out with locals. It's one big Groundhog Day. We drank and did blow from when we woke up until we passed out.

But the show was electric.

The crowd sang along with every song. At one point, banging on the keys, feeling the energy from the audience, I looked up and saw the Christ the Redeemer statue on the opposite hill. Built between 1922 and 1931, it was voted as one of the New Seven Wonders of the World. It was just about too much and I almost cried right there onstage.

We finished our set and made drinks back at the dressing room. Tonight we're going to watch INXS. At showtime we're escorted to a designated area stage right. INXS went on. Fans about lost their minds. The band sounded great and Michael was on fire. He was Mick Jagger incarnate. He had the crowd in the palms of his hands. They played hit after hit, did two encores, then they left the stage, fans went home, and we went back to the dressing room to hang out when a rep from the INXS camp came in and told us that the band wanted to party with us tonight. He gave us the address to a chic disco club and said to meet them there in an hour.

Bill led the way into the disco to bullshit our way in without paying a cover charge. I don't know what he said but it worked and we were in.

The club was everything I hated about clubs. Too crowded, hard to get a drink, and loud dance music playing constantly. Michael and the band were in a roped-off area near the back. They saw us and waved us to their side of the velvet rope. We met everybody in the band, but I couldn't tell you their names now — just like they couldn't tell you mine.

We ordered a round of drinks on them and mingled and chatted. Michael showed us a back way to an outside balcony. That's where he went when he wanted to do some blow, you see. It's windy outside and felt kind of good. He offered us some from his personal stash. I went first, but when I dipped the guitar pick into the bag and lifted it up to my nose the wind took all the blow off the pick.

Major party foul! I was mortified.

Michael laughed really hard and says Not to worry. Then everybody's laughing because there was plenty more where that came from. So, I tried it again and this time was successful. Thanked him and stepped away to make room for the next contestant.

I thought we could drink. But these Aussie boys could flat-out fucking drink. I can't keep up. We stayed at the club for three hours continuously rotating out for blow and inside for shots. Then back to the hotel. INXS was staying at the same place and insisted we drink in the hotel bar with them. The human body can only take so much before it starts to shut down. I'd had very little sleep the last three days and been partying hard. I needed sleep and slipped out of the bar. When I got to the elevators the drummer for INXS was half in and passed out. The elevator doors kept opening and closing on him. I thought it was pretty cold to leave their bandmate at the mercy of the elevator door but apparently this happened all the time. Not wanting to interfere with band ritual lest it hurt their success, I left him there.

Finally got to my room and scheduled a wake-up call. We were playing a stadium in São Paulo tomorrow night. With an afternoon flight, I had to get some sleep. I took a whole Xanax bar and laid down on the bed, turned on the TV for company, and went to sleep. The last thing I remembered was the sun peeking its way through my curtains.

The phone ringing scared me out of a peaceful sleep. The passenger van was leaving in twenty minutes. I threw on some clothes, brushed at my teeth, packed my shit, and headed for the lobby, making it just in time to grab a seat before the van sped off. We arrived, checked in, and found the nearest bar. Had the usual. You know what that was by now, right?

We made it to São Paulo two hours after the sun was highest in the sky and rested at the hotel before the 6:00 p.m. departure to the show. An hour before leaving, after showering and dressing, I did the last of my blow. Time to re-up. I was ready for a drink. Then and only then we'd bring the Rock & Roll to the people.

Arriving at the venue, we went straight to the dressing room and mixed drinks to get in the vibe. At times we've been known to finish off two two-liter bottles of vodka before a show. This is not bragging. I look back and realize all that is just sad. Anyway, we hit the stage feeling good, again to a crowd of over one hundred thousand fans. The show felt inspired and we were well received by the audience.

I asked Bruster if he can score some more dope from the local guy like he had before. He said he'd try. We went back to the hotel and hit the bar. Didn't even go upstairs to change and freshen up. Found a comfortable place in the back and ordered the usual.

We'd been in São Paulo so long fans started showing up at the hotel. They were very polite and respectful. The band didn't mind; they knew where their bread was buttered. An hour later, Bruster showed up with the blow. I went to the restroom and did two guitar picks full. Perked right up. The blow seemed to heighten my senses. I promised myself to go to bed early.

But that promise blew up in smoke. There comes a point in time when an addict is using that he has to make the choice: Do I get sleep or do I stay up? This decision is clouded by drugs and alcohol and usually the wrong choice is made.

I chose to stay up.

We had a 10:30 a.m. flight to Curitiba tomorrow to do another festival with INXS. Curitiba is one of the smaller cities in Brazil but we're told it was very beautiful and picturesque. So here it was, around midnight, and no end to the party was in sight. Everybody drinking and chatting and having a good time. There's a camaraderie between the band and most oftentimes we commiserated after a show. In any case, the party kept rolling way into the night. I met two locals and talked with them for about an hour. They explained where to go — and where not to! — in the city. They were a sweet couple.

The hotel bar closed a couple of hours before dawn and the party moved to Bruster's room. We had a bottle of Absolut lifted from a dressing room and a bottle of cranberry juice, too. Dave and Murph came to party. We mixed the usuals and did more blow.

We were saying I love you man! That would've been embarrassing had we not been so high. Soon the sun would be up. We were partied out, said goodbye, and went to our rooms. We had to meet in the lobby at 9:00 a.m. There's no way I was going to sleep. So, I just turned on the TV and laid down on the bed and rested my eyes.

But nine o'clock came fast and it came hard.

We landed in Curitiba at half past noon. Hyatt Regency check-in done and me starving, I went to my room and immediately ordered that which, as you know, is The Yardstick By Which All Other Food Is Measured, and woofed down the meal when it came.

I was hung over again. I know it seems excessive, but four ibuprofen equal one prescription-strength Motrin. I thought about doing a bump but doing cocaine before the sun goes down feels trashy…unless you've been up all night then what is time, right?

Washing off last night's party funk, and hangover fading away, it was time to prep for the show. We had to be at the venue by 6:00 p.m. Pedreira Paulo Leminski had a capacity of twenty-five thousand and was built in an old stone quarry surrounded by a wall of rock thirty meters high.

The dressing room pre-show ritual of vodka, cocaine, and camaraderie began with the ever-present nervous energy rearing its head. It doesn't matter how many shows I've played, I still get nervous. It's the reptilian brain sending fight-or-flight signals. When standing in the wings, my brain says Run like hell! But once I play that first note that feeling dissipates and everything is alright.

Showtime. We file out of the door and down a paved path toward the rim of the quarry. At its edge is an old decrepit elevator that looked like a small steel cage in ill repair with peeling yellow paint and missing the steel mesh where the door was supposed to be. It seemed as rickety as an old wooden rollercoaster. It can only hold four and was the only way to negotiate the thirty meters — that's ninety-eight feet, y'all! — down to the stage.

This next bit is being said by the same man who jumped in tandem out of a perfectly good airplane at fifteen thousand feet for the one simple reason that he didn't want to be his girlfriend's bitch, namely:

I have a prodigious fear of heights.

Oh, hell no! I say aloud to no one in particular and slowly walked backward away from that contraption. Bill Sullivan gently took hold saying calmly It will be alright, Joey.

And now he's using Calm Reassuring Voice on me? I created CRV, but could I tell him that little fact? No, I could not because I cannot speak. Like a child, eyes closed, I held on to Bill's arm and squeezed for dear life as we stepped into the death trap.

Gears grinded like a death rattle.

Things went dangerously thump and thud.

Herky-jerky we jostled all the way to the bottom.

Every slip of the chain clanking like the ghost I was soon to become.

The ride down took forever. Karl, Grant, Bill, and I hit bottom and I jumped out. Shook all over with shivers that wouldn't stop. The other guys laughed. Called me a pussy.

But we had a show to do, so I somehow managed to shake off the fear and got my mind focused. The house lights went down, and Bill Sullivan introduced the band.

We walked onstage, got to our instruments, and Dave started Somebody To Shove. The song starts with Dave getting feedback from his guitar cabinet and then Grant counts off the song. The adrenaline my body produced from the elevator ride manifested into positive energy for the stage. I was playing very precisely but also with feel. It felt good. There's a lot of energy all around the stage and the band gave the people their money's worth. We ended with Black Gold, walked offstage, drained but satisfied.

Then I remembered the elevator. By now, though, I was too tired to be afraid. I got on with Dave, Danny, and Brendan. The elevator started its ascent. I hear the chain grinding. Halfway up Danny grabs the steel bars, shaking them like an ape in a cage. I'm mortified and begged him to stop which only made him do it more. I was convinced I was going to die in that elevator that night. But to my relief, it stopped at the top. Who was the first to jump off?

I was.

And I'm not too proud to say I almost went to my knees to kiss the ground.

Back to the dressing room for more drinks and cocaine. Everybody was holding. Danny started throwing chairs around the room. He was just letting off a little steam. We're acting like Rock Stars are supposed to, right?

At 9:45 p.m. the runner was ready to take us back to The Hyatt. I grabbed a bottle of Absolut, we climbed in, and headed to the hotel where the band made a beeline for the bar. I took the bottle of Absolut to my room, but once I got there no longer felt like partying. Drained from the show and tired of doing blow and drinking, I needed a night off.

We were scheduled to fly back to São Paulo tomorrow at noon, so after a diet cola and a Xanax bar, I laid back and snuggled under the covers with the air conditioner so cold you could hang meat. CNN International on in the background, I slowly closed my eyes and drifted off to sleep.

So, there I was being intimate with my wife. We were holding each other and kissing passionately. It's dark outside, late. Suddenly the phone is ringing. I get angry. Who'd be calling at this time of night and ruining our time together? But the phone won't stop ringing and ringing and…

I opened my eyes and try to focus on the ceiling. The ringing was a wake-up call on this March 13 and Kim was not in my arms. Damn it.

So, back to work, boys and girls. Showering, dressing, and packing done, I made sure I knew where my blow was. I took it out and opened the bag, dipped the guitar pick, scooped up a bump, and carefully-carefully brought it to Nostril One and snorted. Did the same thing for Nostril Two. I folded the baggie and put it away by which time about thirty seconds had passed and here it came. One hell of a rush. I grabbed luggage and headed down. I saw Danny and Dave at the bar looking like they hadn't had any sleep, each drinking a Bloody Mary. Bill was settling with the front desk.

We arrived at the airport at 10:30 a.m., checked in, and headed for security but, interestingly, there was none. Okay, it was a small airport, but no security? I'd never seen an airport without a security check. It's all tumbleweeds and swinging doors at this *aeroporto*. Unimpeded, we walked directly to our gate, but nobody was there, either. The bars and restaurants were closed. It was a ghost town.

Eventually and slowly, other passengers began showing up. This gave us hope we were in the right place. At 11:30, a flight attendant opened the walkway door and people lined up. They never announced for people to board. People just lined up and the agent took their ticket. We did the same. Found our seats. The airline even ran a food service, but it was unrecognizable. Another white meat I say to Bill, who laughs at my joke.

I swear I hear a chicken cackle. Were there other livestock aboard?

By mid-afternoon we're back at the Maksoud. Man, it felt like coming home. One more day in São Paulo, then off to London, the one in the U.K., where the band would do a bit of press and try to rest. Our first show of the European leg of the tour was in Dublin, the one in Ireland, on March 17, and we were due to travel there the day before.

I went to my room and settled in. It was still early and I hadn't eaten that day. I settled on room service and ordered spaghetti bolognese and a diet cola. It's good. It's hard to fuck up spaghetti, but you'd be surprised at how it can be done.

Being in Brazil for just one more day, the band had a unique problem. It seems we bought too much cocaine. We couldn't take it with us to Europe and there was too much left to do it all while still in Brazil. We can give it away but didn't know who to and we certainly couldn't sell it.

I was sure we'd certainly try to do it all and stay up all night. We'd certainly not sleep and without a doubt feel like shit on the transatlantic flight, but the math was indisputable: We were all holding — a lot. I called Bruster to talk over the problem. He said he'd been thinking about it too and had come to the same conclusion.

So that's what we did. Gathered around a table, dumped our blow on it, and stayed up all night. It wasn't as much fun as it sounds. In fact, it was more like a chore. What was left we left for the maid to figure out.

When we met at the lobby for departure, we looked like shit but we're feeling not so bad. Did we regret it? No. Would we do it again? Definitely. We had fun in South America and certainly left our mark. But now it was time to get to Heathrow.

1994: WITH KARL MUELLER ON JAPAN TOUR
SADLY, KARL PASSED AWAY IN 2005 FROM THROAT CANCER.

DUBLIN, IRELAND

It's 1994 and I'm somewhere over the Irish Sea, which separates Ireland from Great Britain, on Aer Lingus flight #529 from Paris, France, to Dublin, Ireland, scheduled to arrive at 22:15 hours, military time, the preferred format in Europe. Scattered around the plane are various members of Soul Asylum, fresh from doing a TV show in France. Some slept, others gathered around Bill Sullivan, the band's tour manager, placing bets on college basketball. It's March and that means March Madness. The band always had a pool to pick the winners at each elimination. I never win at this shit, but I put my $20 in the pool and picked some names. All I remember is I bet on Kentucky to win it all, and lost.

The plane made its final approach and there we were landed, in the eastern city on the bay at the mouth of the River Liffey. We cleared customs with a stamp and a wave of a hand not interested in giving a Rock & Roll band a hard time. Outside the airport, those who smoked, did. On the way to the hotel in the van, Karl Mueller, bass player and founding member of Soul Asylum, used food color to dye his winkie green in honor of his late grandfather, who also dyed his winkie green every Saint Patrick's Day. Karl was a little tipsy, as we all were, so with great vigor — but not a lot of finesse — he completed his mission.

We arrived at the Westbury hotel on Grafton Street three quarters of an hour later. The hotel was a Victorian affair with contemporary furniture and was centrally located. One could take a short walk and find all the Irish culture one desired. There's a seven-foot Steinway piano near the bar adjacent to the lobby. It looked like a hotel one would imagine if imagining a four-star hotel in Dublin, Ireland. The concierge remembers your name. Everything's available 24/7. It is one of the nicest hotels I ever had the pleasure to stay in. Definitely in my top ten.

We were scheduled to spend three days in Dublin. Our first show was at the SFX Center the next day, Saint Patrick's Day, with departure the morning of the 18th. After checking in, we quickly reconvened in the lobby and headed out for a night of drinking, mischief, and mayhem.

First stop: The pub on the corner.

We wanted to belly-up to the bar and drink a pint of Guinness Stout with real Irish people. These people were friendlier than those in the U.K. or Europe — and they loved to drink. It's cool sitting in a bar with the sound of an Irish brogue in the air. Life was good. I could sleep until at least noon the next day so we're in for a late night. I wish I could remember the name of that pub.

Second and third stops: We left the first pub and dropped into a couple more as we walked along Grafton Street. None of these were as happening as the first. We had heard a rumor that U2 owned a nightclub in Dublin. We inquired and found out that U2's nightclub was in the basement of The Clarence Hotel, which they had also bought and renovated. So —

Fourth stop: Off we went to find U2's club. The place was called The Kitchen. We arrived and talked our way inside. We didn't know what to expect. It's very dark and cave-like. Techno and house music blared through the speakers at an almost unbearable level. There's a moderate crowd dressed like Eurotrash, but that's what you get on a Wednesday night in Dublin, Ireland. Soul Asylum hadn't broken in Europe at that point so we weren't recognized. We couldn't play the Rock Star card. No one noticed us or seemed to care. Tired from travel and too much to drink, we fled The Kitchen and grabbed a cab to —

Fifth stop: The Westbury, where the bar was still open, and had a nightcap before heading up to our rooms and passing out.

Thursday, March 17th, Saint Patrick's Day: I awoke around 13:00 hours with head pounding, so I was on a mission for ibuprofen, which I always carry. I took four pills and choked them down with water and gas, or club soda as we know it here in the States. I laid back down and let the pills start to work. We didn't have soundcheck until 16:00 hours. Room service, read the paper, shower, TV, then lobby call at 15:30. Soundcheck went off without a hitch. I remember we played this really moody song that Dave Pirner wrote during our time off. The song was called I Should Have Stayed in Bed All Day. I like that song a lot.

After soundcheck, dinner was served. The catering crew that traveled with us on this tour was excellent. Good food while traveling abroad makes for happy campers. Bad food can ruin a whole tour. I believe they served a delicious Shepherd's Pie. The band that opened for us on this leg of the tour was the Meat Puppets. I became very good friends with Curt Kirkwood, and later played on a Meat Puppets record as well as a solo project with Curt. We also wrote songs together around 2003. One of them is on his solo album Snow. The Meat Puppets took the stage to a crowd of about 1500 punters ready to rock. They sometimes played a George Jones song, and I'd play piano with them, but not that night. The Meat Puppets ripped through their set with enthusiasm and really got the crowd on their side. They rocked. Soul Asylum had to follow that.

HANGING WITH BONO

Backstage in the dressing room, Bill Sullivan comes in and says we have a surprise guest for the show. Bono, singer/songwriter from U2, is here. Bill proceeds to tell us that Bono's a fan of the band and wants to meet us after the show.

Wow. Could it get any better or nerve-wracking than that?

We had fifteen hundred screaming fans to play for, Bono waiting to meet us, and it's Saint Patrick's Day in Dublin. It's like we're getting the key to the city. Thank God we had vodka. Soul Asylum takes the stage at 21:00. We play like we're playing these songs for the first time. We even tried new material, and it went over well. The crowd was over the top. It felt like home. We were nervous, but it didn't show. Dave had a false start on Somebody To Shove, but that just added to the show's charm. You have to be able to laugh at yourself. We did two encores. I think we played a cover of Rhinestone Cowboy to end the set. We did a good job and felt good about it. Now we're ready to meet The Man.

In our dressing room, I was taken aback when I saw Bono in person for the first time. U2 was between tours and writing another record. He'd gained weight, maybe thirty pounds, and had a very thick beard as well. He looked more like Van Morrison than himself, but there was no mistaking it was him when he spoke.

Going around the room, Bill Sullivan introduced us one at a time. Bono had a really cool vibe about him, and I remember thinking He's the Rick Richards of Dublin. We talked about music and politics (we'd just been to the White House). He listened to each intently and addressed us sociably. He was just a guy out on the town (granted, his town) on Saint Patrick's Day, meeting new people, and the world was a better place for it. Bono told us that his brother, Norman, owned an Italian restaurant called Tosca. He invited the whole band and crew out to dinner there.

At Tosca we filed in and sat at a huge table in the middle of the room. Apparently, Bono had phoned ahead and they were expecting us. The restaurant was typical of any upscale Italian restaurant. Cozy, not too dark, not too bright. You had to look closely, but the walls were adorned with original paintings. Some of the artwork was Bono's, and the rest were from other promising artists of Dublin.

I can't remember where everybody sat, but I do remember Bono sat at the middle of the table with Dave Pirner on one side and Bill Sullivan on the other. I sat next to Dave so I might get in on the conversation every now and then. My favorite song by U2 is One. I love that song, and I love the lyrics. I had one burning question that I wanted to ask Bono, and it's the one question you're not supposed to ask songwriters.

I screwed up my nerve and told him that I liked One. He said Thank you. Then I asked him what the song was about. What he said was surprising. It's about a couple, one is HIV positive. The one singing the song is the infected partner. When I listen now, knowing what they were inspired by, it brings new meaning to the lyrics. I can only muster up a Wow.

We had several bottles of really good wine with the meal and were feeling a nice glow. A couple of more bottles and we're ready to go pub-crawling. A pub crawl is where you go to one pub, have a drink and check out the scene, then immediately go to the next pub and repeat. Everywhere we went the people practically worshipped Bono, but they kept their distance and showed him respect. He hugged a few people and laughed a lot. He seemed to be totally in his element. I lost track of how many pubs we visited. The night seemed to last forever, but all good things must come to an end.

We ended up at the Westbury hotel where shots at the bar were chased with beer. I eventually found the Steinway Grand and played. Everybody gathered around the piano and sang. What a great moment of camaraderie; we all seemed to bond. I can't remember what I played, but I'm sure I included some Stones, Faces,

Badfinger, and Beatles. The highlight of our Instant Concert was Fairytale of New York by The Pogues.

We took turns playing and singing. Bono played for awhile. Though he seemed to have a penchant for Motown, he played a couple of songs he'd been working on in the studio, too. That was cool. Dave played Piano Man by Billy Joel to which we all sang along loudly. The Instant Concert wound down and people said goodnight with hugs all around.

We had a plane to catch at 14:45 and it was already 06:00. I barely remember going to my room and passing out. Traveling is tough when hung over. I took my usual ibuprofen as a preemptive measure to dull the pain and drifted off to sleep with the sights and sounds of the night's activities running through my head.

Friday, March 18. I slept until the very last minute possible, then showered, packed, and met the band in the lobby, sights and sounds of our time in Dublin still running fresh in my mind. Everyone was quiet on the ride to the airport. I guess they were reflecting on how cool the night before had been. Like me, maybe they realized last night was one of those once-in-a-lifetime hangs. It's a good thing to meet someone you admire and find out he's just a guy like you, motivated by the same basic needs, and has the same feelings. I've had evenings that could compare to Saint Patrick's Day 1994, but none have ever topped it.

Sad to say, Karl Mueller would pass away from esophageal cancer in 2005. But that would be eleven years on, so back to the recollections of this Accidental Rock Star we go.

Picture if you will a pair of pants. The pants are Levi's blue jeans...at least, one can only suppose so. It's hard to tell, see, because you really don't want to get that close to them. Threadbare and worn to the point of barely qualifying as a garment of any kind, these pants have never been washed or mended in any way. They were much more worn than just having holes in the knees. No, they would be lucky to be that intact.

Strings of white fringe hung like decorations on a military uniform down both legs. They smelled like a skunk and had a texture more like the oily skin of a small mammal, not unlike a ferret without its fur. The word musky comes to mind. One time on the tour bus, I opened the bathroom door and was overwhelmed by an odor smelling like somebody combined an ass with a skunk and then killed and field-dressed it right there.

These pants were part of Dave Pirner's wardrobe. He wore them every Soul Asylum show. They were part of his machinations of bringing Rock to the people. He sweated in them every night to the point they were more than wet. Sweat poured through them like a rainstorm in the desert.

I have searched the dictionary and thesaurus for just the right word to describe these pants, and here are just a few of the many to describe them: Foul-smelling, reeking, fetid, malodorous, pungent, rank, noxious, mephitic, off, gamy, high, musty, STINKY!

But they were loved by many.

You really had to experience them up close and in person to appreciate them. They were so ragged Dave had to wear boxer shorts to keep from showing off his meat and two veg. One would find those pants in the most bizarre places. You'd be in the dressing room looking for bottled water under the catering table and there they'd be, smell hitting you before you actually made eye contact. Dave wore them on their 1993 Rolling Stone cover. They are actually held together not by cotton fibers but funk, body oil, and the screams of rabid female fans.

I figured he was the right man to ask because of all of his responsibilities he was the pants' personal valet. He managed to keep them close — but not too close. I finally caught him alone in the dressing room or the back lounge and casually asked for the backstory.

He drew me close, saying in hushed tones Joey, those are The Pants That Feed Us.

I don't understand.

He drew me even closer as if to tell me something of great importance. With as much reverence one can achieve in a whisper he says Without those pants the show won't go on. Dave performs in those pants every night. All the ladies expect to see those pants.

Thus, they truly are The Pants That Feed Us.

That's right. Without the pants there would be no show. No shows meant we had to stop being Rock Stars. Then, gentlemen, by all means and personal sacrifices, we had to protect our phony baloney jobs and The Pants That Feed Us!

I was first introduced to The Pants That Feed Us in 1993. Held together by pure funk, miraculously they lasted through that year and the next and into the one following. I swear that after everyone was asleep on the bus The Pants That Feed Us roamed the hall and lounges of the bus looking for another gig to play. By this time the pants had a preternatural aura around them. Sometimes I even smelled the faint odor of gasoline.

To change up Charles Dickens' famous words to fit The Pants That Feed Us, I quote thusly:

"It was the best of times, it was the stinkiest of times, it was the age of international travel, it was the age of foolish excess, it was the epoch of confidence, it was the epoch of devotion to rituals, it was the season of spotlights, it was the season of highlights, it was the spring of aspirations, it was the winter of torture."
— Joey Huffman, misquoting Dickens, 2023

Spring of 1995 saw the Europe tour before embarking on a headlining tour of America in support of the new album Let Your Dim Light Shine. We had spent about a year recording it and were tired of the studio, eager to play the new record live. We released a single, Misery, and it was climbing the charts on both sides of the Atlantic. We played Germany, France, Spain, and the U.K.

One day, we found ourselves in Amsterdam playing a show at the Paradiso. We paid a visit to The Bulldog and played the parts of the ugly Americans who can't tolerate good weed. Oh yes, add to The Pants That Feed Us the odor of serious skunkweed. We played a fun-bordering-on-stupid show that night. We were stoned and Dave was telling jokes like he's Shecky Greene to a Dutch audience that wasn't in on the joke. We finished the show and took two vans back to the Amsterdam Hilton.

You just knew it had to happen.

It was long overdue.

Perhaps we should have paid more attention.

But the events of that night will be forever unclear. Not unlike the JFK assassination, there were conflicting versions of what went down. I shall do my best to recount what I remember.

We arrive at the hotel after the gig. My room's next to Dave's. Bill's was down the hall. We'd been at the hotel for about twenty minutes when I hear a commotion and Bill Sullivan's voice in the hall. I open the door and take a peek. There's smoke coming from Dave's room and Bill is talking excitedly to a hotel employee, apparently trying to talk him out of calling the fire department. I hear water running in Dave's bathroom, the smell of burnt hair and skunk permeating the air. I walk into Dave's room where I see a frantic Dave wearing only a hotel hospitality robe. I follow the sound of water running and turn the corner into Dave's bathroom and had to do a double take at what I saw.

The Pants That Feed Us were on fire!

And they were burning underwater!

The water seemed to be fueling the fire. Like sulfur in water, The Pants That Feed Us smoked and burned. The pants were evil. Soaked with sweat, body oil, and dope, they can't be extinguished! For awhile the fire would seem to go out only to flame up again and again when the water was turned off. It's like they refused to die! It took fifteen minutes for them to give up the ghost.

I can only speculate at what happened prior to my entering the room to watch the flaming and subsequent demise of The Pants That Feed Us. Here's my speculation:

Dave arrives at his room still wet and sweaty from the gig. He undresses and lays The Pants That Feed Us over a lamp to dry. The pair is sweat-soaked and even funkier. He goes about his business not paying any attention to the pants over the lamp. Perhaps he makes a phone call to his girlfriend.

End Speculation: What is clear is that The Pants That Feed Us must have begun to smolder and smoke a bit.

Speculation Back On: Dave is still oblivious to this. He's kind of like that. I'd been in the band for five years and was talking about my kids one day, and Dave looked up and says I didn't know you were a father. Anyway, he keeps on doing whatever he's doing. Changing his shirt? Then, suddenly the pants burst into flames scaring the shit out of him and setting the lampshade on fire. Smoke is everywhere.

Again, End Speculation: He grabs a wooden hotel hanger to get the pants from the lamp to the bathtub. He threw it into the bathtub along with the remains of The Pants That Feed Us.

Begin Speculation Again: He probably tried to beat the fire out with the hanger. When that doesn't work, and flames getting higher, at some point, he calls Bill Sullivan for help and he comes running. Bill calms Dave down, hopefully using his CRV.

End Speculation Yet Once More and Lastly: Bill explains to the hotel manager what has transpired. He probably slipped the hotel manager 100 kroner for his trouble and for not calling the fire department.

Now, people, don't be sad. The Pants That Feed Us had a good run and did their jobs of marketing and magically producing success. They're in a better place. I don't know how they were disposed of, but I'm sure it involved some kind of ceremony. Nobody talked about it afterward. It's like it never happened. Sometimes I can get a whiff of some pong today and have a flashback to The Pants That Feed Us.

God bless The Pants That Feed Us.

May they rest in peace.

MILAN, ITALY

Amsterdam. The city from which when one departs chances are very high there will be a delayed search and many questions asked at customs. Especially for Rock Bands. I was moving a little slow because I didn't get much sleep the night before because of The Incident of The Pants That Feed Us.

Everyone was dragging ass and grouchy because of the early flight from Amsterdam Airport Schiphol to the Milan Malpensa Airport. In the shuttle, nobody says much as this is the time on the road that inevitably surfaces where one hasn't had enough time to shake off the homesick blues.

In 1994, the European Union (EU) had just been formed the year before but wasn't quite fully operational yet. Therefore, one still had to show a passport and clear customs at every border crossing. Checking in wasn't very eventful and security was a swinging door so we had time to have breakfast or, more likely, a morning drink. Vodka wasn't just for drinking at the show. I had a stiff Bloody Mary and everyone else had a drink or two. All except for Bill Sullivan, the band's tour manager. That seemed strange, but whatever.

The flight was on time and we boarded without incident. Everyone had disposed of any weed if they were carrying before boarding. Although I didn't imbibe the stuff myself, I was emotionally moved for my friends when they had to toss their stash.

We boarded the flight to Milan and relaxed in business class. An hour and a half later we landed, cleared passport control with no trouble, collected luggage, and proceeded through customs.

There's something strange going on with Bill Sullivan. Usually he's the first through customs to intervene in case any band member has a problem passing through. This time he's hanging back.

Customs is scary because military guards were everywhere carrying AK-47s and they certainly seemed open for business. There were also a couple of canine units randomly checking bags for bombs or contraband. We had gathered our luggage ready to walk out the door into the real world when we heard the dogs barking and jumping at Bill — particularly his briefcase. I thought that perhaps they just smelled the residue of pot from him smoking a joint from Amsterdam.

The guards proceeded to grab Bill and escort him into a little room sectioned off by an L-shaped curtain adjacent to the customs lobby. Alarmed and, frankly, scared, none of us knew what to do. Bill was the man in charge and, like sheep without a shepherd, we froze and waited.

Five minutes later Bill comes walking toward us. We were very curious and wanted to know what had happened in that cordoned-off room. Bill just walked on saying Let's get the fuck out of here. At the Milan Hyatt, Bill checked us in and handed out keys. We parted and went to rooms, desperately wanting to know what transpired at the airport but nothing yet from Bill.

It's the beginning of the week and time for per diem. I went to his room and knocked. He invited me in, handed over an envelope with my name and the amount enclosed on it. Alone, now I asked. This is the synopsis:

The guards escorted Bill into the room and asked him to open his briefcase. He did as instructed. Inside the briefcase was about a pound of weed and ten thousand dollars American. Bill pointed at the pot and says I think you're looking for this, but you're really looking for this — and points at the cash.

The guards stepped aside. After a brief but heated conversation in Italian they take the money from the briefcase and say he's free to go and he went.

I was amazed.

Bill had the biggest balls I'd ever seen. But, he said, that wasn't the first time this had happened. In fact, it was a frequent occurrence when going through customs and crossing borders when the guards wanted to wake us up in the middle of the night and search the tour bus. It all happened so efficiently none of us had ever noticed.

I still think about Bill and that day. He was the best tour manager bar none.

THE BIG EASY

I like waking up on a tour bus. There is a constant hum of generators running and a little vibration from it, too. Curtain drawn, cuddled up with a comforter while the bus air blows cold, feeling like I'm floating on air. I slid the curtain open and rolled out. The cabin wasn't as cold as my bunk, but it was comfortable. I seemed to be the only one there. I take a quick look at the bulletin board and see the day sheet:

Thursday, July 21, 1994

The House of Blues

New Orleans, LA

No soundcheck

I glanced at my watch. 4:30 p.m. Cool. Now all I had to do was go inside the venue and find the runner to take me to the hotel. I find her in the production office, grab my bags, and load them into the van.

A key was waiting at the front desk. Sign here and initial there…aaaand…there, thank you, Mr. Huffman. Bags and I arrive at the assigned room where I throw bags on one bed and face-plant into the other, letting my body assimilate new surroundings.

Outside was 96° and humid, a typical day for New Orleans in the summer. The air conditioner was on high and felt really good. I could've slipped into a coma, but I had other plans. I opened one of my bags and saw what I expected. The bag contained forty-eight hundred in cash, twenty five hits of blotter acid, an eight ball of methamphetamine, forty Valiums, and other assorted items.

I had that much cash because Drivin N Cryin considered me an equal member of the band. Whenever we hit bonus, it was split equally — and we're hitting a lot of bonuses on this tour. The crowds were great. Mostly sold-out shows.

The dope was there because I had a serious drug habit at the time but was having such a great time being a Rock Star and wasn't hurting anyone but myself — or so I thought. I cut a line of meth and snorted it with a rolled-up crisp twenty. That felt so good I did it again. Then I pulled four hits of blotter acid off the page and popped them under my tongue to let them absorb into the bloodstream. I'd keep them in my mouth for a half hour. I took the acid early because it takes about two to three hours to start hitting the system.

I turned on the TV and started watching Judge Judy or some such shit. It's just background noise anyway. So, I look at my watch and an hour has gone by. We don't play until 10:00 p.m., so…time to kill. I wasn't hungry but needed to put something in my stomach. I ordered fries, a diet cola, and The Yardstick By Which All Other Food Is Measured.

Transportation for the night consisted of two trips to the gig. One van was leaving at seven and the other at nine. Feeling restless, I'd take the earlier one, get to the venue, pour Jim Beam, and settle into the vibe.

Room service arrived and I nibbled at it just to get something in my belly. Flipping the channels I hit gold with The Simpsons, laid back, and watched. Time seemed to stop and start. I can feel the earth rotating around the sun. Meth had me resonating at the speed of sound which, as cold as that room was, had to be about 770 mph.

I caught the early van and went straight to the dressing room. The green room was spacious with a long table loaded with food and sodas and a fist of Jim Beam. Tasteful lighting with floor lamps and

Christmas lights strung here and there gave it a festive atmosphere. Absolutely no overhead lights: Nothing is a buzzkill more than overhead lights. Scented candles all about the room. Walls adorned with abstract paintings by Glenn Fox who just so happened to be a friend of mine. Couches and chairs here and there on a hardwood floor with a rug rolled tastefully across it.

I was the only one in the room. It's a moment of calm before the storm. I mixed a drink, sat on a couch, and soaked it all in. I can feel the LSD creeping up. I laid my head back and closed my eyes, content.

Trance broke when the rest of the band came piling in. We greeted each other like family. I didn't tell them I'd taken acid. They didn't need to know. I was starting to feel the acid in my joints. It's called a body high and I loved it when that happened. Every move was an adventure in sensation.

I mixed another drink. Walked out of the green room into a hall that separated two dressing rooms. The lights were bright out there and there was a lot of activity. It was almost too much to digest but I pulled it together. The opening act was getting ready to take the stage.

Then I saw a beautiful girl sitting alone on a bench in the hallway. She had dark wavy hair and a pretty face. She looked fit and well put together. This made me sad and curious about why such a pretty girl was sitting alone on a bench in the hallway. I took a big sip of my drink, went over, plopped down very fast, and say Hi, I'm Joey.

My name is Margaret and I'm the dressing room server.

Hello, Margaret, I play keyboards for Drivin N Cryin.

Cool, Joey.

You must see a lot of bands and have lots of crazy band guys hitting on you, right?

I can take care of myself.

I just bet she could. The opening band went on and I was still in the hall talking to this mysterious woman. With the mixture of LSD, meth, and Jim Beam, I felt free to tell her anything. I was psychedelic with emotion, couldn't come down, and was very attracted to this woman. Sometimes there's a chemistry between two people which is undeniable. While the opening band was playing we sat there chatting like we'd known each other all our lives. I was very animated and told her stories from the road. She seemed to enjoy them. I was afraid I might appear too high-strung and scare her away, but she stayed on that bench in the hallway as the band played on.

She had the most contagious laugh. I loved to make her laugh just so I could hear it. She had a good sense of humor and made me laugh, too. I was smitten. One burning question resonated in my mind, but I kept it to myself. Said I hoped to see her later. The opening band's set was winding down and it was time to get to the dressing room for pre-show rituals with my bandmates.

Sometimes you can tell by the vibe that it's going to be a good show. The show was sold out and we felt the crowd's energy — or maybe it was just me because of my altered state. I had just the right mix of drugs and alcohol coursing through my veins so was feeling really good, but I mixed another drink and was now ready to play. But even getting my game face on and rising to the occasion, I couldn't keep Margaret out of my mind.

On the way to the stage I saw her still sitting on the bench and asked her the question that kept racing through my mind: Did she want to hang out together after the show? She'd be charmed to escort me and hang out together. Okay, I'd see her after the show and, excited, walked through the stage doors.

The acid I'd taken was getting well into my body and when the band hit the stage, I was peaking. My keyboards seemed to droop across the stand like cooked spaghetti. But my hands knew where to go so I wasn't about to resist the will of the trip.

As predicted, the band was spectacular. The setlist melded from song to song. I was playing with a lot of intensity and found myself playing parts I'd never played before. Sometimes that happens when you're in the groove. Artificially high or not, that happens with all musicians at some point and it's a glorious thing. The crowd was with us and we came back for two encores.

Escorted back to our dressing room, it was a time of celebration and decompressing. Everybody in the band was happy. I snuck off to the restroom and did another bump, but came back just in time to join the band as they drank a shot of Jim Beam in a toast to the good performance. It's as close to a victory lap as we can get.

By the time I saw Margaret again it was midnight. She had work to do before she could clock out. I was okay with waiting and went to the dressing room.

Sometimes when you're high, you forget to do important things. I hadn't eaten since room service at the hotel and thought maybe I should eat something now even though I was far from hungry. The food was still out from earlier in the evening. I found the fruit tray. Discovered mixed nuts. Had a few bottles of water so as not to get dehydrated. The fruit and melon flavors exploded in my mouth and I had sensations all over my body. I mixed another Jim Beam and diet cola and sat on the comfy couch, patiently waiting for Margaret.

She showed up right on time. We walked to her car, a blue-green 1966 Plymouth Satellite. It was sweet. In the car we talked about a plan. Margaret says she's hungry so the first thing we do is drive around and look for a place to eat that's still serving food and was not in the French Quarter. But nothing was open, so we gave up and went to my room. The room was like I left it: The bag of money and all the drugs lying open on the bed and fully exposed. I was embarrassed and tried to move it all, but it was too late.

Is that money in your bag?

It is.

I've never seen that much money before.

It only looks like a lot of money because it's mostly twenties.

But how much is there?

I don't know; count it.

She was hesitant at first but I kept telling her it was okay. She slowly gathered the money from the bag. Because I was unable to keep my mouth shut and kept breaking her concentration, she lost count a couple of times. Eventually she counted it all and it came out to forty-eight hundred. She counted it again. Same result. Then in a drug-induced decision, I made her an offer:

You can have half.

That's generous, but I can't take the money in good conscience.

Take it.

No.

Take it.

No, thank you.

Take it!

No.

Okay, take a hundred dollars as a tip for working the green room.

Well, alright.

I showed her that money was not the only thing in the bag. Had she ever done methamphetamine? That was a no. I told her about the blotter acid and how it makes you feel and she seemed interested so I gave her a quarter of a hit and told her to put it under her tongue for thirty minutes. Which she did. I began to talk all about my favorite (or least favorite depending on the day) subject: Me.

I included the good and the bad. She seemed to admire that honesty. Then she talked about herself. Born in New Orleans. Been there all her life. Was an extra in Interview With The Vampire. She'd like to travel one day and envied mine.

I'd left the TV on when leaving the room earlier. I noticed the test pattern with a Native American on it. I was fascinated. The acid I'd taken earlier was now at its peak. Couldn't take eyes off colors swirling and headdress feathers moving as if blowing in the wind.

I'm sorry…what?

I have my place and you won't be distracted by the TV there.

Okay…sure.

We arrive at her apartment in the Lower Garden District, a very pretty historic neighborhood with cobblestoned streets. We climb a dark flight of stairs and go in the large studio apartment with separate kitchenette and hardwood floors. Rugs and curtain panels from the set of Interview With The Vampire were draped all around the many windows in the flat but there was no closet space and her collection of vintage clothing was hung on rolling racks, like the kind used on movie sets, and took up the majority of the space. She took the cushion off the papasan chair and put it on the floor for us to sit on and there were a lot of old-fashioned beeswax candles that smelled like honey. She slowly and unhurriedly lit them all and they were the only source of light in the room.

She opened a bottle of Merlot and poured us each a glass. We sat on the cushion and I turned to face her. I took a sip of wine. She did the same. We looked at each other. We raised our glass in cheer to have met and had another sip.

My body was tingling from the LSD I'd taken. She says she was starting to feel the effect of her dose. There was definitely chemistry between us. I was shy but not afraid. I slowly leaned over and kissed her softly on the lips. She reciprocated. She's a good kisser. The kiss was not sloppy or wet. Nothing dirty about it. It's an innocent kiss that lasted about ten seconds and then I leaned back again.

The kiss sent a burst of chills down my back and made me tingle all over and tugged at me like I was learning about love all over again. I felt as if I was ten and having my first kiss. I changed the mood by asking what all of the clothes hanging in the racks were all about. They were vintage-style clothes from the Fifties, Sixties, and Seventies. She also had period pieces bought after they wrapped up filming the movie she was the extra in when they had an after-production sale, selling wardrobes for pennies on the dollar. You know I've got a love for clothes so when she said Do you want to try any on? of course my answer was Yes, please!

We'd put something on, look in the mirror, and laugh hysterically like two kids playing dress-up. It was all great fun. We'd stop every now and then to pour another glass of wine and then get right back at it. I'd put on a festive hat and she'd put on a French hat that looked like it came from the seventeenth century.

Pleased to meet you, mademoiselle. Are you here for the party?

Well, yes, good sir.

Do you like my chapeau?

Of course, sir, I think it divine.

Then we'd laugh like children. We were having such a great time. Time flew and before we knew it, it was five in the morning. I wasn't tired. Didn't think she was either. But the fashion show was losing its charm, so we sat on the cushion again. She opened another bottle of wine and refilled glasses. We sipped and talked. Neither wanted this night to be over. Makes me sad to think about it still.

When do you have to leave? Bus call's at ten. Do you want to hear any music? Why, yes, that would be lovely. Here's The Psychedelic Furs. Ah, good choice; come back and sit beside me on the cushion.

We snuggled and kept talking about our lives and learning about each other. We'd kiss a bit. Innocent and yet erotic at the same time. The music made me tremble. She felt me shaking and asked if I was okay. I assured her I was and that my body high was taking over. I was hearing every instrument separately and precisely. When I closed my eyes, I watched my own personal light show. Colors blended and every word sung was a visual. Somehow it all made sense and I felt safe and warm. With every sensation all my joints felt like they were throbbing with a ticklish sensation. There was a sexual charge in the room, and it was very erotic. More erotic than any sex I'd ever had. Touching each other and responding, a bit of heavy petting but that's all. We mostly just held each other.

Time continued to fly. We checked the clock and another two hours had fallen off our time together. I'd feel anxious and nervous every time we checked the clock because it was a countdown to the time I must leave and I didn't want ever to leave.

Finally, though, it was time and I had to go. This was before cellphones with cameras, so we didn't get a picture of any of our mischief. We go down the stairs to her car. The day is really hot already plus before we left she'd adorned me with a top hat, black trenchcoat, and a handful of Mardi Gras beads. I broke out in a sweat immediately. She couldn't get the air conditioner on fast enough.

We drove in silence to meet the bus. I was thinking about the night before and already had good memories and was banking them. I think she was doing the same. If we talked it might break the spell. We pulled right up to the bus parked on the street with motor humming, everybody already on it. Hmmm...appears I was late.

Margaret and I had one last kiss and then I hopped out of the car and waved goodbye as she drove away. When I got on the bus everybody was laughing at the way I looked. I admit I looked pretty damn silly the way she had outfitted me. They asked what I did last night but I just didn't have the words to describe it. Told them I'd tell them later, but never did. How do you explain something so otherworldly and strange? But happen it did.

Ah, Margaret. I am most grateful for those memories.

Thank you, dear lady.

MY WIFE WAS ANGRY

Kim could get angry sometimes. She hated when the kids ran in and out of the front door. She hated when the kids couldn't find one shoe in the morning and ran late for school. But that's normal mama stuff. She really hated when I stayed at the studio all night. And she utterly hated when I didn't listen to her.

Granted, she had her reasons to be angry and that's a fact I shall not deny. But this particular time in 1997 she was only angry at me. My day started off okay but then she came out of the bedroom and saw how messed up the living room and kitchen were and demanded to know why I was not watching the kids and how did I let this happen?

Just missing stepping on a Lego helicopter, which would've pushed her threshold of tolerance deep into the red, she sat on the couch between all the stuffed animals. A lesson we men have to learn is that telling a woman to calm down — and her going quiet — is never a good thing. I had not yet learned that and so told her to just calm down after which, that's right…yeah…she got very quiet.

I, being a problem-solver at my very core, got to thinking: What is making her so irritable? Ah-ha! I know. She's irritable because she's hungry. You know what? I'll make her a sandwich and off I went into the kitchen. While making it, I hear her mumbling under her breath like a pot beginning to boil. Something like Uuuugh! I do everything. No one ever helps me.

I wanted to tell her I was helping by making her a sandwich but, smart man about women that I am, let that sleeping dog lie and thought I'd just let my actions speak loudest in this situation. Oh, yeah. Her sandwich was going to be awesome. I toasted the bread and everything. Cut a fresh ripe tomato. Got out cheese and meat. She's still talking to herself but now louder than before, working herself up.

Damn, I better get this sandwich in her hands and quick.

When the toast was ready, I set the oven on broil and took a piece of toast and put the cheese on it and back into the oven better than a Quiznos. On the other piece of toast, I spread Hellman's mayonnaise and a spicy mustard...forgot the brand. Added a big handful of turkey.

I hear my wife starting a conversation with herself which was always a bad thing because she'd start arguing with herself. Her voice was rising and she was winning every argument.

Got to get this sandwich done, Joey boy. Faster I went, slicing the tomato nice and thin. Put three slices on the turkey. Then when the cheese had melted in the oven, it went on top of the pile and was pressed down a little so the flavors would marry.

SunChips on the plate with the sammich, grab a diet cola, and walk to the living room tactically dodging Legos and Play-Doh. Stood by the couch directly in front of her where I swear it had gotten ten degrees colder. She's sitting all the way back into the couch, eyes closed.

I didn't want to interrupt her contemplation but I needed to get her to eat her sandwich. Right? That would solve everything. So, very quietly I say Dear, your sandwich is ready.

No response.

Of course, being the man who understands what women need, I nudged her a little bit and said it again only this time slightly louder to get through her contemplative state. Without warning she shakes herself awake, looks directly in my eyes. I hand her the sandwich and she takes it although eating was the farthest thing from her mind at the moment. I mean, who knew? I certainly didn't.

With a great building anger, she starts spitting words like bullets, yelling You don't do anything around here. You're selfish. You lock yourself in your office and sometimes don't come out all day. You leave all the cleaning to me.

Deliberately she rises from the sofa, sandwich in left hand, right forefinger pointing at me in little stabbing motions punctuating her angry litany of things I never did for her. Screaming louder and getting closer, she continues.

You use the bathroom, but do you ever clean up after yourself? No! I get down on my hands and knees and scrub the floor.

She points her finger into my chest to make her point: Who do you think cleans the toilets in this house? Is it you? Is it you?!?

She's standing close, rigid and stiff, and waiting for an answer. I said the first thing I thought, which is not the best thing to do at such moments. But after all, I knew how to handle women so, if she isn't hungry, make her laugh, right? Doesn't it always work out well to make a furious woman laugh? Of course it does. Naturally, I answered Jeopardy style:

Who is the Tidy Bowl Man?

We stood rooted in place for what seemed like hours. Then she grabbed the sandwich and, James Cagney style, rubbed it in my face. Storming off to our room, she slammed the door. There I stood with sandwich smashed into my face so went to the kitchen and cleaned it off, but I didn't try to go talk her down. No, I wasn't that clueless. Now was not the time for anything but a fast détente. I cleaned up the living room and put everything in its place. Washed the dishes and cleaned up in the kitchen. Everything was quiet. Like a forest after a mighty oak falls.

Everything she said was true.

I was never there.

I wasn't a part of their lives.

I was either out on the road for ten months a year or staying for days at the studio when I was supposed to be at home. I always had something going on to take me away from them. In more sober moments I regretted not being at home and would tell myself this time it's going to be different.

But get meth and pills in me and suddenly it was all about Me, **ME, *ME!*** All drug users are selfish and I was at fault. Chose music and drugs over family so I understand why she was angry and I know why she'd eventually file for divorce. It took me a long time to come to grips with reality.

But I faced my demons and fought them off. It took almost five years, but I got clean in February 2004. I've been trying to make up for that lost time with my kids, Whitney and Joey, and that's going good lately. I'm so proud of them. Even their mother is forgiving. It's kind of like we started over. When she reads this — and I know she will — I just want to let her know one more time that I truly am sorry.

EVERY GREAT DREAM BEGINS WITH A DREAMER

I played with Soul Asylum from 1993 through 1997. They are a great band. It was an honor to have been a part of it. The ride was wild. They were the first band I played with that was just starting their rise to the pinnacle of success and stardom. It's a thrill.

I have a recurring dream about Soul Asylum. In my dream I'm backstage at a concert and trying to find the stage. Soul Asylum is about to start but I'm eternally lost, panicking, and running out of time. Then I hear the band starting the opening song Without a Trace. I'm running up and down corridors and slinging open every creepy door I come to. There's not a single person in sight. No one to ask where the stage is. I'm at the top of my stress level and —

Then I wake, sweating, heart racing, realizing it's only a dream, eventually calm down. But it seems so real. I know it's a variety of the classic go to school/work naked dream. I still dream it every now and then, but why it's always with Soul Asylum I have no clue.

Moving forward to 1998. I'm touring with Matchbox Twenty. They were a great band to tour with. Again, another awesome band I got in on the ground floor with. We'd always get to the venue a couple hours before we played so we can go to Catering and relax before the show. I get nervous before shows. It's just my nature what with my reptilian brain episodes I'm always wrestling with.

Soul Asylum is the opening act for this leg of the tour. It's good to see them and catch up. It was weird being around them while being in another band. I felt like a traitor but there were no bad feelings. There's a reason I'm telling you all this history.

I normally stay in the dressing room when the opening band goes on. I might have a drink to calm my nerves. Sometimes I had to drink to get the spiders off. To say it in a short, simple sentence: I was always wound tight before a show.

Why, I do not know, but during that whole tour, without warning, I'd hear Soul Asylum playing Without a Trace off in the distance. I'd go into panic mode and get the urge to bolt and go find the stage. My mouth goes dry and I start shaking. My legs feel like they're made of rubber like they do after almost having a car crash. It's my nightmares come true. About that time someone in the band says Joey! You okay?

It'd take a good five or six minutes to get out of that trance and get thoughts together. I'd think over and over: I play with Matchbox Twenty now. I don't play with Soul Asylum anymore. Then a rush of calm runs through and my legs still. Breath returns to normal. Elated I wasn't living my nightmare again, I laughed and say Guys, you won't believe what just happened.

It got to the point that Rob would come to me around five minutes before Soul Asylum's show started and — using his Calm Reassuring Voice — say Joey, it's about time. Remember: You're with Matchbox Twenty and not them anymore, okay, Joey? Joey? Okay?

Sometimes I think I need therapy.

MATCHBOX TWENTY

Someone once asked what was the coolest thing about playing with MB20. I'm sure you won't believe me, but it's true:

I never had to carry my luggage.

Atlantic Records arranged a vacation as a reward for our success in Australia in 1998. As we came in for a landing we see the beautiful blue water of the Great Barrier Reef. The plane lands and taxis to a spot on the tarmac where there was a train of golf carts, only those were the luggage carts. The crew unloads luggage and sweeps it away to sort.

It'd probably be in our rooms before we arrive at the hotel.

Another golf cart train takes us to check in. The scenery's beautiful. The sun's shining. It's about seventy degrees. On the five-minute ride to the hotel we're silent, simply taking in the beauty of Hamilton Island, a resort on the upper east coast of Australia. Perfect place to go on vacation. All we had to do was play one acoustic set for the island guests, which we did on our first night there. Not a bad deal for a bunch of road-ravaged musicians.

Sure enough, when we arrive they're waiting on us with keys at the ready and a packet with information on things to do. There are no cars. Not even maintenance vehicles. Catalina Island is similar. So, for better or worse we each received our own golf cart.

We follow a bellman in his golf cart to our rooms. And what rooms they were. Each of us — including the crew — had their own two-story suite. I was speechless. Never had I ever stayed in a suite bigger than my apartment. It opened onto a foyer which led into the living room. The kitchen was off to the left. Bathroom adjacent to the living room. Upstairs, the master was very sizable with a double king-sized bed, TV with cable, a Nintendo Game Boy.

And it was en suite.

I wandered downstairs to acclimate myself to the space and found a mini bar. Fixed a drink and snared a handful of M&M's then went out on the balcony. There were white cockatiels everywhere. They'd land on the balcony rail. One even climbed onto my forearm. I felt like a pirate. When I fed them M&M's, they swarmed like in The Birds movie. I ran inside for cover.

Every place we toured around the world there was always one suite booked at every hotel. And every time we checked in somebody was going to get lucky and get the suite. It was that way and had been that way since the discovery of fire and the invention of the submarine. So how did it happen that we all got beautiful, luxurious, and cool suites this time?

It happened in a big way. You see, there was this one suite against which all the other suites paled in comparison. This suite was just too much. Twice the size of the others. Master bedroom downstairs and a living area you can land a plane in. Upstairs was another luxurious bedroom and bathroom. But the thing that made that place swing more than any of the others was this suite had it's very own swimming pool.

Jason, our security guy, got the luck of the draw. It's his room...well, for now. As soon as Rob and Kyle saw it they declared that this was going to be the party room. Jason was still the occupant, but he was going to have to entertain about twenty to twenty-five: Some drunk, most loud, and a few blotter-acid-tripping.

He wasn't very happy about that, but he couldn't say no to Rob.

So here's the deal: Never travel with any kind of dope. It's too dangerous and they're always looking for a Rock Star to bust. Instead, you let your crew hook up with the local crew to supply drugs. Crash had close ties with this one guy in the local crew he'd worked with before who had meth for Crash, weed for most everybody, a sundry of prescription pills, and a final act of kindness at the end of the tour he'd been saving as a surprise: Four sheets of blotter acid with twenty-five hits per sheet. That was more than enough for us. We had some left over, but we'd leave it for the maid to deal with after our departure.

Now the plan was that everybody was going to take a hit or two. But when it came time to drop, several chickened out. That made it difficult because there were those who did and those that didn't. And to top it off, tour manager Dean planned to ruin our buzz trying to catch us doing something devious.

I showed up at Crash's room in the middle of the afternoon and scored two hits that I did immediately and two more as chasers in case two weren't enough. The funny thing about acid is that it can take from one to over three hours to get in your system. In other words, when and how it works varies every time.

I went to my room and had a nice long shower and dressed. It's early, I don't think we were supposed to meet for dinner until six. So, I went across the street where they had more than enough whiskey to defile myself. Dean and Paul were having themselves a cocktail, so I joined them, ordering a double Jim Beam with a water back. I was already trying to take the edge off the acid by drinking.

You see, the mysterious part about this caper is nobody knows who dropped and who didn't. I'm sitting there having a cocktail and I'm wondering about Paul. Did he drop? He didn't seem to show any symptoms, but I wasn't feeling it either. I knew for a fact that Dean didn't dose because he's the sort that needs a drink to kill the bug up his ass.

I found out later that Joey, Rob, Kyle, Crash, Doug, Kenny, and a few Australian girls and dudes wanted to party. Fine by me. We had the party room from Hell, much to Jason's chagrin. But now it was time to go to dinner. Kenny shared my ride to the French restaurant down by the water where the shops and stuff were. We go inside. Our party is already seated: Dean, Paul, Kyle, and Pookie, and now Kenny and me.

We're at the point of ordering when the LSD starts creeping up. Nothing on the menu looks good. I order a filet with vegetables. Our waiter goes around the table taking orders. It's then I noticed our waiter's head. Pulsating cycled from normal and then the top part of his head would pulsate like a lightbulb. It's weirding me out. I look over at Kenny, who had dropped around the same time I did. He wasn't looking too good. Was he seeing it, too? A case of mass hysteria maybe? Kyle seemed fine but he probably dosed later than we did.

I killed my drink, stood up awkwardly and say in a voice a little too loud I'm going to the bathroom. Kenny stood up and says Me, too. We manage to get to the bathroom without incident.

Man oh man, I can feel it coming on. Me too. I'm not hungry anymore. Me neither. Dean's being creepy; wanna ditch this place and find a safer place to ride the psychedelic wave? Yes. Me too. Let's go. Okay. Sneak out the front door? Yes. Who's driving? Me? You? Me. Faster. My room? Yes. Drinkees? Yes. Alison? Yes. Paint? Yes. Laptop? Okay. Alison? Yes. Alison? Yes. Alison? Yes. Pink background. Hey, that's our waiter; oooo that's good. My aim is true, no tip for YOU! All together now: My aim is true! No tip for YOU! Alison? Yes. Yes. Yes. Let's ride golf cart. How fast are we going? Ninety.

Well, what seemed like four hours turned out to be only one. Anyway, there's only one road on the island that begins where the hotels are and winds down three quarters of a mile to a fork. Left fork, restaurants, shops, activities, and the airstrip. Right, go up the hill to the top of the mountain. The road up was about a half mile long.

At the top is a radio telescope. Giving evidence people had been there way before us, there was a firepit and graffiti. One by one the people on LSD show up and hang out with us. The stars were like…like we're next to them. Supposedly George Harrison had a house down the hill. I started singing Don't Let Me Down and everybody joined in. We were more yelling than singing. I hope we didn't ruin George's evening.

Seemed like it took forever to get to the top but it was a damn rollercoaster coming down. Kenny and I rode around for about another hour giggling a lot and trying not to hit the wallabies. Wallabies come out at dusk and are everywhere. They're like midget kangaroos and are oblivious. We were in no danger of hitting one, though. Remember twenty miles per hour seems like ninety when you're tripping. They'd easily step out of our way. I thought I heard them laugh as we passed. I was probably just hearing the acid.

Rob bought me a little present at the airport gift shop before we flew to Hamilton Island: A stuffed toad with its arms hugging an airplane bottle of Jack Daniel's on a wooden base I can proudly display at home. I took that thing with me everywhere. I'd hold it on the roof of the cart like a police siren.

I was starting to get the body high that good LSD gives: Pleasant feelings in the joints. I was really high but not in a bad way and give myself over to the drug. I don't fight it but enjoy where it takes me. Maybe that's why I've never had a bad trip. Kenny and I go back to our rooms and get ready to visit the designated party pad. I change my shirt and fluff my hair, and head up to the party room not knowing what I'd find. I found Apocalypse Now.

BEGIN SCENE

SCENE: Joey arrives at suite. Door is ajar. He pushes it open slowly but we can't make out anything at first. All lights are off in the suite. Through a sliding glass door leading to a lighted pool we hear sounds of the party. We see a lot of people.

JOEY: That's him. There he is.

SCENE: We see Joey focusing on a bald head glistening in the moonlight. We see crew member Jason who is not moving or making a sound. Joey's acid brain translates that as extreme passive-aggressive behavior of film icon Marlon Brando in his famous role from that movie.

JOEY: [Joey stops dead in the darkness, eyes grow manic and he quietly whispers.] That's Colonel Kurtz. I'm sure of it! Oh, God! Oh, God! Colonel Kurtz is here.

SCENE: We see the band and crew and others who've joined the crowd, male and female, gathered around the pool where the party is in full mellow roast. We see Kyle singing and playing guitar. We see a normal situation. But Joey, reacting to his acid-peaking brain, focuses on Jason who he believes is the evil Colonel Kurtz. Naturally, it follows Joey becomes Photojournalist, played in the film by Dennis Hopper. Freaked, Joey leaps out of the darkness through the door and crashes onto the patio. He begins a word-for-word recitation of Photojournalist's rants, looking at no one in particular.

JOEY: Hey, man, you don't *talk* to the Colonel. You *listen* to him. The man's *enlarged* my mind. He's a poet-warrior in the *classic* sense. I mean sometimes he'll, uh, well, you'll say hello to him, right? And he'll just *walk right by* you, and he *won't even notice* you.

SCENE: Kyle stops playing and singing and stares at Joey. All eyes have turned and also focused on Joey. Joey continues the recitation.

JOEY: And suddenly he'll grab you, and he'll throw you in a corner, and he'll say Do you know that *if* is the middle word in life?

SCENE: Joey pauses. Crowd stares.

JOEY: *If* you can keep your head when all about you are losing theirs and blaming it on you. *If* you can trust yourself when all men doubt you — I mean I'm no, I can't —

SCENE: Even in mellow-roast mode, alarm now shows on all faces and bodies tense as they wait for what they know not. Some in the crowd rise from their seats waiting to see what Joey will do. Will they need to rescue him or restrain him? These are ready for action. Joey turns right and focuses on those people.

JOEY: I'm a little man, I'm a little man, he's, he's a great man. I should have been a pair of ragged claws scuttling across floors of silent seas — I mean…

SCENE: Joey pauses. Looks around. Takes in the scene by the pool where he sees everybody is shocked, worried, and afraid. They are confused, not understanding Joey's frame of reference. Some come near to calm him down. Joey turns to his left to address those people.

JOEY: Do you *know* what the man is saying? *Do you!?* This is dialectics. It's very simple *dialectics*. One through nine, no maybes, no supposes, no fractions…you can't travel in space, you can't go out into space, you know, without, like, you know, with *fractions*…what are you going to land on, one quarter, three-eighths…

SCENE: Joey turns back to his right.

JOEY: What are you going to do when you go from here to Venus or something…that's *dialectic physics*, OK? *Dialectic logic* is there's only love and hate, you either love somebody or you hate them. He's clear in his mind, but his soul is mad.

SCENE: Joey stops talking and breaks a huge sweat. Some continue to calm him further. Finally calmed, he sits hard into an empty seat. He looks at Jason. Jason is staring at him, still silent and not moving.

JOEY: [Smiles gently and speaks almost serenely] Jason, you look just like Colonel Kurtz from Apocalypse Now. Hey. Listen y'all, I'm peaking and I'm Dennis Hopper and you need to go to the sliding glass door and look out this way.

SCENE: A few get up, walk to the darkened room and step in. They turn and look out at the pool from inside the darkened room. We see them nodding and speaking over each other as they come out to find their seats.

CROWD: It's creepy. It's creepy and weird. Yeah, man, he looks like Marlon Brando's Kurtz.

SCENE: The tension breaks as everyone laughs uncontrollably. The party settles back into a mellow roast. Kyle picks up his guitar and sings. Joey talks to a pretty Australian girl the rest of the night. Dawn rears its ugly head and the party winds down. Joey walks the girl to her car and says goodbye.

END SCENE

That was intense, but I'm beginning to wind down, too. I always get a little sad when I'm coming down, so went to my suite and tried to sleep, but couldn't. As they always do, events of yesterday and last night keep running through my head. I feel content and finally sleep soundly for eight hours. Woke up feeling surprisingly good. Very clean acid. We're all signed up to go snorkeling on the Great Barrier Reef. God bless Crash because he was the only one of us party animals who made it to the reef.

1998: SYDNEY TOUR. MATCHBOX TWENTY

SHRINERS ARE FINER

I have been a bad boy. I am going to Hell.

It all started out as an irritatingly normal day in 1999. Mari and I went out in the car for a ride. I'm quite partial to car rides. Anything can happen on a car ride. A car ride is an adventure and we are pirates sailing the open seas looking for a bounty.

Our trip was simple. We needed a couple of bottles of Cabernet and cigarettes (this is before I quit smoking which I did in 2005) and to see what the day had to offer. The plan was to get the wine and come back to her house and enjoy it in the sun on the back deck.

The trip to Kroger is uneventful. We didn't even talk on this beautiful, sunny, autumn day with the temperature in the low seventies. Transcendental Blues by Steve Earle, one of my all-time favorites, is playing in the car. The windows are down and my hair's blowing like a pirate in a storm. Aargh, me maties, all's right with the world!

And isn't that always when misfortune happens? Yes, it is. If one wakes up and feels the best they have felt in a long time, one should watch one's back because dark clouds are just over the horizon.

We pull into the parking lot and get lucky because when we arrive a car's backing out of a spot close to the door. We park, get out, and walk toward the entrance. Then I notice a Shriner collecting money for the Scottish Rite Hospital. I tell Mari to go on without me because I was going to go talk to the Shriner and donate a few dollars for a good cause. I won't be long, I tell her. She goes in because she believes what I say.

I approach the Shriner, happy to help, but was suddenly overcome with a sense of impending doom. I get to his station, which consisted of a bucket on a stand and a table with purple cloth. The Shriner had it strategically placed between him and the people who were kind enough to make donations. He wore a purple fez with an emblem on it, a striped button-up shirt, a red vest which clashed with the hat, nondescript trousers, and old-man white shoes like you get at the mom-and-pop drugstore. Shirt tucked in pants and a brown belt made his belly hang over the front of his pants like Santa Claus. He must've been about fifty-five or sixty. He did not seem to be a happy man.

I watch him at a distance for to soak in his demeanor. He never engaged in conversations with any who donated to the cause. All he'd said is thank you and looks away when someone drops money in the bucket. I walk up and said hello. He just nods. I put a dollar in the bucket and received the requisite thank you. I asked him how things were going. He nods and grunts something under his breath. I was thinking he's acting a little morose and I had another sudden sense of impending doom.

I told him he had a cool hat. He nods but is now rocking back and forth slightly on his feet. I put another dollar into the bucket and asked what was the significance of the gold emblem on his fez. He was silent for a second. Irritated, he says it's called a yearb and it's a sacred Shriner emblem.

I admired the gold gleaming in the sun as if on its volition.

I dropped another dollar in the bucket and stand there quiet for a moment as the Shriner stilled like a wax figure and I looked him over again. I notice a solid gold Shriner ring on his right hand opposite of where one wears a wedding band. It's unusually large. He spoke not a word. I told him that big gold ring he was flashing sure was pretty. Naturally I ask my second question: All I need is a ballpark figure — how much money do you make after taxes?

He stands as still as Kaw-Liga did in front of the general store. Stiff and stoic, the man says nothing at all but he's getting irritated. Then I thought that, well, maybe that question was a little personal and excused his response because after all I have no filter.

I drop another dollar in the bucket and stare at him. He didn't make eye contact. So I lean in closer and whisper What kind of gas mileage does one of those clown cars get?

He stiffens not wanting to be seen being angry at a patron outside the entrance of a Kroger in Duluth, Georgia. In a whisper out of the side of his mouth he says Go away. Obviously, he wasn't grasping my dollar-a-question technique. I dropped another dollar in the bucket and stared again. He was rolling to a boil but I was also getting a bit miffed.

I wad up a dollar and threw it into the bucket and tried to look him straight in his eyes but he wouldn't make eye contact. I got louder. Whoa, this situation was escalating quickly. We were drawing attention from shoppers. Aggravated, I asked if Shriners had a secret handshake. Finally I asked something that got a reaction. He was like a statue suddenly coming to life and says sternly Go a-WAY!

My anger surfaces and off come my sunglasses. Louder I say Look, Clown, if you're gonna take my money, ride around in clown cars in stupid parades — I hate parades! — and wear a funny hat in public and not answer a few simple questions, then you need to find another line of work.

A crowd is gathering; as well they should because when was the last time they saw an Accidental Rock Star (ARS) in the middle of a bipolar mania picking a fight in a grocery store parking lot with a Yaarab Temple Man (YTM) who's yelling to the ARS You're a reprobate and a degenerate and ARS is yelling back to YTM You're an old fucker that needs a drink to kill the bug up your ass?

Exactly! Never.

What happens next will be talked about long after YTM and ARS leave this earth. Even passed down in Shriner history from generation to generation.

Now there's a highly interested audience therefore, logically, at this point ARS wants his money back. YTM must have sensed something because as soon as ARS moves toward the bucket YTM dives toward it to protect it. They reach the bucket at the same time and collide with it and each other causing the bucket to come tumbling down spilling bills and coins everywhere.

Thief! shouts ARS grabbing at a wad of bills and walking away pleading his case with anyone who'd listen that YTM was a bad man. YTM quickly herds the money back in the bucket and comes with purpose after ARS who was speed-walking back to the parking lot and circling back to the entrance with a crazy YTM behind him. At this point people are hiding their children, gasping in shock and awe, and quickly walking in any direction that's not toward ARS who is running back to the entrance yelling Anarchy! Anarchy!

Just then an unsuspecting Mari walks out of Kroger with her hands full of Cabernet and our smokes. ARS watches bags fall in slow motion, bottles shattering and wine splattering and cigarettes flying all over the pavement. This just made the whole thing seem surreal to ARS. Mari, being the voice of reason, grabs ARS' arm.

Joey! What's going on? Why are you running and yelling? Come on, let's get the hell out of here.

She pulls ARS toward the car by one arm and ARS is waving his free hand and flipping the bird to anyone who cares to watch.

Reaching the car, Mari and ARS jump in. ARS is trying to calm down and suddenly I realize I'm sweating profusely and out of breath. Don't smoke, kids. Mari puts the pedal to the metal and we leave like we just robbed a bank.

Geez, Joey, what the hell happened out there?

I hate that fucking Shriner, I HATE that fucking Shriner. Never take me to Kroger again.

She readily agrees. It was not her fault I created a scene but next time it will be an adventure at a Publix.

D-I-V-O-R-C-E

I take the blame for our divorce in 1998.

Kim and I had a healthy marriage for seven years but drugs disconnected reality from my priorities. A polydrug user that self-medicated my bipolarism, by whatever name I called myself or reasons I gave for doing it, it badly impaired my ability to be a good husband and father. Then, when I started having success, I saw less and less of Kim. I'd stay at Triclops Studio days in a row, only coming home to crash and shower.

I pushed her away. We grew apart. Naturally, it was only a matter of time before she'd find someone else.

I saw other women during this time, though not as many as you might expect of an Accidental Rock Star. In this book I hardly ever mention other women because there really weren't that many. Sequestered as we were to hotels, tour buses, and venues, there was next to no time to meet women.

Besides, drugs were my most attentive mistress. No female could even come close. It's a full-time job being a drug addict. Women were ancillary. It's too bad that drinking and drugs are cornerstones of the music industry. In 2019, Paul Saintilan (University of New South Wales Sydney) did a study on the phenomenon. He noted in the abstract of his research paper the five pressures that influence the vulnerability of musicians to alcohol and drug dependence. They are:

1) Pressure to be creative.

2) Pressures generated by performance anxiety.

3) Challenge of managing emotional turbulence such as doubts and fears while living a hectic, pressured life.

4) Social, cultural, and workplace pressures to drink or use drugs.

5) Dealing with identity issues (public persona versus private self, subcultural identity, and issues with fame and celebrity).

My drug use was fueled by monotony, a DNA-deep loneliness, and the need to self-medicate my bipolar condition. I accept full responsibility for my actions but if I had to do it all again I believe I would. That sounds terrible, doesn't it? I don't say that lightly. All my experiences made me who I am now and, honestly, I can't imagine myself any different or taking any other path to have arrived here.

For a long time drugs were a big part of my life. I'm not going to apologize for any of it except in this: I mightily regret that Kim and my children had to suffer through the pain of my addiction. But one thing is for certain: I've been clean since 2004 and proud of it.

This has allowed me to make up for lost time with my children. Hasn't been easy. They've got a lot to forgive. But I do love them. And I hope they can see I am still trying to be better for them.

Me and CeeLo (2000) working on his first solo record

CeeLo Green and His Perfect Imperfections

COCK OF THE WALK STUDIOS

April 11, 2000, 12:00 a.m., Kennesaw, Georgia

He was late. He was always late. I tried to talk to him about it and he'd say he'd be on time from now on, promise. Not that it bothered me anymore. Maybe I was a little bit irritated, but all would be forgiven when he walked through the studio door.

I looked at the clock. Midnight. He was later than usual. The session was booked for eight so I picked up my cellphone and tried to call K.C., but it went straight to voicemail.

I decided I'd given them enough time. After all, four hours lost that I could've spent lying in bed and watching cartoons. But just when I pushed the first switch to power down, K.C. and CeeLo burst through the studio door. They looked to be laughing very loud, but I couldn't hear them in the control room.

They staggered through the door hanging onto each other, not knowing who was holding up whom. CeeLo had the biggest bottle of Sky Vodka I'd ever seen in my life. It's larger than life. It looked like something a venue would hang over the bar to advertise. But on closer inspection it was full of vodka. Nice.

K.C. and CeeLo were pretty wobbly. They stumbled into the control room still laughing. CeeLo gave me a drunken hug and apologized for being late. He sat on the couch next to K.C., wrestling the giant bottle of vodka the whole time and throwing a Whattup, Dawg? my way.

Nothin' but a thang, but I don't think he heard that because he wanted another drink. They had orange juice in the car to mix with the vodka but no cups. K.C. went to the car for the OJ. I went to the kitchen and looked for cups, but to no avail. K.C. came back in with the juice and one super-sized cup from McDonald's.

There was discussion back and forth among the three of us about the cup situation and after several hits-and-misses at solutions I ask Why don't we mix one big, strong drink in the double-size cup and share it?

We nod approval and patted each other on the back to empathize with our decisions. I wanted to take a victory lap but that would've been too much. So, I mixed the biggest show drink I'd ever mixed, making sure the amount of vodka was representative of the size of the bottle. I took a sip. It's strong but manageable. I got lucky and got my shivers again.

We passed the drink around five times until I interrupted the ritual when the producer/engineer in me asked if we're going to record or not. By this time I was cool either way. CeeLo said to load the song Getting Grown. That song was nominated for a Grammy in 2002.

This was the first time I'd ever seen CeeLo drunk. They always had weed with them and smoked it constantly, but never drunk. It was funny to see him like this. Still, CeeLo had a great work ethic. If he had to finish lyrics, I'd loop the music and he'd get it done. We worked better when it was just me and him; I played piano, guitar, and bass on certain tracks. For a year we worked together during which time we tracked about fifty songs not counting the artists on his label. I always felt satisfied when we were finished recording.

Sometimes he'd bring his posse to the session. Maybe fifteen people. Most were artists CeeLo signed to his record label and the rest were just bitches. Hey, don't holler at me; that was the parlance of the time and I'm merely quoting popular usage. CeeLo prohibited anyone from saying The N Word out of respect for me. He didn't want me to get uncomfortable, which I appreciated.

They'd order pizza and make a mess. Sometimes they'd try to talk above the music, making it hard to hear. I'd have to turn the console halfway up before they'd shut up and even then I'd have to walk out of the control room and stay gone five minutes — just enough time for CeeLo to put the fear of God into them. Then back into the control room where I'd be met with dead silence. Could've heard a pin drop.

CeeLo, where do you want to start?

The first time I met CeeLo was when Britt Turner called saying CeeLo wanted to come up and check out the studio that very night. We say that's cool. The studio was on the grounds with Jesse James Dupree's house, which house came with lawn jockeys. Jesse had never really thought about that. But suddenly it came to him: That could've been awkward to explain. We go outside, grab lawn jockeys, and hide them.

So, CeeLo gets to the studio and loads his keyboard in. He wants to track right now which took us aback for a moment, but hey, that's cool. He wanted to record old school with the two-inch tape machine. We got him patched in and up and rolling in about ten minutes.

He had a song he wanted to track a piano solo for. Does anyone in here play piano? I slowly raise my hand and say I do. I get my piano from the car.

He just wanted a solo, so I listen to the track and say I can do that. We start running the track while I play along. I nailed it the second time around. CeeLo was impressed. At that moment, we cemented a good relationship.

But I digress. On this night of the single large drink cup, I load the session into Pro Tools. CeeLo was now going to sing background vocals. The U87 was already set up from the session the day before. I patch it into the Avalon 737 and patch that straight into a channel on Pro Tools. I'd create six tracks because he likes to work fast. He'd sing and right after the take say Give me another track.

So, I'd go to the patchbay, unplug the cable, plug it into the next track. And so on and so forth. But before we start tracking, I set the level on the 737. Some people don't like the 737 because they say they can't get enough gain from them. I have to say forget about the VU meters and crank it up so you can hear the tube compressor. Don't look, just listen.

I pressed the record button and off we went. He'd have me play it over a couple times so he could find the part. We tracked vocals for about fifteen minutes and then decide to just hang and get drunk.

After awhile we needed a refill, so I mixed another, stronger than the last. We passed it around and talked. It soon became clear CeeLo's wife kicked him out of the house earlier that day after a fight of Biblical proportions.

I point and say See those garbage bags on the couch in front of the console; all my clothes are in them; wife dumped them in the driveway and I'm sleeping on the couch, pretty much living here; I'll call her in the morning and see what it was I did this time.

K.C. says his woman was tripping and giving him grief about staying out late and going to the clubs. The three of us cry like babies when CeeLo says he loves his wife and wants to go home. We talk and drink until sunrise, though with no windows it's hard to confirm the time. But we came to the conclusion we all had the same problems and our lives weren't different at all.

HYPNOTHERAPY

Best thing for him really, his therapy was going nowhere.

Hannibal Lecter – Silence of the Lambs

On a humid June day in 2003, a former girlfriend and I took a ride up to Norcross, Georgia, to see a hypnotherapist. It would seem that the anti-depressants I was taking for my bipolarism weren't working and we were seeking alternative treatment to alleviate symptoms. The girlfriend and I weren't getting along; we were willing to try anything if it would help. She'd been taking classes from the Doctor — that word needs ironic quotation marks around it! — and thought hypnotherapy might work. I was skeptical but willing to try anything, especially since she was footing the seven-hundred-dollar bill for the session.

We arrived at a Tudor-style house. It's pleasant enough but I sense a foreboding. Ringing the bell, I expected Lurch from The Addams Family to answer. But when the door hinges creak open, a sweet old lady answered and bid us to please come inside. The man's wife? I look around. It seemed like a normal dwelling. There were no chicken feet or talismans hanging around. I don't have time to drink it all in because once we entered the foyer, the nice lady yells Charles, they're here.

A muffled voice from upstairs says Send them on up.

Up a flight of stairs, then we walk through an open door into a large office filled with a desk, filing cabinets, and other various office miscellanea. Off to the right was a comfortable chair conspicuously facing a very comfortable-looking couch with pillows from end to end. Copious diplomas, certificates, and awards adorn the good

Doctor's wall. It's designed to make a person feel comfortable. But on me? It had the opposite effect.

I was introduced to the Doctor. Pleasantries exchanged, my girlfriend took a seat to observe the proceedings, her being a protégé of the good Doctor and all. He began to explain the procedure and what to expect. The Doctor began with:

In the universe and on earth there are energies, spirits, demons, and other earthbound entities that can psychologically and physically attach themselves to a person and drain them of their energy. There are many different reasons why this happens. Earthbound spirits are ghosts that attach themselves to you because they are attracted to your life energy. Demons and other Satanic forces attach themselves to you for the sake of evil. Past life attachments are past life experiences attached to your psyche trying to right a wrong that has happened in the past.

He went on.

There are other entities or clusters, elementals, and earth energies that attach to you for various reasons. It isn't really necessary for you to understand them all. You just need to understand the concept, and any of these earthbound entities could be the cause your depression, anger, confusion, erratic behavior, and other afflictions.

I will be performing a series of non-invasive tests on you to determine what kind of entity or entities had attached themselves.

Alrighty then. Let's get started.

First, he had me stand facing him with my feet shoulder width apart and raise my left arm into the air over my head and extend my right arm perpendicular to my body forming what resembled a backward L. He felt my left armpit as if to feel the lymph nodes. He then checked the strength and firmness of my left arm by trying to move it back and forth. He then did the same to the other arm.

Next, he held his hands about three inches from the top of my head and moved them around as if to examine some invisible energy field or aura and would occasionally utter Hmmm or That's interesting.

He had me open my mouth and looked at my tongue. He shined a flashlight in my eyes and examined them from a mere three inches away. Then he made me jump out of my skin when he startled me by exclaiming loudly:

Ah ha!

After that, the Doctor took two small iron rods from a felt bag. The rods were twelve inches long and curved ninety degrees at one end for another two inches forming an L. He stood five feet away. Facing me, he held the rods so that the small part of each L was between his thumb and forefinger and extended straight out from his body pointing at me. He then walked very slowly toward me until the rods crossed each other at two feet away.

That's odd, he says, and does it again with the same result. Ten times he did this. He looked very serious. The premise of this exercise is similar to that of a Ouija board. The rods were, in theory, crossing each other when my energy field was strong enough to repel them. It would have been just as easy to manipulate them with thumbs and forefingers as one would move the planchette on a Ouija board.

I went into this therapy session with an open mind and was a willing subject. I wanted it to work. I thought he'd just hypnotize me and suggest I not be depressed just as one would suggest one stop smoking if that was their affliction. Open to the point of being naïve about the spirits but…those divining rods were a red flag and that's when my radar pinged.

As abruptly as the tests began, they were over. The Doctor was satisfied. He had his diagnosis. He had me sit in a chair and stood in front of me to deliver his opinion. I was thinking, okay, maybe he has found a ghost or a dead relative attached to me. Never in my wildest dreams would have expected what came out of the Doctor's mouth next. He shocked me with:

Son, what we have here is a clear and classic manifestation of demon possession.

He went straight to demonic possession without passing go or collecting two hundred dollars? True, I felt bad, but not possessed by an unholy entity from the bowels of Hell bad. Still, my girlfriend paid big bucks for this so I was determined to see it through and played along.

Doctor, what do you want from me?

I was simply to lie on the couch and get comfortable. He was going to sit in the chair and hypnotize me and when I was fully under he was going to exorcise the demon and send it back to Hell where it belonged. I said I was okay with that as long as nothing creepy *a la* The Exorcist happens, though in my opinion we had already crossed the line into creepy hocus-pocus. Still, I got comfortable on the couch while the Doctor took a seat. I gotta say that couch was one of the most comfortable I've ever been exorcised on. The Doctor tells me to relax and then began talking to me in what I politely am referring to as the CRV as he says —

Joey, picture a lake with no ripples on the surface.

I picture a smooth lake.

Joey, picture a lake totally devoid of motion.

I picture that.

Joey, relax your fingers. Feel the tension release from your fingers.

I pretend to do that.

Joey, concentrate on your....

He walks me through my entire anatomy instructing how to concentrate on relaxing each part.

Joey, your mind should be blank.

It is not. It never can be.

Joey, you should put all thoughts aside.

I don't. I can't.

This went on for about twenty minutes and as God as my witness I was an eager subject trying hard to do what he was suggesting. I did feel relaxed and had a sense of well-being. But then he tells me he's going to count backward from ten to one and that when he reaches one he'd clap his hands three times and I'd be hypnotized. So I thought Okay, here we go.

Ten, nine, eight, seven, six, five, four, three, two, one.

He claps three times. The sound reverberates in the room.

I'm no longer talking to Joey, I'm talking to the demon who has taken possession of his body. Do you hear me, demon?

Now at this point I had a choice. I could've told them that I really didn't think this was working. Maybe we should try it again. I don't think I'm hypnotized. But where is the fun in that? So, I conjured up the scariest and most demonic sounding voice I could and said:

Yes, I hear you, asshole.

You are in this body without permission and an abomination. I command you to come out and go back to Hell where you belong.

No, I like it in here.

I command you demon, leave this body and return to Hell.

Fuck you, asshole. You're not the boss of me.

Demon, identify yourself. By what name are you called?

Ask your mother, asshole! I fucked her last night.

What gives you the right to possess this body?

Look, y'all, I even spoke some Latin to really convince him he was conversing with a demon and answered thusly:

Deus ex machina, motherfucker!

The Doctor and I went back and forth in his manner for thirty minutes at least. It was exhausting. I was about to break character and laugh because it was so absurd, but then I thought my girlfriend needed to get her money's worth so I never relented. Finally, after another ten minutes of back and forth, another option for the demon appeared on the table.

Demon, if you won't go back to Hell, will you travel beyond the astral plains, sit on a rock and contemplate your existence for eternity?

Really? A loophole? That was rich. But okay. So, the demon replies

That sounds nice. Okay, I'll do that.

Then it is done. I will count to three and you will leave this body and contemplate your existence for eternity. One, two, three…be gone!

Silence… then:

Joey, you are clean.

Joey, I will count backward from ten to one and you will feel fresh and wide awake. Joey, your afflictions will afflict you no more. Ten, nine, eight, seven, six, five, four, three, two, one.

He clapped his hands and I pretended to wake up and innocent-like ask what happened. They relay the story and I feign disbelief. I told my girlfriend that I felt like a great weight had been lifted from my shoulders and I was upbeat and happy. I shook the Doctor's hand all the while knowing he was a charlatan and a snake oil salesman. I wanted to hit him, but my girlfriend was so overjoyed I resisted the urge. Besides, it was funnier to just let it ride. I wish I could remember his name so I could expose him for the quack that he is, but I can't recall. I chalk it up to experience and laugh to myself and had seven hundred bucks worth of fun in any case.

If you steer clear of new age hypnotherapist types then my story will have not been in vain. I just hope it made you laugh as much as the Doctor laughs on the way to the bank.

Postscript: After a little research I do know his name. Look, if you decide to see a hypnotherapist located in Norcross, Georgia, and you want to know if the one you've chosen is the same one I went to, feel free to get in touch and I'll tell you his name.

KEITH RICHARDS CHRONICLES — 4 OF 4

2001. Crash calls. He was the guitar tech for Matchbox Twenty. Said he'd be out of town for a few days because he was going to Nashville with MB20 for a TV special starring Willie Nelson. The Night of Stars and Guitars was to be shot at Ryman Auditorium, the original place of the Grand Ole Opry before it moved. There are a lot of stories in that old church, and I vow out loud to do that show.

I immediately call Rob Thomas and leave a message: I'd love to do the show with them because I found out Kyle was not going to be there. Rob calls back almost instantly saying that's a great idea. We'd do a duet with Willie Nelson on the song written by Ed Bruce and Patsy Bruce: Mammas Don't Let Your Babies Grow Up To Be Cowboys. That song is right up my piano-playing alley. He says the office will call and work out details. I was excited and happy.

The office calls and we haggle over rate and I'm happy with it because I was also getting union scale from the TV show. The thrill of playing with MB20 and Willie Nelson was so great I'd have done it for free — not that I told them that and I hope you don't either. A room at Loews and a first-class ticket to Nashville and get to play at the Ryman with Willie? How could this get any better?

We rehearse and do a dress run-through all day Thursday. A run-through the next afternoon then open doors and live broadcast of the show. Back to Atlanta the day after. It's looking like a nice three-day vacation.

And here came the silent treatment from Sherry, my girlfriend at the time. I had to pry the problem out of her. Her feelings were hurt because I didn't invite her to come, too. I forgot that it'd be exciting for her. So I say fuck the first-class ticket and we'll just drive up to Nashville. She's happy…for a while.

We planned to leave around two the afternoon on the departure date. Then, for no apparent reason, I decide to tint my hair red. I believe drug use played a part in that decision. That pushed us back to six. Sherry was packing like she was going to be gone for a month. I only packed a shaving kit, three shirts, socks, and a pair of Gap jeans. Her packing pushed departure time back to eight. My acoustic guitar, her luggage, and my bag went in her Mercedes and then we remembered snacks. We'd get snacks and drinks when we fill up. So we headed out on our adventure.

When we gassed up the car we discovered we left the dope at the house and had to turn around and scoop it up. We were now on a ten o'clock departure time, fast heading to midnight. Sherry drove first. She is a Type A personality, flashing high beams at slower traffic. No patience at all. Drove me crazy and finally I'd had all I could stand and by the time we went through Chattanooga I took over driving and listened to Tom Petty and the Heartbreakers' box set. My mania had hit full throttle.

We arrived in Nashville and get lost. I called Jason, MB20's security guy. He was trying to guide us to the hotel. We made a wrong turn, had to turn around. Of course this was my fault — according to my girlfriend, at least. We finally pulled into the hotel, unload, and check in. Loews is equivalent to the Ritz-Carlton and Four Seasons. By the time we arrived it was two in the morning. We were high, so we ordered room service and I played guitar and such and we stayed up all night.

MB20's people got in touch at ten that morning: Lobby call was at noon. The band arrives at the Ryman, then an hour to fill out paperwork, get credentials, and be shown to our dressing room. Things were running late, as things seem to do with All-Star shows. I went roaming to see who was there that I might know. I saw Crash in his guitar station in the wings of stage right. Then out of the corner of my eye I saw Jane Rose, Keith Richards' manager.

I made my way over and hugged her neck. I didn't know Keith was on the bill. She says Oh yes! How could he miss this?

I told her I was there playing with MB20 and we talked business for a short time and then it was time to do our rehearsal without Willie. Jane says to get in touch with Tony Russell and we could probably hang out with Keith at some point. We did a rehearsal then went upstairs to our dressing room. I saw Tony and it turned out that Keith was in the dressing room across the hall from us. I went in to say hi. Keith is a sweetheart. He hugged my neck and we talked about shit that had happened since the last time we hung out. I told him I hadn't slept in three days and had to get a nap soon. Keith said The thing about sleep, Joey, is it'll always creep up on ya!

We say goodbye and promise to get together after the show aired the next day. We ran through the song with Willie and headed back to the hotel. MB20 had reservations at a four-star Italian restaurant later that night. So we all met in the lobby around nine and headed to dinner in two passenger vans. We had a dining room all to ourselves. Antipasto and wine to start. I had three glasses of wine. Out of the blue I declared that if you name a city, any city, I can tell you what county it's in. Kids, stay away from drugs. Anyway, people start naming cities and I'm nailing it. This went on for fifteen minutes before I finally missed one. The city was Phoenix and I guessed Mesa County.

I. Was. Wrong.

Still, I was the king of random information for fifteen minutes. I take what attention I can get. Guess I didn't get enough good attention from Mommy when I was a child. So, over the course of the evening we talk music. We talk songs. We talk studio stuff and Mac vs PC. It's a lovely evening with old friends. We headed back to the hotel, but it was too early and I was too high so into to the hotel bar I went; Sherry went to the room. It's good to see people I hadn't seen in a while. We had a swell night at the bar, but the evening wound down so I fucked off to my room. Sherry was asleep when I got there and I lay down beside her to rest.

I awoke at nine. Did a couple of bumps to wake up and then started writing on the guitar. We ordered room service and it was nibbled on. Drank the pot of coffee, though. There's nothing to put the edge on a crystal meth buzz like room service coffee. I picked out my wardrobe and took a shower and Sherry did my hair and I dressed. Time for lobby call.

We load in the van and off to the Ryman we go. It takes an hour to check in and get new credentials. We scampered to dressing rooms where gift bags from Willie awaited. They contained a fifth of Willie's signature bourbon, red bandanna, bottle opener, trucker hat, Willie T-shirt, and an Apple device I'd never seen before. It's called an iPod, one of the first ones on the market. It had 20 GB storage and a navigation wheel that actually turned. The geek in me couldn't wait to get home and fill it with music.

We waited around a lot. That's what happens when you're doing a live broadcast.

Wait, wait, wait...

Rush to the stage.

Hurry up! You're on next!

All the artists had their own minder. We did our run-through with Willie and it sounded great. I love the piano at the Opry.

I loved the stories, too. I heard one about Porter Wagoner and George Jones. Porter's in the bathroom and George walks in and takes the stall beside Porter. Then out of nowhere George grabs Porter's penis. I mean, grabs it hard. He put Porter in great pain for thirty seconds and then let go. George says to Porter I just wanted to see what Tammy was fucking, and walks out.

Another story I'm fond of is this one. Johnny Cash, Waylon Jennings, and Willie Nelson were standing around side stage. Dolly Parton's performing onstage. Johnny says Look at the tits on her. Waylon replies I'd like to fuck her. Willie says I wonder if she has any rolling papers?

Real stories, apocryphal, or just jokes? Who knows, but by whatever name they were called, they made me laugh.

That night Willie's guests also included Ryan Adams, Jon Bon Jovi, Sheryl Crow, Bill Evans, Vince Gill, Patty Griffin, Emmylou

Harris, Norah Jones, Toby Keith, Brian McKnight, Aaron Neville, Ray Price, Keith Richards, Richie Sambora (who I like to refer to as Itchy Sombrero), Hank Williams III, and Lee Ann Womack. It's a star-studded evening and I enjoyed watching them. Ryan Adams, Emmylou Harris, Ray Price, Sheryl Crow, and Keith Richards were my favorites that evening, but all artists performed well.

I saw a lot of people I knew including my friend Peter Stroud playing with Sheryl Crow. The Ryman Auditorium has three stories of dressing rooms on both sides of the stage. There's also a green room where one can mingle. Seeing Keith for a moment was cool. Hanging with MB20 was a thrill as well. The show started and we watched other artists from the wings or on TV monitors in every dressing room. It's a good show. Willie was spot on. Our minder came and got us two acts before we were on.

We went on and started playing. Willie makes his appearance during the second verse. It was a privilege to be onstage with him. When the song was over, Willie dedicated it to Waylon. I was touched. Keith did The Worst off of Voodoo Lounge.

Ah man, it sure was good to hear him.

I love the excitement live TV. But then the show was over and we hung around and chatted with other artists. I met Ryan Adams, which was cool because I'm a fan. He'd been in a bar fight the night before and had a black eye. He told one of those You should see the other guy stories. We went through the infamous alley behind the Ryman to Tootsies Orchid Lounge and had a drink. Signed a few things for fans. Then back to the hotel.

We arrive at the hotel around midnight. I drank with friends for a while then slipped up to my room at half past one to wait for Tony's call to hang with Keith. I was to wait in my room and he'd come get us when it was time. We hung out drinking from the mini bar when there came a knock at the door. It's Tony. Sherry had just ordered room service so Tony tells her to call down and have it delivered to Keith's room. He thought Keith would get a kick out of that. So she did. Then we all did a bump or two and rode elevators up to Keith's.

Before we got to Keith's suite, I hear music and smell pot. We get to the door, Tony knocks, then uses his key. Keith's sitting in a comfortable chair with his legs crossed yoga-style and having a drink. Most people think Keith drinks bourbon but he actually drinks vodka mixed with Orange Crush. He says he drinks something so disgusting that few people dare to try it, so he never runs out of vodka. Tony motions us into the room and follows us in. When Keith sees us he says excitedly:

Ah, fresh meat!

Reggae music is playing. My friend Pierre is nodded out in a chair beside Keith. Rob Fraboni is asleep in Keith's bed. We take a seat on a small sofa against the wall at a 90° angle to the left of Keith. Tony sits down next to Keith in another chair. Keith says Joey, nice to see you…and who are you, my dear? Sherry! Delighted to meet you.

For Sherry, the very first look she had into my life was me being on live TV with Willie Nelson and going out to dinner with MB20 et al., and hanging with Keith Richards in his suite. After that, whenever I'd ask if she wanted to come to Opp, Alabama, to see me play with The Georgia Satellites, she always declined.

Keith says the reggae music playing is music he's writing for the new album. The same thing repeated over and over for about thirty minutes. Then another reggae song, only a little different, would play. Joey, you should've been there because this cat playing keyboards gets up in the middle of recording and makes himself a sandwich, then comes back and starts playing again.

We laughed at that pretty hard. Keith always listens to songs like this and through it somehow he sees a song that will be a song for the Rolling Stones.

Keith was in rare form this night. At one point Keith stands and says Lead Singers. Ha! Mick Jagger, David Bowie, Roger Daltrey, and Robert Plant…they're all poofsters! He did his best imitation of

Mick Jagger's rooster walk and we all cracked up. Then he went to his Dr. bag and pulled out his Jamaican knife. If you don't know, Keith carries a Dr. bag that has a .38 revolver, brass knuckles, and a Jamaican knife. Tony was on the room phone talking to room service and Keith goes over beside him and tries to cut the telephone line. Alas he doesn't have the strength he used to. So instead of one clean cut he had to saw it off. I laughed at that, too.

Then from his position at the phone, Keith sees Rob sleeping in his bed, charges into the bedroom and yells Find your own bed, you arsehole. Seriously, get the fuck up and out of my bed.

Rob wakes up and comes shuffling out looking like a kid getting up for school. The funny thing about Keith is people hang out with him and end up thinking they are him and party too hard and sometimes end up in his bed. Keith tells us why he must shoot his gun every three or four years. He says:

For example, I was in the tuning room with Ronnie at the Spectrum in Philadelphia and Mick's vocal warm-up room was right next door. I called Tony and told him to move this fucking *c**t* to the other side of the building. They were taking too long, so I pulled out me old .38 and fired off about five rounds into a concrete building. They got it done then, man. Management by gunfire. They pay attention for a while after that.

Sherry's room service eventually arrives and we attack it. It's something Southwestern. I don't recall what specifically, but we all eat some of it. Around seven we get up and leave with Tony. Didn't want to wear out our welcome. We go to my room where Tony, Sherry, and I do more meth and we stay up talking about firewalls and Internet security. Why?

I do not remember why.

Tony stayed until we checked out. We had valet-parked the Mercedes and walked out with him to have our car brought around. We were packing the small car with our stuff when I hear a honk. I look up to see a white passenger van and Keith yelling out the van window at me. I go over and he gets out and hugs me and says You're part of the family so don't be a stranger; love you, man.

I said I felt the same.

Tony had his hands full on that visit, for sure, but later tells me Keith was acting up for the benefit of Sherry.

We hop in our car and head out on the highway. We passed a car dealer called Beaman Autos. The sign was a giant neon Native American. I tell Sherry that the Beamans were my people and how they had come down from the mountains to settle the fertile land. I told her that white buffalo came and rubbed us out. I'm the only Beaman left to tell the tales of woe and darkness. We were on I-24 by that time and Sherry says Joey, ninety-five percent of what you say is bullshit...but I love you for the five percent that says heartfelt and profound stuff.

We took the cork out of Willie's whiskey and drank a toast to the last evening there and drove into the sun on our way home to Atlanta.

THE GEORGIA SATELLITES

Todd Johnston, Rick Richards,
Joey Huffman, Rick Price

AN EPIPHANY

Some say addiction is a disease, and that may be so in some cases. But they call it a habit for a reason.

In 2004 my girlfriend and I were fighting so I was sleeping on the couch when I sat straight up because an undeniable, profound moment of clarity — an epiphany, if you will — was upon me:

If I didn't stop using, I'd be kissing my life goodbye.

I'd already destroyed certain business relationships. But if I wanted to pick up the pieces and repair singed bridges of business and family, I couldn't do an eight ball of meth every other day. I called my friend Ted and asked him to take me to an Alcoholics Anonymous meeting, which he did the next day.

I went every day for a year and got my blue chip.

It says in AA's The Big Book to go out and try controlled drinking. Alcoholics can't do it. I can have two drinks and go home with no problems. I stopped going to AA after that because I realized I wasn't an alcoholic and, come to find out, I wasn't addicted to drugs either.

Meth, benzodiazepines, cocaine, heroin, MDMA, and alcohol were tools I was using to manage my bipolar. That I was using them badly was my fault. It was my fault because I had gotten into bad habits.

Getting clean and sober, well, the hardest thing about that is having to deal with feelings I'd been repressing by drinking and drug use. So, metaphorically speaking, I put my hand down my pants, grabbed my balls, and said Man up, boy.

That worked and I faced those feelings head on.

I forgave myself first.

Then I forgave people that had hurt me in the past.

I didn't forgive them for them, I forgave them for me. It felt like I'd been carrying a load of bricks around forever and all I had to do was set them down. My choice. I stopped resenting people and things. I became a better person. Have I relapsed? Of course, such as that is part of recovery and changing bad habits. But it was never for long and always made me remember why I stopped in the first place. I suffer from bipolar disorder and people like me often self-medicate. When the party was over and the drugs all used up, I slept it off.

But if I tried to keep the party rolling, it would've rolled over me. When I was done I was done.

No looking back, no regrets.

But that was the drugs. I continued to self-medicate with alcohol but — yes, there's hope! — while not technically an alcoholic, I did realize even that needed to be under better control. And I did get that under control.

Now I only have maybe a double shot before a show.

PAJAMARAMA

Still in my pajamas on a mid-afternoon in 2006. People may say four o'clock is way too late to be dressed in sleeping attire, but I must differ. It may be a lazy way to spend the day *oooorrrr* there just might be more important shit to do than getting dressed. Example: Counting how many outdated hard drives I have. I bet if I gave you one of my hard drives for your birthday every year before you left your mortal coil behind, my hard drives would still not be depleted.

Then I felt the urge to write a song and think about income taxes and how I was going to use a Schedule C to set up all my equipment that I bought for the last five years and depreciate it all at the same time. But I'm wandering away from the storyline.

You see, most people usually change their pajamas for other types of clothes before driving off to work. But I had a vision of a better plan. By saying I had a vision, what I really meant was I going to conserve as much energy as possible. I was going to push the envelope of being lazy in all matters concerning wardrobe. So, I kept the pajama pants on, pulled on my maroon woobie sweater, wrapped my neck with a scarf adorned with little black skulls I found at Target in the Junior Department, and top it all off with my Doc's and shades.

My hair looked better than the day before, too. Perhaps I wiggled around in my bed just enough to give it more body. I code-named my hairstyle The Night Sweats.

Ready to rumble, I walked out of my front door into a sun shining like it was only shining on me. I heard birds chirping and I swear I was going to break into a song at any minute.

Task #1: Drop someone off in Smyrna. But she was hungry, so…

Task #2: Stop at Publix and get her a protein bar. Task #2 was performed flawlessly in my pajama pants and without Siri's help, thank you very much. Then...

Task #1: Off to Smyrna to complete said dropping off but Siri, still mad at me, is not saying where to turn until right before I have to make that turn. I swear I heard her sigh passive-aggressively before she bellowed the directions in a pissed-off voice: Turn left NOW!

Task #3: Stop by the studio to see how mixing was progressing, but I managed to get terribly lost. It's then I remembered I didn't have my wallet with me because it's still in my big boy pants right where I left them. Siri was ignoring me and I was on Powder Springs Road before I realized I was driving in the polar opposite direction I should be. I figured it out and made it to the studio. Thanks a lot, Siri.

The freedom of pajamas and the warm sweater and scarf made me think I should make this a regular thing. It's kind of like casual Friday for people with ADHD. I walked into the studio where all were impressed with my juvenile yet Continental ensemble.

It's casual Friday. Didn't you get the memo?

Hey, Joey...it's Monday, buddy.

I had to think about that for a few seconds. Then it was on to business. I talked with the client about the mix, saying we should mute the out-of-tune guitar and replace it with a B3 track. And it became so.

My first public session in pajamas. I can scratch that off the bucket list.

After handling work, I picked up my passenger and proceeded home to the compound. Stopped for gas at QuikTrip. In full Pajamarama regalia, including sunglasses at night, I get out of the car and, because I'm one wallet short, scraped up enough change to get two bucks worth of gas. This way I knew I could make it back to QT the next morning with my wallet for a proper tankful.

People are looking at me and probably thinking I was just another derelict out for some mischief. But I was not. I was ARS Man feeling like The Dude in The Big Lebowski going to the grocery store in his robe and sandals to get Half and Half to mix his Caucasians with. Today I was The Dude! It's not every day you can be The Dude. I was free of responsibility, money issues, rent, and blue jeans.

Either way it was funny to me. What a wonderful twilight I had as the moon passed the sun on its way down. I just had one of those days that are The Yardstick For How All Other Days Are Measured. Now to end it in perfect symmetry, I needed The Yardstick By Which All Other Food Is Measured, but where would I get it?

I was filled with joy and sadness.

The Dancing Outlaw: Jesco White

(2011. Photo credit Storm Taylor)

Joey & Jesco

JESCO WHITE

You can take the boy out of his hillbilly culture but it's nigh on impossible to take the hillbilly out of the boy. I met Neal Spears around 2008 when I was in a short-term relationship with Dea Riley who was running for lieutenant governor of Kentucky with author, attorney, and five-time-loser gubernatorial candidate Gatewood Galbraith. She broke up with me when I posted on my blog:

It's hotter than two rats fucking in a wool sock.

She wanted her Rock Star but couldn't face the reality of me not having a filter. Still, she had me playing a rally for her at The Mineshaft in my hometown of Pikeville, Kentucky. I agreed to do it but I can't sing much, so I needed someone who could. Neal came highly recommended. Without rehearsing, we did a fantastic set at the political rally to a massive crowd of five.

Neal and I hit it off immediately. I was ten years his senior, but he reminded me of me. We had the same tastes in music and the same sense of humor. Even though the relationship with Dea ended, Neal and I got along so great that I regularly drove to Pikeville to do gigs with him. Wasn't much pay but lots of fun. We played as a duo, though sometimes Dave Prince and his guitar sat in.

We played clubs and restaurants but mostly we played The Mineshaft. On this one particular weekend they had also booked a special guest for us: The Dancing Outlaw Jesco White who was to dance while we played.

You don't know who Jesco White is? Let's just say briefly that Jesco liked to dance and do drugs — be it huffing glue or something else. The boy liked to party, to put it lightly. The Wild and Wonderful Whites of West Virginia was a 2009 film Johnny Knoxville produced about the whole White family, including Jesco. If you have one thing on your to-do list, let it be to check out the videos of the amazing White family on YouTube.

The one thing I love about playing Pikeville is that I can leave my SUV in the parking lot after the show and pick it up the next day. This means I can drink Jim Beam and diet cola all night and not have to drive. Neal didn't drink so he didn't mind driving. After the shows, we'd go to his apartment and smoke weed (Neal) and drink (Joey). We'd talk about anything and everything and solve the world's problems and by the next day forget how we did it. We had all day to sleep but usually woke around noon. I was able to visit my hometown and get paid. Life was good then.

But back to Jesco. He was booked to clog and dance to the music for this weekend engagement. Neal and I arrived at the venue by eight to begin playing by nine-ish. It took ten minutes to set up. Neal, ever the perfectionist, took longer but he was dealing with the front of house and our monitors.

The club wasn't very crowded at eight, but people were drifting in. I grabbed a Jim Beam and diet cola from the bar and went to sit in the corner where I can see everything. Jesco came in with his small entourage which consisted of his girlfriend, sister, and a little boy about ten. No one seemed alarmed that an underage child was at a wild bar. They went straight to the office.

The Mineshaft was about half full when Neal and I began playing. We started on time but I'm sure we could've started anytime and none would've noticed or cared. So we start our set and halfway through the first song the crowd parts and in comes Jesco already a-dancin'. The crowd gathers to watch and cheer him on. People took selfies with him and got his autograph.

We played our set and took a break. Jesco never stopped dancing. It was sad, really. He didn't seem to know some people were laughing *at* him and not *with* him. To the people at the club he was their own private freak show. I had a hard time with that. Then again, freak shows have been around for hundreds, maybe thousands, of years and they always get an audience and make some money, so maybe it wasn't as bad as I thought. At any rate, Jesco seemed to enjoy the attention. He was a star and these were his fans and he was going to entertain them.

Neal and I started the second set and there was Jesco, clogging like his life depended on it. He has talent. His dancing is not bad.

As the evening wore on a crowd mentality took over. People were drunk and going up to Jesco while he was dancing and invading his space. They started being rude to him. Some were yelling at him. Some were trying to dance around him. But he took it all like a soldier and just kept dancing.

I wanted to meet Jesco but they were out of there before we finished our set. We finished for the night, got a bottle from the bar, and took it to Neal's where I put a good dent in it. We stayed up all night talking. I didn't think to ask Neal what he thought about Jesco.

The next night was a repeat of the previous except we got there later because we didn't have to set up. Neal and I sat and talked to a few folks. I even saw some people I hadn't seen in years and enjoyed catching up with them.

We started the first set and here comes Jesco dancing his heart out. The crowd's bigger than the night before so there wasn't as much room for him to pull out all the stops in his repertoire. Pretty much the same as the first night, though: Selfies, handshakes, and autographs. Then it turned ugly again but nothing too bad. Neal and I decide to break down and load out the next day so we can stay and press the flesh and get gloriously drunk.

I missed Jesco again. Was he just being mysterious or what? Figured I'd see him at settlement the next day, so I was cool. We closed the place down. A few friends and I met up at Neal's for the after-party. I drink. I don't smoke weed, but that didn't stop everybody else from partaking.

We listened to music and partied all night. I woke up at noon on a couch, looked around, saw bodies on the other couch and all over the floor. No one made it out alive. People started waking up and getting their wits about them. Some say goodbye and leave. Neal and I were scheduled to be at The Mineshaft to break down and load out at two. We made it a little after that. I was wondering if people get as hung over from weed as they do from drinking because I was feeling the drink which caused us to slowly and carefully walk to the club's back door where the bartender let us in. While I was breaking down, I heard voices in the bar area, but didn't think much about it.

Neal and I loaded out and all was fine, but we had to go back inside to settle our gigs. I heard the same voices that were talking earlier but in hushed tones. We didn't know what to do. We needed to settle up but the conversation in the other room seemed very private. Then a kid's screaming Goddamn it, Jesco, get your motherfucking cocaine so we can go home!

Getting called out by a ten-year-old about your drugs has to be the worst. But it got Jesco's attention, and he and his cocaine and entourage slunk back to West Virginia and now we can go in, settle our shows, and even get a little bonus. Neal and I get into our separate cars and say goodbye.

I went to see family and spend time with them.

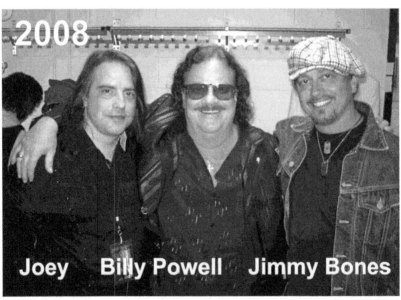

Joey   Billy Powell   Jimmy Bones

Madison Square Garden

SHOW DRINKS, THE LEGEND, AND THE BIG BAD TROUBLE WITH A WILD BOAR

Hank's playing Bama Jam in the sweltering June heat of Rural Alabama in 2009. I drive to the gig with my friends Val King and Angie Alex, then of the online magazine The Backstage Beat. I was doing a blog for them called Postcards From The Road at the time; the idea was to interview me backstage for a video blog. You know what they say about the best-laid plans of mice and men, not to mention Accidental Rock Stars and journalists.

We were supposed to leave Angie's house at seven that morning. I arrive on time then realize I'd forgotten a bag of cords I needed for the show so had to drive back home and get it, which put our departure time more around quarter past eight. It was hotter than two rats...well, you know the rest. Thank God and Jesus for A/C.

We hit the road, Val and Alex in the front of Val's son's Jeep, and me laid out in the back. We drive for what seemed like hours. Felt like we were in Rural Alabama longer than Moses and the Israelites wandered in the desert. I went without cell service for over three hours. Even satellites couldn't find us and we got lost because the GPS lost signal. GPS isn't supposed to lose signal. There should have been a sign that read You are now entering Rural Alabama. Please set your technology clocks back twenty years and pull out your paper map.

Yes, thank God, we stumble across a liquor store and finally make it to our destination after asking directions twenty different times. We found our way backstage. While waiting for credentials, Bob Smith, tour manager, sensed something in the air, dubbing Val and Angie The Troublemakers. Bob warned me to not turn the day into The Joey Huffman Show. I assured him I wouldn't and all would be well. I lied to Bob — but not on purpose. The Troublemakers lived up to their new sobriquet and I had a new nickname by day's end. Here's what happened.

The sun's over the yardarm somewhere, so the first order of business was to find Jim Beam and start drinking. We found it on the band bus being guarded by Bob. Angie asked him for a tour of the bus while Val and I quickly and stealthily mixed three show drinks.

A show drink consists of a little bit of ice in a red Solo cup filled to the top with Jim Beam and a splash of diet cola for color. We absconded with the drinks and hit the stage to watch Blackberry Smoke.

By the end of their blazing set, I'd already sucked the bottom out of my show drink and was ready for another. The Troublemakers and I thought it might be a good time to film the interview, so we retired to the bus again. Bob was nowhere to be found so we mixed more show drinks without any surreptitiousness involved. Now, I have a high tolerance for liquor but after two show drinks, besides becoming infinitely more charming — at least I think so, onlookers' opinions may vary! — I start to slur but only a little bit. It doesn't take a prognosticator to predict that maybe a drunk, slurring Joey might not make for the best video interview. But if two show drinks are good then three must be better. I might add The Troublemakers were just as tipsy. Luckily, we had a video camera to capture the comedy that ensued.

Angie set up the camera and put me between her and Val. They are both very attractive girls, well-endowed, and wearing shirts featuring said endowments. I felt like Hugh Hefner being interviewed at the Playboy Mansion. I honestly don't remember much about the interview. It's online on YouTube somewhere. If you can find it, please share the link on my FB page because I haven't been able to get to it.

I prattled on and on like a complete jackass. But we trudged through. I'm not embarrassed, though I think I should be. I remember it was hilarious. Well, Bob reappears on the bus because it had to be cleaned and ready for Hank's arrival in less than an hour. So he not so subtly reminds us there's food and liquor in the dressing room. In other words, Get the fuck off my bus.

So off we head for the dressing room. Bob was correct, there was copious alcohol and snack foods. We mixed another show drink and settled in. It's dinnertime and, instead of going to Catering, we got a menu for a nearby restaurant to order from. Lindsey, our caregiver/minder, provided us with a piece of paper and a pen on which to put orders with names written beside the ones we chose.

This is where the trouble really started. You see, I wanted the filet mignon. Not a problem. But on the menu the filet mignon was called The Legend. So to keep the orders straight, logic dictates I write Joey Huffman, The Legend. Lindsey saw this and it was all over. And thus I became The Legend.

The nickname spread like wildfire. Even Hank called me The Legend. It's funny and I really didn't mind. After all, there are worse nicknames. In time I managed to get it shortened to TL. That nickname stuck for three years.

Anyway, I ate The Legend, had another show drink, and it was time for the show. But I was comfortable on the couch and complained about going to work. Everybody in the room collectively said Oh, poor Joey has to do what he loves in front of a festival crowd, boo-hoo, waah-waah-waah.

I was feeling no pain and, having found a blanket in the dressing room, turned it into a cape. I agreed to perform but only if I could wear my cape. Someone consented but somehow it vanished before we hit the stage. I know we had a good show in front of a crowd of about thirty thousand people. I wish I could remember more about it but it was a while back and I was lit like a Christmas tree. After the show, we retired to the bus for another show drink.

The bus parked next to ours was Travis Tritt's, where on display at the front was a stuffed wild boar. The story of the boar is as follows: The night before, Kid Rock shot the wild boar on Hank's property in Apalachicola, Florida. Hank called his personal taxidermist and had him do a rush job on the boar. Hank then flew it in his jet, transferred it to his limo, and personally delivered it to Travis because Travis was going to see Kid Rock the following evening. The Troublemakers, now dubbed by the band The Party Girls From Mount Pilot, didn't know the history of the boar when they decided that it'd be a good idea to go pose provocatively with it while I took pictures. When Bob saw what was transpiring, he lost his mind. How dare we desecrate the wild boar? How disrespectful! What if Hank finds out? But all was well. No harm, no foul. We left the boar in peace although I'm sure it would've been blushing had it had a pulse.

In the end all had fun, even Bob. We decided to spend the night. It took another two hours to find the hotel but that's another story.

Hey, wanna hear a joke?

If UUUUU have a personal taxidermist on call, UUUUU just might be a redneck.

I MET AND TALKED WITH GOD AT DENNY'S ON CHRISTMAS EVE

God is not scary at all. I met him at a Denny's where He ordered the Club Sandwich with fries and unsweetened tea. He came to me as an elderly gentleman, a tailor by trade, explaining life in terms a tailor used.

Life is like a quality garment. You have to care for it, otherwise it will start to unravel and become threadbare.

A suit must be dry-cleaned often and hung in the closet after you've worn it. Try not to stain it or rip it. The garment has many colors all woven together. When the woven parts that make up the garment separate or rip, it affects the whole garment.

One's responsibility is to mend the garment when damaged and keep it together.

Then God gave me His final words of wisdom:

You only get one garment in your lifetime. Take great care of yours and be respectful of all the threads that bind it together.

Then again, maybe this whole story is because I was tripping and only thought I met God.

2017 Backstage at Lakewood (Atlanta): Bella Clifton, Rob Thomas, Joey, and Kimberly Charick

2012

JT Longoria

Taz Bentley

Izzy Stradlin

Joey

Ocean Way Studios

JOEY and
DAVE PIRNER

2013

NERVES AND TUMORS

It's September of 2013 and the headaches came and went so bad that sometimes I lay in the dark and suffered all day. They were becoming more frequent and severe. It was not fun.

My girlfriend Kimberly — we were living together — was frustrated because she didn't understand the scope of my headaches. It wasn't her fault she didn't understand. I wasn't one to complain or explain the pain, so for all she knew I was just slacking off and avoiding my career and life...and her. She's tired of me and my headaches and, needing some time apart, suggested I spend time with my daughter Whitney. That was Tuesday. I talked to her every day while I was away. Apparently, she missed me because I was invited back home on Saturday. I was so happy to see her and gave her a big hug.

My headache was there all the time. The only thing that changed was its intensity. I feel like I have an ice cream headache that won't go away.

She says she wants to understand. Then I did what men don't usually do: I asked her to take me to the Emergency Room. Yeah. I was at that point. She got really concerned when she heard moaning.

When do you want to go?

Right now!

The gravity of the situation hit and she quickly drove me to the ER at Kennestone. When asked if symptoms were life-threatening, I took it to mean was I going to keel over and die right there so I said they weren't. They produced a ream of paper but I gave it all to Kimberly, who asked the questions and quickly filled it out. I signed and she gave it all to the nurse who told us to have a seat.

Thirty minutes later we go through double doors into the ER lobby. I brought Kimberly back because I didn't want to be alone. We went to a room. I changed into a hospital gown, crawled into bed, and covered up with sheets and blanket. Kimberly pulled her chair close, held my hand, and comforted me with talk to ease my mind's anxiety and fear:

Everything's going to be okay, Joey. I'm here for you, Joey. I won't let them hurt you, Joey.

Nurse Mandy was in a good mood which helped mine. She got an IV going and fanned it out to four inputs which allowed them to give shots and not have to stick the patient again. She started a saline IV and checked vitals. They were stable.

Have you ever had an MRI?

I have not.

Well, it isn't that big of a deal.

I'm claustrophobic.

Don't worry about that; we'll give you something to help the nerves.

She left and came back shortly with two Ativan. I removed all earrings, bracelets, necklaces, and rings. She put them in a plastic bag with Huffman A-4 written across it.

Kimberly had been watching and listening to what was going on and had questions: Is MRI radioactive? Are there other diagnostic options? Can I go with Joey to MRI? The answers: No. No. And No.

Yay on not being radioactive. Seems head pain is hard to diagnose with any other diagnostic tool, so MRI was best. And I'd just have to suck up my claustrophobia.

The nurse left and Kimberly, now assured, continued to comfort so well I closed my eyes and almost drifted off to sleep. About an hour later a porter helps me out of bed, sits me in a wheelchair, and off we go to MRI.

The examination was performed in a special room that houses the MRI system. Strategically placed lighting was only where they needed it, so overall it was dark inside the lab. The MRI machine itself was lit up and looked like a rocket laying on its side with a comfortably padded table gently gliding in and out.

That room was cold, so they provided a blanket and a pillow and told me to lay down on the padded table and get comfortable. They offered a blindfold and earplugs. I declined. They offered an attachment that worked like a periscope where I can see them in the booth. That was an option I could go for. The periscope got me out of the tube visually thus helping with claustrophobia and, curious as I always am, I wanted to watch them do their job.

They were ready to start so a nurse made sure I was comfortable and ready. The MRI procedure takes around forty to forty-five minutes. At three quarters of the way through, they pull the patient out and inject a contrast solution, like a dye. Then back in for ten more minutes and then out and it's over.

Almost immediately the table began sliding into the tube until I was four fifths of the way in. I had to put my arms up on my body. It was so tight I felt like I was in a torpedo tube and had to concentrate using breathing exercises to keep from hyperventilating.

Sound like all hell breaking loose as if they were beating on the side of the tube was followed by the sound of silence. An alarm buzzed loud for a minute followed by a hydraulic noise that sounds like when you adjust your office chair after you let it go all the way up then pull the lever and it makes a hissing sound on the way down. Next came the very loud clamor sounding like an electric saw on metal.

That series happened four or five times after which they took me halfway out to administer the contrast. While the nurse was checking vitals, they shot the dye in the peripheral IV. I feel the dye creeping all through my body. Then back inside the torpedo tube where I heard the same cacophony as before. The session with the contrast only lasted ten minutes and, as promised, they pulled me out and I sit up. They removed the periscope device and helped me stand, but I got to keep the blanket because I was cold.

Then back to A-4 with the porter and into the bed. Kimberly was there waiting for answers but there were none yet. She crawled up in the bed and cuddled. I tell her an overly dramatic yet mysterious story of the MRI experience. I gave her a play-by-play.

It's good to have something to talk about while waiting and an hour and a half passes. Each time the nurse came in to check vitals, we'd ask if there was news. No news yet, she'd say. Finally, though, a resident shows up. Introductions were made and I got right down to it: What's the diagnosis?

It's a tumor called a schwannoma, an abnormal lump or growth of cells, he says.

A tumor is considered benign when the cells in the tumor are normal, that is, the cells simply got a wrong message to replicate themselves and turn into a lump, but do not spread to or destroy other cells. A tumor is considered as malignant cancer when the cells are abnormal, that is, they replicate and spread (metastasize) and destroy other cells and don't stop growing.

But at that moment, I didn't know all that. All I heard was tumor. Is it cancer, Doctor?

No. The tumor is benign, so it'd be best to contact a neurosurgeon and have it taken out sooner rather than later. That means surgery. The schwannoma is about the size of a tennis ball and probably pushing against a nerve so, more than likely, that's where all the pain is coming from.

Too stunned to react quickly, Kimberly and I couldn't ask questions. The resident quietly excused himself saying he'd be right back, and he was...with a prescription for twenty Percocet, a business card for a neurologist, and instructions:

Contact a neurosurgeon. It doesn't have to be the one on the card; any neurosurgeon you are comfortable with and trust. You are now free to leave.

He exited the room leaving us with many questions only a neurosurgeon can answer. We fill the prescription, getting home at dark. We had been at the hospital for five hours and were numb. I took two Percocet and went to bed.

Kimberly went online and started researching. She identified the cause of the headaches: Trigeminal Neuralgia. The schwannoma tumor was putting pressure on the trigeminal nerve.

The Percocet helped with the pain, but I ran out in about a week. I went to Doctor B— for pain relief. He prescribed twenty more Percocet. I went to Dr. T— for pain relief and he prescribed twenty Percocet. I went to Dr K— and he wrote a prescription for twenty Percocet.

The reason they only prescribed once is because they are under the eye of the FDA and only allowed to prescribe that way. The DEA wanted opioids prescribed only to cancer patients and terminal patients. They were cracking down hard on doctors. Break the FDA rules and a doctor could have their license revoked.

Val:
Little sister
I never had
and best
friend.

I called Val King — my very best friend, we're like brother and sister — and told her the news about the tumor and the pain. She came right over and I filled her in and said I didn't know what to do. The brain surgeon the hospital recommended has only been practicing three years and I didn't want an inexperienced neurologist poking around in my brain.

We talk about which hospital's best and figured Emory University Hospital. Val sprang into action. She called her doctor, part of the Emory Healthcare Network, and left a message. He returned her call that evening. The doc knew the best and promised to call and give a referral. Which he did. I'm very grateful for that.

When Val called, the receptionist at the neurosurgeon's office informed her they weren't taking any new patients for six months. But Val worked her magic and asked to speak to the office manager. The office manager came on the line. Val explained who made the referral, that he was a member of the Emory network, and was supposed to have already called and made the referral. Not only that, Joey is in a lot of pain. Val got them to agree to an appointment for Tuesday, October 8th. Val doesn't take no for an answer.

Val is badass.

She came over every day after that allowing Kimberly to be able to work from home and not feel like she had to worry every minute. Kimberly regularly came from downstairs to check on me, but Val was my day-to-day friend and confidante. Kimberly was very busy working hard to pay bills and taking care of her three children. We saw each other at bedtime, and she loved me, but she couldn't be there constantly. She had to conserve her energies, too.

This is the face of four-oxy-per-day PAIN.

Tuesday, October 8th

Val and Kimberly took me to the appointment with a neurosurgeon in downtown Atlanta. Since I was a new patient, there was more paperwork. Kimberly and Val double-teamed it. I couldn't do anything but rock back and forth in pain. Finally, we're called back where a nurse took vitals. Blood pressure 120/80, just like clockwork. We waited about ten minutes and in walks Dr. H —. He was tall with black hair and brown eyes and wearing a lab coat. Introductions were made, then Dr. H— got to the point:

There usually isn't any pain related to tumors. The brain itself feels no pain. So where is the pain and what is it like?

I point to the front of my skull about two inches to the left of the top, and about two inches above my left eyebrow. Then I explain: It's constant, Doctor. Sometimes the pain comes from the top of my head, down through my forehead, through my eye and down through my cheek and into my teeth.

He looked at the MRI, studying something, and says it sounded like Trigeminal Neuralgia. It's a chronic pain condition that affects the trigeminal nerve which carries sensation from your face to your brain. Because the pain is so bad and doesn't go away, it's also known as the suicide disease. One or more of these symptoms may be experienced:

- Episodes of severe, shooting, or jabbing pain that may feel like an electric shock.
- Spontaneous attacks of pain.
- Pain triggered by touching the face, chewing, speaking, or brushing teeth.
- Bouts of excruciating pain lasting from a few seconds to several minutes.
- Episodes of several attacks lasting days, weeks, months, or longer.
- Constant aching.

- A burning feeling that may occur before it erupts into painful spasms.
- Pain in areas supplied by the trigeminal nerve, including the cheek, jaw, teeth, gums, lips and, less often, the eyes and forehead.
- Pain affecting one side of the face at a time, though rarely may affect both sides of the face.
- Pain focused in one spot or spreading in a wider pattern.
- Attacks that become more frequent and intense over time.

Dr. H— said they'd give something for the pain, but it would only reduce it, not make it go away. I'd need to see a pain management doctor to prescribe dose amounts that will help until surgery could be performed. This was somewhat concerning because I'd been clean since 2004 and didn't want it to lead me into any darker places.

The doc came back with a prescription for twenty Percocet and tells me to make an appointment for surgery with the receptionist behind the desk. So, we made an appointment for November 21.

We got back home, and Val and I go upstairs to the bedroom. I laid down as Val sat in the middle of the bed, phone in hand. She knew a pain management clinic down by the airport she took her mother and ex-boyfriend to. Appointment made with Dr. S— for two days away made me feel a little better.

It's a sunny day when Val and I ventured out to see Dr. S— at his Hapeville office. While I slumped in pain, Val finished the paperwork and gave it to the nurse. Fifteen minutes later they called my name and we walk in on Dr. S— arguing with a nurse because he was not going to treat me since it looked like I'd been doctor-shopping. Before I understood what was going on, Val ran through an armed Atlanta police officer and two nurses to get to Dr. S—. She pleaded with him to listen. Explained the whole situation. The tumor. Trigeminal nerve. Surgery. Her mother's pain and her boyfriend's pain and the referral to him by my neurologist…well, that last part wasn't exactly true. Sure, Dr. H— had said to find a pain management doctor but had never gotten around to giving a referral.

Dr. S— put all that together and agreed to see me. Val thanked him over and over. Without her pleading I certainly wouldn't have been treated by him. I'm glad she's on my side.

Val is badass.

Dr. S— came into the room and sat across from me. Which drugs are you doing or have ever done?

I began ticking off one by one all I'd ever used: Marijuana. Methamphetamine. Cocaine. Benzodiazepine, or benzos for short. Amphetamines. Heroin. Methylenedioxymethamphetamine, also known as MDMA and includes Ecstasy and Molly. Mushrooms. Acid. Then added: Oh, plus I still drink more than a little vodka and Jim Beam at times.

That puts you in a very high-risk category. Does anyone in the family do drugs?

My brother abused painkillers and is an alcoholic, but he got treatment and has been sober more than thirty years.

Symptoms?

I list them. He says the next time I come in the first thing to do is give a urine sample. Fill it, give it to the nurse, register and wait to be called.

He hands me the prescription and says he'd see me in one month. I pay and make the next appointment. As we wait for the car to warm up, I looked at the prescription. It was for one hundred twenty 30 mg oxycodone pills, one pill four times per day. On the street those cost eighty bucks per, so this prescription was worth ten thousand dollars in street value, but they were more valuable as something to kill my damn pain.

Getting the prescription filled involved some drama. Pharmacists also have to worry about the FDA so they are wary of prescriptions for pain that may end up being used for recreation or sold. I don't blame them for their wariness at all, but Val proved I was truly a patient, not a user. Twenty minutes later we're on our way home, but I took the first pill right there in the car.

Ten minutes later we get to the house. The oxy was getting into my system. I'd never felt that way before. I was getting sleepy and itching a little bit like a heroin addict. Felt warm. Felt a sense of well-being. I fell into bed. This medicine was definitely helping.

Val told Kimberly all about our day, all the drama, and all the close calls. Kimberly thanked Val for being there. Val would be here same time tomorrow.

For the next three weeks, I was almost painless, but the oxycodone had me on my ass, sleeping a lot, unable to do much but watch cartoons. Val came every day and ran errands.

Then a bomb dropped.

A healthcare manager from Emory Hospital Midtown called and wanted to know how we were going to pay the twenty thousand down payment. I said I thought they had to take all patients and she said that it's only if its imminently life-threatening. I handed the phone to Val. But badass as she is, she couldn't twist a deal with the hospital. It looked like my surgery was canceled. Even if we managed to raise twenty thousand dollars, we'd still owe a hundred and seventy thousand. Things were looking dark. I needed a miracle.

Then a miracle did happen at the end of October. An angel called with good news.

Joey. This is Tatum. I heard about you from a mutual friend in Nashville. The best thing you can do is not to worry about money. We are going to handle everything. We will get you health insurance that Emory will take. So stop worrying.

Tatum Allsep founded Music Health Alliance. [Their website has a lot more information: musichealthalliance.com]. She began documenting the music industry's need for healthcare support using a new model that simplified the process of access. So, there she is, just launching Music Health Alliance to the public in January of

2013, and who gets a call from her in November? That's right. Me — who, I later found out, was their first client.

She went on about help to get my bills paid while I was ill. She talked to the doctors and rebooked the surgery for January 7th, 2014. Music Health Alliance did all of this at no charge to me. Tatum was a true advocate and very nice on top of that. Now I could really relax knowing that everything was taken care of. Now all my worries and energies were focused on the surgery.

But even surgery worries can break through the oxy shell and let me tell you, I was worried.

Thursday, November 7th

At Dr. S— again. Fill cup, put in door, register, and wait. Should be easy, but try as I might, I can't make water. I felt an imaginary stress from the nurse outside the door. I turned on the water. No help there! I tried to relax and just let it flow. Fifteen minutes later I managed enough for the cup and turned it over to the nurse and wait to be called.

I look around the room and notice most of the people there look dopesick and were there for their fix. The agony for which they started coming to a pain management clinic was long gone and now they looked defeated, lost, and miserable. I turn to Val.

Val, I do not want to end up like these people. Please help me to get off the opioids, okay? Remind me when it's time to start weaning myself off the oxy. Promise?

I promise, Joey.

Name called, I go to an examination room where a nurse takes vitals, fills out paperwork, and says Dr. S— will see you soon. She leaves. A few moments later in he came.

Hello. How's the medication working? Any side effects or changes you might be concerned about?

Assured the meds were working and there were no problems, he writes a prescription and says See you next month. I make payment and book an appointment. We leave to get prescription filled. No problems with that. After paying, we go home, I kiss Kimberly, give her the prescription, then head up to bed.

Friday, November 8th

Val and my daughter Whitney throw a benefit at 120 Café off Roswell Road near The Big Chicken. They only had two or three days to get it together. They secured the venue and made posters, got it mentioned on Atlanta's 97.1 a few times thanks to Kaedy Kiely, and promoted it on Facebook. Many bands donated their time to play; some I knew, others I didn't. They were all heroes in my book. I was humbled and moved by their goodwill. There were:

Drivin N Cryin, Angie Aparo, Peter Stroud, Davin McCoy, Uberstout, Gasoline Bros, South City Riot, Liz Melendez, The Higher Choir, Hailey Fletcher, David T & Friends, Mike Martin, and The Athens Band.

People want me to come out and talk but all I want to do is sit on this way-comfortable couch with Monkey Man and relax. I had had a couple of oxycodone pills and a couple of drinks and man I was floating just about pain-free six inches above that comfy couch. I could've stayed there all night.

Monkey Man and I chatted about his bar — Monkey Man's — that had been located in a strip mall on the corner of Windy Hill and U.S. 41. Monkey Man's bar got hit directly by a tornado. I mean, the whole strip mall was leveled. I mean, like there had never been anything there at all. Terrible. The HellHounds had played his club a few times and always enjoyed it.

Kim, my ex-wife, took me off the comfy couch and introduced me around, dragging me like a toy on a string. I met so many people

I can't remember them all. Whitney saved me. She assigned Kim something to do regarding the raffle later that night and I was able to get back to the comfy couch.

But Monkey Man was gone. He's mysterious that way.

You might think the loud music would make my headache worse, but it didn't. My pain level was about a three because of the oxycodone buffering my body from the world.

End of the night, it was time to sit in with Drivin N Cryin and Peter Stroud. I went to the stage when they called my name. I was playing someone else's keyboard, and it sounded good. I have to say this night was about the haziest of my illness. I can hardly remember anything of what happened. The memories are fuzzy but good all the same.

The benefit was a success. Hats off to Val and Whitney. They worked hard with only three days to get it all together. The show was sold out, and a lot of great bands donated their time to play. I think everyone had a good time. I know I did…at least, the parts I can remember.

Three Weeks Into November

I'm feeling strange sensations. Can't sleep; anxious. One night it got so bad I couldn't stay in bed with Kimberly. I didn't want to wake her, so I snuck downstairs, feeling really bad but hard to explain the sensations. I sat on the couch ensconced in a blanket just rocking back and forth as the pain hit wave after wave sometimes feeling like my brain was caving in on itself.

I tried eating…to no avail.

I tried to go to the bathroom…but couldn't.

I tried walking around the house…but nothing helped.

So, I sat, wrapped in a blanket, and rocked. It's the only thing that helped. Then the hallucinations started. Geometric shapes and faces flew all around as I rocked, rocked, rocked, rocked, rocked. Then it happened.

A seizure.

I simply lay writhing on the floor for…I can only guess: Thirty seconds maybe? After the seizure, I stayed on the floor, afraid to move. Finally, whole body shaking, I managed to get up. I thought maybe I could now lay in bed, so I took an oxy and slept.

When Kimberly got up, I woke and followed her downstairs trying to tell her what happened, but the words wouldn't come. I got frustrated and that was scaring her a bit. I couldn't tell her about the horror show last night was. She called Val. The first thing out of Val's mouth: Has he been forgetting to take his Klonopin?

I'd forgotten to refill the prescription. Mystery solved.

Kimberly gets the prescription refilled. I took two pills and thirty minutes later I was back to normal. Kimberly hugged me hard and says Don't ever scare me like that again; I love you.

It's no joke: Benzo withdrawal makes heroin withdrawal look like a carnival ride.

The thing about laying around all day and watching cartoons is it manifests itself into a feeling of low self-esteem and depression. I saw myself as a burden to others and felt sorry for myself. Why would God do this to me? Am I a bad person? There's a lot of time to think about these things and get more depressed.

It's always better to keep Joey occupied, so sometimes Val came and scooped me up to ride around and pass the time and I'd feel like I was in a parade no one was watching. Sometimes I'd drift in and out of consciousness. At times I'd nod off mid-sentence. Other times I'd be fully awake and ready to go. It all depended on when I took my meds.

When my buddy Rick Meyer found out about my illness, he called regularly just to talk and came over every Wednesday and took me out to eat. He helped me stay happy. Rick is a good friend.

The days passed slowly. Still, every day that fell off was one day closer to surgery. I didn't know what was going to happen, so the fear of the great unknown loomed large.

(Rick Meyer passed away in 2020.)

Thursday, December 12th

Time to see Dr. S—. Val took me, like always, and everything went fine. Got the prescription and had it filled with no snags.

Still, I was so lonely and wanted to see all my friends, so out of the blue I announced on Thursday I was having a Christmas party the next day, which was crazy and impossible. Kimberly and Val tried to talk me out of it. There's not enough time, they say. People already have plans for the weekend, they insist.

But I was heavily medicated and would not be deterred. I spent the rest of Thursday and a goodly part of Friday calling people and inviting them to the little get-together. If I couldn't get them on the phone, I left a message.

Kimberly brought up two good points: What are we going to feed them? And what will we have for them to drink?

I thought for a moment. Can't go wrong with a couple of large cheese-and-cracker plates, a veggie plate, and two or three bottles of wine. Besides, most are gonna bring their favorite something to drink anyway. Planning: Done!

Kimberly took me to Kroger to get the food and wine. She stayed in the car while I ventured in. At checkout I got carded for the wine.

I know they card everybody, but it still made me feel good.

When we got home, Kimberly helped carry in the food and wine. She knows the drugs make for a clumsiness looking for a place to happen, so she took all the trays into the kitchen by herself and put them in the refrigerator. I carried the wine and sat it on the counter — undropped and unbroken.

Afternoon

Kimberly picks up and straightens. I run the Hoover and make sure dishes are done and stored. Kimberly cleans counters and stovetop. We finish around 5:00 and let me tell you:

That house sparkled.

Guests are supposed to arrive around 8:00, so I had time to get ready and took a long, hot shower and began to figure out what I was going to wear. I started with a black T-shirt and favorite jeans, a maroon paisley button-down shirt unbuttoned over the T-shirt. I finished the wardrobe with my trusty Doc Martens; you would've thought it was 1995. I took the next oxycodone and went downstairs.

Kimberly told me to turn around. She played with my hair a little. I shook my head and my hair looked like it did before she adjusted it. She smiled and gave me a hug:

You look very handsome, Joey.

6:30 p.m.

Kimberly's turn to shower and get ready. She disappears upstairs. I open a bottle of Merlot and pour a glass before it had a chance to breathe. It was sweet but had a tart aftertaste. It was good enough for me and as you've learned by now: It's all about me.

Kimberly came back down in tight jeans, a lavender sweater, and comfortable shoes. I told her she looked gorgeous. She says thank you, poured a glass of wine, tasted, and declared it good. I finished mine and poured another. We were just waiting for guests to arrive now. I remembered the cheese and veggie platters in the refrigerator and hurried to take them out. Kimberly tells me to let her do it, took three platters from me, and lined them up on the counter.

The doorbell rang and there was my friend Marlin Brackett with a bottle of wine and a six-pack of Samuel Adams. I invited him to come in. Kimberly took his coat and we retired to the kitchen. Does he want a beer? He did, so I hand him a beer and put the rest in the refrigerator and give him the bottle opener.

Marlin and I chat a little bit, catching up, then the doorbell rings. I was surprised to see my friend and attorney, McCracken Poston, with a twelve-pack of Miller Lite and a bottle of Cabernet in his hands. I take the beer and lead him to the kitchen where the party is.

Does McCracken want a beer? He did, so I handed him a beer and put the rest in the refrigerator, make introductions between the first two guests, and they exchange pleasantries. As they talk, I pour another glass of wine and offer cheese and crackers, but they decline.

8:30 p.m.

Surely more guests will start showing up soon. I crack open the door and peek out then go back to the kitchen where there was a party. McCracken and Marlin are conversing. I listen. They're just talking about what they do for a living. I was waiting for a place to jump into the conversation, but the doorbell rings.

I open the door for a third time. There is my friend Peter Stroud with a twelve-pack of Pabst Blue Ribbon in one hand and a bottle of Merlot in the other. I take the beer and invite him on in. Does he want a beer? He did, so I gave him one from the twelve-pack he brought and put the rest in the refrigerator, introduce him to McCracken and Marlin, and they shake hands and start talking.

9:15 p.m.

No other guests had arrived. I was disappointed...but mostly embarrassed. I went back to the kitchen where Kimberly had joined the party. I thought that was a good thing. For one, I enjoyed her company, and secondly, she was not shy at all. She's a great match for me because when I don't know what to say she steps in and says the right thing. She'd never met these friends of mine, so she stepped up and introduced herself which — Joey, Joey, Joey! — is something I should've done.

We were sharing stories in the kitchen, just drinking and enjoying ourselves. I poured another glass of wine. The party was turning into a success. I was no longer embarrassed. It somehow seemed like just the right number of guests.

McCracken told us a true story about an old man in Ringgold, Georgia, and his young bride. Everybody thought the old man was crazy and holding the young woman hostage. He was very private, and they did not receive visitors. He was mysterious but extremely adroit at fixing mechanical things like lawnmowers and tractors. That's how he survived. He could be seen out walking and visiting pawn shops to ask if there was something they needed repairing. Somebody usually had something.

He didn't have a car and walked everywhere he went. Sometimes he had a wheelbarrow with him, sometimes he didn't. But he was out at dawn and back home at dusk.

Sewing circle ladies kept rumors flying around. One heard the old man chained the poor young thing to a bed. Another heard he was starving her near to death. Rumors got worse with each telling.

One morning the man showed up early at McCracken's office and told him his wife passed away during the night. He'd contacted McCracken before he called the police. McCracken says he'd represent him, but they had to call the police. So, they did.

McCracken gave the old man a ride to his house, arriving just as police and EMCs were showing up. Detectives and forensic experts were the first to enter, followed by McCracken and the newly widowed. Once inside, McCracken scanned the house. The man was a borderline hoarder, but the bedroom was clean.

McCracken noticed the walls were lined with notes and the walls were written on, too. McCracken pulled one note off and examined it. To his shock it was a love letter to the man. McCracken examined other notes on the wall. All love letters to her husband. Some were taped, others held by thumbtacks. There must have been a thousand, maybe more. And under the notes were love letters written on the walls. It was a lot to take in.

The coroner arrived at the scene and once all the evidence was processed would examine the body and give a preliminary cause of death. There was no blood. No lacerations. No bruises on her body. She lay there, appearing peaceful. The coroner determined no signs of foul play but couldn't verify it wasn't murder or natural causes until he performed an autopsy.

McCracken asked the old man if he wanted to get something to eat. He did. So they climbed into McCracken's car and headed toward the Waffle House. He couldn't believe his wife was gone. She was his little angel. They were still in love after all these years.

The coroner did the autopsy and found absolutely nothing pointing to foul play. He did confirm natural causes: She'd died from an aneurism of the artery attached to her left ventricle. He said it had probably been weak from birth.

The man was cleared of any crime or other nefariousness.

McCracken knew the editor of the local newspaper and gave him the information about the love notes and how much in love they were. The editor agreed to run the story about the couple on page one and set up an interview with the old man. The editor went to their house to see the letters and take a few for reference. He also took a photographer with him to document the small house.

The people of the town had been gossiping for years. It's high time for them to have their comeuppances. The couple was probably the happiest in Ringgold. The article came out in the next edition of the morning paper. It sweetly told the story of a man and woman in love. The man knew what people thought of him and simply decided to ignore them. He knew what was waiting for him at home.

Knowing that the man had to be grieving, McCracken often took him for a Waffle House breakfast. He eventually opened up to McCracken and they became friends. McCracken always checked to see if he had groceries and made sure that he was comfortable before he said goodnight.

Damn.

I think I had a tear in my eye.

We all commiserated with the man and talked about how good the story was.

1:30 a.m.

It's getting late and the party was winding down. McCracken had to drive back to Ringgold, Marlin also had a long drive, and Peter headed on out, too. We say our goodbyes and watch them walk out to their cars and get in. We didn't stop watching until their taillights disappeared over the hill.

Kimberly says it had been the perfect party: We all truly enjoyed ourselves. I was feeling pretty good about it. She tells me to take my meds and go to bed. She'd clean and be right up. I went upstairs, took the meds, and got into our comfortable bed. I watched South Park until the drugs put me to sleep. I'm pretty sure she kissed me and said I love you. Then she hit the hay.

Kimberly is Jewish so she usually didn't have a Christmas tree. But I wore a yarmulke every Friday for Shabbat and participated in every Seder including Passover, so I wasn't wrong for wanting a Christmas tree even if she didn't celebrate. We went to Pike Nursery and found a tree we both agreed on — after much discussion. We only had to wait ten minutes until the man tied our tree to the car roof and off we headed for home.

We had cleared a place for the Christmas tree in the corner next to the television. Now we just had to get it off the car. I had a box cutter and finally it was free. I was too fucked up and couldn't carry it into the house by myself. Kimberly helped and we got it in. I placed it in the corner and tried to straighten it, but Kimberly had to make the final adjustments.

She found ornaments but the lights didn't work and the wires were so tangled you couldn't tell the start from the end. Kimberly went to Target and got more. I think she was enjoying this bit of fun as much as I was.

She got back with three boxes of lights. We plugged them up in series so all the lights would come to life at once then strung them on the tree, but she didn't like the way I was doing it. I was to sit on the couch and watch. Kimberly did a good job with the lights.

Next, hanging the ornaments. I almost fell into the Christmas tree trying to reach near the top. Again, I was told to sit. When she finished decorating, the tree was beautiful. It reminded me of Christmas trees from my youth definitely putting me into the holiday spirit.

One Week Before Christmas

I called Izzy to come from Huntsville to Marietta to hang out. He could take me Christmas shopping…and other places. I begged and begged him to come and spend Christmas with us. He showed up Wednesday, December 18. He could only stay a few days so wouldn't be here for Christmas, but I was so happy to see him I didn't care. Hugs and kisses all around.

Izzy and I rode around and laughed about the good old days. We stopped at Chili's to get a bite to eat and sat at the bar looking at menus and in general doing and saying things men like to say when their women aren't around to scold them. Neither of us knew what we wanted. Then here came a bright idea.

Izzy, listen to me for thirty seconds: What if we don't get an entrée but just order two Chocolate Volcano cakes and make the biggest mess we can?

That sounds awesome!

Do not tell Kimberly about this; you swear?

I swear!

We readied ourselves for battle. But when the cakes arrive they didn't look anything like the picture on the menu. Still, they were chocolate and full of warm chocolate syrup and topped with vanilla ice cream. We ate it all and were thinking of splitting another, but cooler heads prevailed.

2016: Izzy Miller and Joey at Hank Rehearsal and Soundcheck: Nashville

I suggested we go Christmas shopping. A discount chain store was just down Roswell Road. The Christmas spirit was alive and well there, but we couldn't find anything we wanted. It's as if they did it on purpose. Then at the corner of an aisle was a display of Christmas stuff. Damned if I didn't get dizzy, fall into the display, and knock the whole thing over.

Way to go, Izzy Miller from Huntsville, Alabama, that drives a Honda Accord!

We were drawing attention and so double-timed it out the door and kept up that pace until we got in the car.

Why did you pull such a dick move like that, Joey?

We started giggling and couldn't stop.

I'm going to stop giggling; Izzy, stop your gigglin'!

He started giggling again. We were grown men and finally got the giggling incident behind us and headed home. I passed out early and slept on the couch.

The next morning I cooked scrambled eggs with cheese, toast, grits, and turkey sausage. It felt good to cook. When doing normal things, I forgot about the surgery. Everybody was happy with breakfast. I cleaned up the mess and washed the dishes, put everything back in its place.

I got Izzy to just drive around so we could hang out. We had no particular place to go, just wheels on the road. I intended to buy Christmas presents for Kimberly and her children Annalia, Bella, and Connor, but had no idea what to get them. Gift cards are lazy, sure, but Connor liked to play video games so I bought him a gift card to GameStop. GameStop was right next to Chili's, so we grab a bite to eat first. It was two o'clock and we're hungry. Chili's is a ghost town. I mean it. Two swinging doors and tumbleweeds. We were the only costumers in the whole building.

Joey, you can drink as many Bloody Marys as you want but I have to stop at two because I have to drive your janky ass around.

Understood, Izzy.

The cheeseburger tasted like freedom and made me feel alive. Juices flowed from the burger randomly like everything real. Exactly the opposite of what was waiting for me on January 7: Bright surgical steel, sterilized instruments, static patient monitors, and a menagerie of medical machines relegated to their specific tasks.

We ate in silence as if we couldn't eat fast enough to satisfy our appetites. I finished the second Bloody Mary and started on the third and last. I had to be awake enough to go Christmas shopping. Izzy paid and we strutted out of the swinging doors like two gunfighters ready to draw.

There's a place called Lizard's Thicket that Kimberly liked to shop at. I liked that boutique because it had a couple of comfortable chairs for men to sit in while their women shopped. What a great idea. But on this day, it was me shopping. I found a rust-brown and ivory, two-toned cashmere scarf I thought she'd like. It was long and soft with frizzy ends. I held it up for Izzy to see and he gave me the look that said Don't ask me.

They gift-wrapped it at no charge. One down, more to go.

We headed to Town Center at Cobb to check out what was happening there. After window shopping, we ended up at the food court. I had a craving for a soft pretzel. It tasted awesome. We looked around some more. There's a long line at the Apple store. There always was. We went to Macy's at the far end of the mall. We looked at earrings and bracelets; saw sunglasses and spent forty-five minutes trying on Ray-Bans. We spent a couple of hours at the mall and all I got was a soft pretzel.

I was looking for a necklace for Kimberly, so naturally we ended up at a jewelry store. Of course, everything I liked was too expensive. I couldn't find anything to fit my budget. The salesman said he had something in the back on which he'd make me an exceedingly good deal. I thought, you know, I might not even be here next Christmas to buy something for Kimberly. Gift-wrapped jewelry box in a bag and off we went.

Almost 7:30

Kimberly and the kids were probably hungry. Time to head home. I had presents to put under the Christmas tree. So, I did. Now it looked a little more like Christmas. Kimberly had been worried about us. I'd taken my phone but didn't think to call her. She's just happy we were home and all right. I was right: She and the kids were starving. We ordered pizza from Mellow Mushroom. Kimberly called it in and was going to pick it up, so I rode to have some alone time with her. I told her about my day…well, all except for the Bloody Marys. Seemed like I hadn't talked to her in months. She was glad I seemed happy.

Back home, I got out and insisted on carrying the pizza inside. She said You'll drop it. After a convincing argument to the contrary, she relinquished and gave me the pizza box. I walked into the house and went to the kitchen and put the undropped pizza on the counter. I yelled Pizza's here!

The rumble of feet on the stairs signaled hungry kids arriving. When they reached the kitchen and saw the pizza, they opened the box and each grabbed a slice. I figured we should have ordered two because with the kids grabbing at it, I wondered if Kimberly, Izzy, and I were even going to get any. The pieces were pretty big, so it was satisfying. We drank water. It's a good thing the kids ate most of it because I was watching my girlish figure. I'm kidding. Actually, I'd lost weight because I wasn't eating much. I didn't have much of an appetite and for the most part was barely eating once a day.

The Next Morning

Izzy and I set off on a mission. We had to go back to the mall to get gift cards for Kimberly's daughters, Bella and Annalia, so Izzy and I took off to The Dress Barn in the same strip mall as Chili's. The lady behind the counter took one look at me and says I know that look, you're buying a gift card; I can help you.

The deal was done. Christmas shopping was complete. And we went to Marlow's Tavern. There's no wait, so we were seated right away. Unfortunately, Izzy had to leave for Huntsville in the morning. It's already 5:00 p.m. I paid the tab this time. We arrived at the house forty minutes later. I put the gift cards in Christmas bags and put them under the tree. Other presents were under the tree, too, making it look a lot like Christmas.

I decided I was going to make my world-famous spaghetti. Out the door Izzy and I went again, this time to Publix to pick up the ingredients. I have a known hatred for prep, so I purchased onions and mushrooms already chopped and sliced.

When we got home, I carried the groceries straight to the kitchen and started cooking. As it simmered, I poured a glass of Merlot, an Australian vintage called Yellow Tail. It tasted good and it's very affordable. Drinking wine while cooking is the chef's prerogative.

I used the simmer time to clean the kitchen and wash the pans and utensils, clean the counter, and put a paper towel down to lay the wooden spoon on. Started the pasta to cooking. Then it was time to make the big announcement: Ready in twelve!

JOEY'S GUARANTEED TO TASTE SPECTACULAR EASY-PEASY SPAGHETTI SAUCE RECIPE

One onion, chopped
Fresh basil
Mushrooms, sliced
Garlic cloves, to taste
Stewed tomatoes, two medium cans
Tomato paste, two small cans
Ground beef, lowest fat content
Two boxes of vermicelli
Parmesan cheese, grated
Merlot
Olive oil, virgin

In one pan, put in enough olive oil to sauté one large, chopped onion, seven cloves of garlic (chopped or whole, your choice), and one pound of sliced mushrooms. Let that sauté until they are done. As that is cooking, in another pot add two regular cans of stewed tomatoes and two small cans of tomato paste. When the sautéed vegetables are done, add all to the sauce. Cook up one pound of hamburger in the sauté pan and cook till done, then add to the sauce. Chop up a package of fresh basil and add it to the sauce. Add Merlot (to taste) to the sauce. Stir well. Cover and let simmer on very low burner for at least two hours and stir occasionally. While it is simmering, cook up spaghetti noodles and drain. Make a plate of it. Salt to taste. Eat and enjoy.

Dinner was served buffet-style. Everybody grabbed a plate and lined up. I put the Parmesan out. We were all seated and began to eat. Everybody said how good it was. Annalia got sneaky and put sauce in a bowl; the sauce was better on the second day and we had a lot left over. When Kimberly put the sauce in Tupperware and put it in the refrigerator, dinner was officially over. Kimberly and I drank the whole bottle of wine. Izzy didn't want any.

We all watched TV for a bit, but it was getting late and Izzy wanted to sleep. Sleep sounded good, so Kimberly and I went upstairs and went to bed. The tumor didn't get in the way of us getting in bed and cuddling until I fell asleep.

December 21st: Three Weeks Until Surgery

Kimberly woke up and that woke me. She put on her robe and went downstairs. I took my meds and went after her. Kimberly was making coffee. Izzy was already up and packing. He had planned to leave by 9:00 a.m. I offered breakfast, but he declined, needed to get on the road. I believe he hadn't even had the time to come visit at all but had made the time. He's one of my best friends, and I enjoyed his company.

Bag in the backseat, he came back to the door, and I hugged him goodbye like a man hugs another man where you hug for a second and start slapping each other on the back. He hugged Kimberly and thanked us for the hospitality, walked to his car and drove off.

I missed him immediately.

It's the first day of winter. The sun is peeking from behind clouds and it's unseasonably cold. Christmas shopping done, I was looking forward to the holiday and couldn't believe it was so close I could reach out and touch it. And then…it was Christmas. We were up before Kimberly's kids. She made the morning coffee strong like I like it. Our coffeemaker was an all-in-one unit with a grinder and could make cappuccino and espresso. All we had to do was make sure there were coffee beans in the reservoir and it was turned on. It was the best coffeemaker in the world...until it broke.

We opened presents. Kimberly gave me a sweater that would become my wobbie sweater. I wore it all the time; it's my favorite. The kids were happy with their gift cards. Connor bought me The Best of Queen 8-CD box set. I don't know where he got it, but it was a way-cool gift. It had all their American releases; I had a good time with that. Kimberly opened her gifts: Card first, scarf second, and the necklace last which she declared she loved and was going to wear with everything.

I cooked breakfast, then we got ready to go for Christmas dinner in a nice neighborhood off Ponce de Leon Avenue to the house of Margaret, Kimberly's friend from work. We parked on the street and carried in the macaroni and cheese I'd made from scratch. There was a lot of it in a big Tupperware container. They met us at the door with Christmas cheer. I'm always embarrassed meeting new people, but these people were all very kind and festive. Kimberly introduced me and I soon felt right at home.

For somebody who wasn't very hungry from the oxycodone, I sure ate plenty and it was all good. White-meat turkey, stuffing, and garlic mashed potatoes, and everything covered with gravy. I even went back for a helping of my macaroni and cheese.

Now, time for dessert. I scooped up a piece of cheesecake. At the first bite, I was stunned at how good it was and snuck around Kimberly to get more. I finished that and got chocolate cake with chocolate frosting. It's damn good, too. Now some brownies. They were awesome, too.

I started talking about the music business with Margaret's husband. He had a Fender Precision Bass in his music room but didn't know how to play it. It felt good; the weight was dispersed making the neck not want to fall when you take your hand off it. I taught him a few things and said he should learn a few songs, but he didn't have an ear for it quite yet.

All good things must come to an end. The couples were leaving; we followed suit. We made a big plate to-go. In fact, we made two. It was all so good. Goodbyes said, we meandered to the car and headed for home, me holding plates in lap. We came close to losing them a couple of times, but I kept them secure. When we got home Kimberly came around the front of the car, opened my door, and took one plate.

Food stored in the refrigerator, I went to the TV room and proclaimed I was in charge of the remote. I found It's a Wonderful Life and we all watched. Made us feel good. When the movie was over, I tried to get everybody to stay up and watch another, but everybody was going to bed. I surrendered and went to bed, too. Soon this night became memories existing only in the shadowy mists of time.

Day after day ticked by slowly and then it was New Year's Eve. Kimberly had been invited to a party. I went along so I wouldn't be alone. Kimberley's friend had cooked dinner, too. Grilled steaks, baked potatoes, salad, and corn on the cob.

Everything was delicious.

After we ate, we went outside to watch fireworks. I'm not really a fan of fireworks but waited around with a stout Jim Beam for them to start. I also dislike parades if that helps. The celebratory fireworks were over before they'd barely started, but the kids enjoyed them.

I finished my drink just as it was time to go. Everybody said their pleasantries and we loaded up the car and went home. Frazzled and a little tipsy, I headed straight up and face-planted in bed. Couldn't move. Stayed that way until Kimberly came in.

I heard Oh no, even your shoes are still on, then felt her taking them off and helping me undress and get ready for bed. She turned out the lights but left the TV on because she knew I found that soothing. We cuddled up and I felt safe. I tried not to think of the surgery. It's getting too damn close and yet not coming fast enough.

On New Year's Day, I stayed in bed all day and watched TV. Kimberly came in and kept me company sometimes. For dinner she made chicken soup and brought it up on a tray. It was great.

Val came a couple of times the week before my surgery. We figured I didn't need to pack because they'd take what I was wearing before surgery and give them back when I was discharged. We planned to put all my meds in something like a carry-on along with my shaving kit. I had a blanket I slept with, so we packed it, too. I really didn't need all that much and it didn't really need to be packed until the night before surgery.

And the week crawled by.

The night before, Kimberly helped organize everything we had to pack but it wouldn't be packed until early morning because I had medication to swallow, a shower to take, and the blanket I slept with. Kimberly set aside meds to take in the morning and packed the rest. Shaving kit and blanket would go in the bag after a shower.

I talked a lot that night. Kimberly was a good listener. She knew when to listen and when to say something comforting. She was being strong for me and made me feel safe. Even with all the medication, I still had trouble sleeping the night before the surgery.

Tossed and turned.

Was hot, then cold.

Slept with one foot out of the covers to regulate temperature and finally drifted off to sleep.

January 7th: Surgery Day

Tuned to a pop station in Atlanta, Kimberly's radio alarm was set to wake us up at 4:30 the morning of surgery. I still remember the song that was playing: Royals by Lorde.

We had to be there right before 6:00 a.m.

We drove to the downtown Emory where Val met us. We valet-parked and walked through the sliding glass doors to the second-floor surgery check-in where we said goodbye, though I'd see them again when getting prepped. I hugged Kimberly for a minute, gave her a kiss on the lips. Hugged Val. Got a wristband with my name and such on it. Waved and went back to a pre-op cubicle and put on a hospital gown. Took off all jewelry and street clothes, put all that in a plastic bag dutifully marked Huffman.

The peripheral IV line for all injections, saline, morphine drip, and any other injectable medications was installed. The nurse gave me a couple of Ativan to calm nerves, then took my clothes and other personal items out of the cubicle to store until I checked out of the hospital.

Another nurse took me to surgery prep on a gurney. I was comforted by Kimberly and Val. We three shared a personal moment, all trying not to cry. Then I was rolled away.

Down a hall somewhere an anesthesiologist slowly put the mask over my face. I breathed in and thought I heard Dr. H— say By the way, you may never be able to talk again.

Then I was out.

Six Hours Later

I was admitted to ICU with a titanium plate where part of my skull used to be. A morphine drip, saline, catheter, Intermittent Pneumatic Compression (IPC) on legs to prevent blood clots, External Ventricular Drain (EVD) to remove excess fluid from brain, blood pressure cuff on arm, a finger clip-on called pulse oximetry to check heart rate and oxygen levels, and sticky pads on chest called ECG leads monitored the heart: All to keep me alive.

A whole staff was committed to my care: Nurses, a resident, porters, a psychiatrist, and patient services assistants. I don't remember seeing Dr. H— after he checked on me that first night after surgery, but the staff were doing their jobs well and he probably had more patients and more surgeries to attend to.

There I was. Hooked to machines and monitored by nurses. Where with a push of a button pain relief could be self-administered through a morphine drip every fifteen minutes if I wanted. I usually stayed asleep longer than that though and only came to consciousness when pain woke me. Then I'd hit the button on the morphine drip and drift off to sleep again.

I came to enough to open eyes and stare at the ceiling trying to figure out where I was. Turned my head. Saw Val in a chair.

I need a hotdog and a Frisbee! I say and go back to sleep. Later that night I woke up again and shout Lucille, I need my microphone. Where is my microphone?

Your microphone, Joey? Don't know what you mean. What microphone?

You know, my microphone; do you have it, Lucille?

No, I don't have it, Joey.

I want to watch TV, Lucy, help me find my microphone.

You mean the remote?

You know what I mean, Lucille, give me my microphone.

It's right here on the bed next to you.

I don't see it; where?

Val hands me the remote. She said I turned on the TV and changed channels until I found something to watch, then fell back to sleep. Later she tells me I woke up and said Owwww, it's pinching my damn dick.

I was referring to the IPC keeping my legs from getting blood clots. I can't remember much of the first night I was awake. When Dr. H— popped in to check on me after the surgery he asked questions. My answers were funny. Val tells me all about them. I do not remember this at all, so this is straight from Val.

Doc: Do you know your name?

Joey (Delivered as if giving name, rank, and serial number): Joseph Rodney Huffman.

Doc: Do you know what year it is?

Joey: It is in the Year of our Lord, 2014.

Doc: Do you know where you are?

Joey (Like a soldier answering his drill sergeant): Emory University Hospital Midtown 550 Peachtree St. NE Atlanta Georgia 30308!

Doc: Now that's funny.

Joey (Hollering): DO YOU THINK THIS IS FUNNY? WELL, HOW FUNNY DO YOU THINK THIS IS: FUCK YOU! NOT SO FUNNY ANYMORE IS IT. FUCK YOU DR. H—. DO YOU WANT ME TO DO A LITTLE DANCE, TOO? WELL, FUCK YOU.

Dr. H— had a good laugh at that and, unfazed, popped back out the door. I bet he's seen some crazy stuff from people coming out from under anesthesia. Also unfazed? The nurse who took vitals and disappeared out the door.

Every hour on the hour nurses checked and recorded vitals. They worked in eight-hour shifts. I'd go to sleep with one nurse and have another when I woke. But they were all nice and pleasant.

The resident was a black man from the continent of Africa, not sure which country, and the subject never came up. I had the hardest time understanding him because his accent was so thick. He came in two or three times a day checking on my progress. I'm sure he was making decisions because he was in charge right under Dr. H—. He always made sure to check the EVD.

Day Two

I woke at 9:00 a.m., in pain. But not as much as the night before. I reached over for the morphine drip. It was gone. Just then the nurse comes in.

What happened to the morphine drip?

Honey, the resident had it removed this morning.

Well, I need a 30 mg oxycodone for pain now; check my chart; I'm supposed to get four a day.

We thought your chart said Only As Needed.

I need one now and one every four hours after that check my chart I've been taking 30 mg of oxycodone every four hours for the last three months.

Okay, I'll try to get it for you now.

Val had spent the night and was now awake and says Good morning, Sunshine.

Did you hear that?

I told the nurse this morning when they were removing your morphine drip that you needed your pain medication.

Thank you.

You're welcome.

How do you feel, Joey?

Like the floor of a New York cab.

Need anything?

I need to know what's happening to my legs; very aggravating; let's ask the nurse to make that go away.

I was a lot more coherent today than yesterday. At least I remembered Val's name. I still needed pain meds and the nurse was soon back with the oxycodone and a paper cup filled with water. She stayed long enough to see me take it. Still, I was irritated. I am not a good patient. However, as all nurses and wives and mothers the world over know: When the patient is irritated, they aren't at death's door no matter how much they proclaim they are. That meant if I had energy to complain, I had energy to get better.

I'll make sure that this gets on the medication list, Mr. Huffman.

Thank you so much, Nurse.

But what was going on with my legs? I'd been outfitted with an IPC, Intermittent Pneumatic Compression, to make sure blood clots don't get in my legs. Nurse thought it was okay to remove and asked the resident. Somewhat relieved with that news, I nod off. A little while later the nurse came back with a porter to take off the IPC. I cannot tell you what a relief it was to get that thing off. It was the most medieval piece of therapy I'd ever endured.

Still, for now, I can move my legs again. Freedom! I retracted them up as far as they'd go, and crossed them, and bent my knees, so grateful I could move I almost cried. You know what? I take that back. IPC was the second most medieval medical treatment. A catheter had to be the first in that list and it was still attached to my manhood. [Things would get more medieval in a few months putting the IPC and catheter to shame. More on that later.]

The nurse came in with medication; I was probably taking twenty different types. There's seven in a tiny Dixie-type cup; one was the oxycodone; it was a relief they cleared that up. Cup of pills to my lips, I poured them in my mouth, and chased with water. While I was asleep the IV got disconnected, so now I was much more mobile.

Val had been at the hospital since I checked in. She needed a break and got relief when Whitney showed up. She mostly sat and studied, but we talked, too. She'd never seen me more vulnerable than this. I think it took her aback to see me in this condition.

The catheter simply had to come out. I wanted to get out of bed, and it was impeding my efforts. When the nurse came in the next time — she was a sweet, older lady — I asked When do you think I can I get this catheter out? Do you think you can go by yourself? I'm pretty sure I can. I'll check with the resident and make sure it's okay.

Moments later she was back announcing Okay, I'll take it out now; just let me unhook the reservoir; this is going to be a little uncomfortable; ready?

I closed my eyes and nod yes. She jerked the catheter hard. It came out so fast I didn't have time to feel any pain, but now I had to get out of bed to use the bathroom. The nurse helped. Took a minute, but one foot on the floor, then the other, and there I stood, out of the bed, walking stiffly because I'd been in bed so long. I made it to the bathroom. Did my business. Walked back. With the nurse's help and some effort, I maneuvered back into the bed.

Early in the afternoon, a physical therapist, a nurse, and the resident stopped by to test post-surgery motor skills. This consisted of getting out of bed and walking up and down the corridors assisted by a walker.

In stages, I sat up and maneuvered until feet reached the floor; the nurse helped with standing. Walker for support, and not feeling much pain, I start moving. Going for a walk made me happy, even if all they wanted me to do was walk to the end of the hall and back with the nurse and therapist beside me giving positive feedback and asking how I felt the whole time.

Walking was a piece of cake. I could've done it without the walker. When I got back to where I started, the resident asked how I felt. I felt great and can do it again, but that wouldn't be necessary. I'd done good. Back at the bed, a nurse helped me get in. I laid down and covered up. Vitals normal. Notes made. Then it was just me and Whitney again.

A nurse came in with good news: Time to eat real food! It was mid-afternoon, but I ordered scrambled eggs with cheese, whole wheat toast, and grits with a large glass of orange juice. All I had to do was make a call to order. Which I did easily. After all, room service was a skill I was pretty good at.

The food cart arrived shortly. The happy patient services assistant (Happy PSA Man) was a guy who seemed to love his job. He couldn't have gotten the food any faster if he'd have flown. After not having anything solid in over forty-eight hours, the aroma was like nectar of the gods. With a happy smile, Happy PSA Man set the tray down and took off the lid with a little flourish. It all looked so good. Every bite was delicious. But I couldn't eat it all.

When Happy PSA Man came back with his cart to pick up my tray, he gently scolded me for not eating it all. You got to eat to be strong, he says. I acknowledged that and he seemed pleased. He rolled the cart out of the room whistling a happy tune.

Most time in the hospital was spent sleeping, but not getting any rest. Hospitals are not where you get rest. It's where you get

monitored and treated so you can go home and rest. I'd been treated:
The surgery. And now what was I getting a lot of? Monitoring. The
routine was like the old song:

> Vitals in the morning.
> Vitals in the evening.
> Vitals at suppertime.
> Be our little patient and
> Get monitored all the time.
> Put your arm in the cuff.
> We'll write your numbers down.
> You won't be here forever, now
> Smile, Smile, Smile!

I tried to be a good patient, but I admit: I complained about
everything. The schedule. Losing sleep. Being poked and prodded.
The resident finally pointedly scolded me…and rightly so.

We aren't here to facilitate you, Mr. Huffman; we're here to get
you well.

In other words, get a better attitude and cooperate and soon you
will be able to go home. I tried hard to get with the program, which
is difficult because, as all who know me can attest:

It's all about Me, ME, **ME!**

Anyway, it was time to order another meal and when I did…

Wait for it!

WAIT FOR IT!

That's right. I ordered The Yardstick By Which All Other Food Is
Measured and fries. Happy PSA Man delivered it and, with his
typical flourish, presented the meal. I could not open my mouth far
enough to bite so tore the sandwich into small pieces. I found a few
packets of ketchup for the fries, which were easier to eat, but I had to
slide them in my mouth one at a time. It took some time, but I
managed to eat half. Though not the best I'd eaten, I was satisfied.
Just then the nurse came in to check vitals.

Good Lord! What did you do? You're a mess!

Ketchup was everywhere on hands, mouth, and face. She got a warm, wet washcloth and came back to clean me up like I was a baby in a highchair. Yeah, she started with my face first, then mouth, and finally hands. I was so embarrassed, but she didn't seem shocked. I bet they've seen a lot worse. Vitals taken, she left.

Whitney made it back from the cafeteria after enjoying a Chicken Caesar Salad. We watched Family Guy. I can always watch that show. In the middle of the episode the resident came in.

How are you doing, Mr. Huffman? I'm fine. Are you in any pain? The only pain I feel is from the stitches…and…oh, and it hurts my jaw to open my mouth. Yes, that's normal because they disconnect your jaw during the surgery.

Whoa. I did not know that was going to happen. But I told him some good news. For the first time since the surgery, I've noticed I don't have the painful headache I had before. There's pain, but it's a different kind. That moment of realization gave me hope.

The resident examined my External Ventricular Drain. He was looking at it closely. Suddenly he tore it out of my head. Evidently it was not necessary anymore.

Fuck me! How about giving a guy some prior notice? What the hell? Still, I thought happily, it wasn't needed anymore! Yay! That was a good thing. And so Day Two ended with more vitals measured and monitoring and sleep interrupted. But things were looking up.

POST-SURGERY JANUARY 2014

Day Three

Nurse woke me with Time for breakfast!

I placed the order. Somehow Whitney was sleeping in one of the chairs. She was going to be relieved today at noon by McCracken, who was driving all the way from Ringgold to chaperone me.

Breakfast was wheeled in by Happy PSA Man. I only picked at the food; tried to butter the toast but tore a hole in it instead. Orange juice hit the spot. Ate a few eggs. Managed one sausage patty. My appetite was still not what it should be. I say to myself Baby steps, Joey, baby steps.

Whitney woke tired and needing to be relieved. I thought she was brave for spending the night and watching over her dad. I lay there thinking about nothing. Time ticked away slowly, measured by the routines of the hospital patient care. Time for vitals. Time for meds. Time to eat. Time to nap. Time to see the resident.

Oh, here's a change. The daily routine was broken up with a visit from a psychiatrist. Introductions and questioning got underway.

Good morning, Mr. Huffman; have you had any depression; any other things on your mind about the surgery and recovery? I'm bipolar. Okay, well, I will be around if you need to talk; just ask for me; thank you.

That morning I also got a second visit from the team: Physical therapist, nurse, and resident. This time I want to show them I can get out of bed all by myself. So, I got to the edge and lifted myself off with my arms. Of course, better safe than sorry, the nurse grabbed my arm to give some support — I wouldn't be the first patient who thought they could but couldn't. I stood. It must've been a lot better than the day before because they seemed impressed.

Me and the walker headed to the hallway. As before, they wanted me to walk to the end of the hall and back, but this time twice. Again, the nurse and the therapist were beside me, cheering me on — or to catch me if I fell. But I did it easily. Didn't even get out of breath.

I can walk more!

Let's see it!

I go to the end of the hall...turn right. Walked until forced to make another right. Kept walking until I had to take another right and was now back in the same hall I started from and walked up to the resident. I felt great!

Back in the room, they took vitals to make sure I hadn't overdone it. I hadn't. The nurse helped me back into bed, made notes, and everyone disappeared as quickly as they appeared.

Getting close to noon, the nurse came to remind me it was time for lunch. Vitals taken, I ordered the chicken-fried steak and a diet cola. Happy PSA Man showed up twenty minutes later with the tray. I sure did like that guy. I ate the entire steak and most of the mashed potatoes. It felt like comfort food — and I did not have to be cleaned up like a toddler.

The resident came in to say I was being transferred from the ICU to a regular room. That must be a good thing, a sign of improvement. I was going to ask the resident if that was the case, but I looked down for a couple of seconds and when I looked back up, he was gone. He was one non-communicating mysterious man — or just very busy.

I was ready to go now, but we're in a holding pattern. Why the delay? Maybe somebody had to sign off on it. Probably the resident. Whitney packed clothes and cellphone and we were ready to go.

Finally, the nurse, a porter, and the resident came in. The porter had a wheelchair. Whitney followed with my stuff to the other side of the hospital and down a couple of floors.

The room was similar to the one in ICU but much bigger. Felt like an upgrade to a ritzy suite. The nurse helped me into bed and made sure I was comfortable and warm under the covers. Almost immediately she was back with meds. I finished those, she took vitals, and was gone. McCracken arrived around 1:00.

He'd gone to the ICU where they told him I'd been transferred to a regular hospital room, but the nurse couldn't find the transfer papers. They finally told him which room but didn't give any directions. He'd been exploring the hospital for the last forty-five minutes, but better late than never.

I introduced him to Whitney, and they shook hands. She's ready to go home and sleep in a real bed. She told McCracken it was nice to meet him, hugged me, kissed my cheek, and left. McCracken came close to the bed.

How're you feeling, partner? Seen better days, my friend. If you need anything while you're under my watch, just ask and I'll make it happen. How was the ride down from Ringgold? Not bad; hit traffic coming into town but nothing to stress about. Sometimes I nod off because of the medication; if that happens, don't feel like I'm ignoring you. Do what you gotta do, Joey, I brought a book to keep me occupied so don't feel like we have to have a conversation. Thanks, buddy.

A period piece was showing on the TV. I love period pieces. Doesn't matter what it is or what it's about. I watch then nod off. And thusly the rest of the day went: Vitals. Meds. Naps. Dinnertime.

Although every fiber in my body was screaming no — it's always a big gamble — I ordered the spaghetti dinner anyway. Touring around the world and having the spaghetti experience in many countries, I've had good luck each time. It's hard to fuck it up. Even if it's just Prego and noodles, it doesn't taste bad. Mostly it's just pedestrian food. But I figured I could get it in my mouth easily.

Hey, McCracken, you hungry? I can eat. There is a great cafeteria downstairs in the lobby with lots of choices. I'll go down and check it out. Don't wait too long; closes early, like maybe seven; not sure. Okay, I'll go down; you want anything? Could my good buddy ol' pal bring me a piece of chocolate cake even if you have to sneak it up? I'll see what I can do; back shortly.

The call of nature needed answering. By now I can make the round trip all by myself with no problem. Back in bed, Happy PSA

Man shows up and wheels his cart in. The spaghetti smelled good. I was right: It was easy to eat. I made sure to use a napkin after every bite. I didn't want to have the shit-show I had with the French fries. I ate most of the spaghetti and didn't make a mess. I felt like an adult.

McCracken arrives back and from under his jacket produced a piece of chocolate cake on a Styrofoam plate.

Thank you, brother; have to eat this before the nurse comes in. Do you want me to watch the door? Would you do that? Sure, I will.

McCracken goes to the door and cracks it so he can see out like a sniper checking for bad guys. I wiped the spaghetti fork with a napkin and ate the cake and Oh. My. God. It tasted so good. Chocolate cake with chocolate icing. I was not having any trouble eating that and just about inhaled it — or so it seemed — making sure to wipe away any evidence after the last bite.

The eagle has left the nest! What? The eagle has left the nest. Come again? I'm finished with the fucking cake. Oh, okay.

He closed the door and came back in the room and we high-fived each other. He got comfortable on the couch.

Thanks, buddy; that was awesome; I could eat another piece. Do you want me to get you another one? No, no; one is enough; watching my girlish figure. Okay, just let me know; I'm your wingman.

The TV was showing some romantic comedy and I got sucked into it. I started nodding off, but the nurse came through the door happily calling out Vitals!

I went through the cycle. Vitals, vitals, pills, vitals, vitals, vitals and pills. All through the evening. The only thing that broke the cycle was when the resident came in saying Mr. Huffman, you will be discharged tomorrow.

That was great news. In case it was wishful thinking on my part, McCracken heard him say it, too. We got excited. I asked McCracken to call Val and Kimberly and let them know.

Day Four

The vitals-pills cycle continued all night. But around 2:00 a.m. something interesting happened. A nurse came in and woke me up.

Mr. Huffman, I need to give you an injection. Just put it in my IV port. I'm sorry, but this shot must be given in the stomach.

I had to take my hospital gown off from the waist up. Half undressed, I laid back down, she sterilized the area, and delivered the shot to my stomach. It hurt like hell.

What is this shot for? It's just part of the medication plan.

She left and I got dressed. Then the vitals-meds cycle started again. All night long and into the morning. At 8:00 a.m. the nurse came in to remind me about breakfast. McCracken was awake on the couch reading his book. I don't know if he got any sleep.

Joey, I'm going down to the cafeteria to get coffee and maybe some breakfast. Okay, I ordered breakfast, so I'll be fine.

McCracken walked out the door and I waited on breakfast. I didn't know when Val and Kimberly were going to be here today. I was getting impatient. I wanted to get out of here and be in my own bed where I can sleep better.

Happy PSA Man walked into the room pushing his cart and bringing happiness to everyone who saw him. I ate everything. The toast, not so much. Drank the orange juice, best thing ever.

After waffle, eggs, and toast, McCracken came back from the cafeteria with a Styrofoam cup of coffee. McCracken called Val again and she answered. She's having coffee and as soon as she gets ready, she'd come. He calls Kimberly and leaves a message. While I was talking to McCracken, Happy PSA Man snuck in and took my tray. More vitals and then around 10:00 a.m. a nurse came in with a syringe for another shot in my stomach. I protested.

Are you sure you have the right room?

Yes, I just need to give you one more injection.

Jesus Christ, okay…let's do — OWWW…is that the last one or can I expect another surprise?

That's the last one; promise.

Later the resident came in, but I couldn't understand him. It sounded as if he'd said something like They didn't get it all and Still some tumor left. I just nod and say okay. He left frustrated with our conversation or lack of one. While the nurse was checking vitals, Val showed up and took charge. I filled her in on all that had been going on and that I thought checkout time was 1:00 p.m.

An administration representative showed up with a bunch of papers to process. Val jumped on that. One of the nurses was talking about aftercare. No way I can remember all that; talk to Val.

Didn't get it all? More tumor to get?

I didn't want to think about that either. I just wanted to go home. Still, the light at the end of the tunnel was shining. I was almost out of here. Kimberly arrived at half past noon and got into the fray. There's a lot of commotion. A nurse brought the bag that had been dutifully marked Huffman. I went into the bathroom, took off the hospital gown, and put on clothes and jewelry. Unpacking clothes and jewelry made me feel like it was Christmas. I needed help with my necklace, so I found Kimberly and asked her to put it on me. I was ready to go and I was ready to go now.

The nurse gave Val thirty-five different prescriptions to fill. No exaggeration. With a different schedule for each. Damn. There was a lot of paperwork the size of an encyclopedia on aftercare. A nurse gave it to Kimberly to keep up with. We were now waiting for the resident to sign me out.

Finally, he came into the room, trying to tell me something, but still I simply could not understand. None of us could. I kept nodding yes and he finally just gave up, had me sign release paperwork, and we're free to go.

It's 1:00 p.m. on the dot.

Hospital policy dictated a ride in a wheelchair to the door. I'm sure I could walk, but I didn't argue because that'd just make me spend more time in the hospital and I was ready to go. Kimberly went to get the car. Val, McCracken, and I went down together, me pushed by a nurse to the main entrance. Kimberly was there with the car. Val opened the door and I got up and out of the wheelchair and into the car. McCracken had to get back to Ringgold and we said our goodbyes. Val followed us home.

It felt so good to be out of the hospital. I sat quietly looking out my window and twenty-five minutes later we're home. Kimberly freaked out when I opened the car door.

Do not open the door; I'll get it for you.

I'm not an invalid.

Val and Kimberly were trying to escort me into the house. I can do it myself, I kept saying like a little boy, but they kept on escorting me anyway. Kimberly says stones leading up to the door were slippery and they didn't want me to fall. I let them do their thing all the way through the front door, up the stairs, and into the bedroom until I sat on the bed. Kimberly brought me my crab shorts and a T-shirt to change into. She hung my robe on the bedpost. I laid down and turned on the TV.

Val went to fill prescriptions. Kimberly went downstairs and rattled around in the kitchen. I laid in bed for ten minutes, already bored. I got out of bed and slipped into my robe.

I looked out the window. Ooooo. Neighbors raking leaves and talking. I thought that looked like fun. And even though I'd never actually met them before I walked down the stairs, out the front door, over to their yard, and say hello. They hello back. I can only imagine what they must have thought. A virtual stranger, barefoot, wearing a robe in mid-afternoon, in the winter. Head shaved on the left and stitches showing. I had to be off-putting to say the least. Not sure what we talked about, but I was enjoying the interaction.

I must have been out there quite a long time because Val came driving up from getting the prescriptions and freaked out. She got out of the car and shouted.

Joey, what are you doing out of bed and out here with no shoes; get back in bed immediately!

Silently, I trudged back to the house and got in bed while Val apologized to the neighbors. I took another pain pill and was out like a light thirty minutes later.

When I woke, Val and Kimberly were sitting on the bedroom floor with red Solo cups and thirty-five prescription bottles trying to figure out when I needed to take which. They were using the calculator on an iPhone so it must have been complicated. Some were due every four hours, some every eight. Some I took as a single dose in the morning and some at bedtime. It's complicated but they figured it out. By the time they finished, six cups were filled with all scheduled pills.

Now came the sticky problem that must be addressed.

It had been a week since my surgery and the pain from the Trigeminal Neuralgia was gone. I didn't need the pain pills anymore, but my body was now habituated to their presence. Having been clean since 2004, I wanted to get off these things ASAP. I have to admit I was afraid of the weaning and knew cold turkey wouldn't be the best way to go. So, I devised a plan.

I took half of what was prescribed: Two pills per day at the 30 mg instead of four. I was a little uncomfortable from normal pain, but not suffering any withdrawals. When I went to Dr. S—, I tossed him the rest of those pills and told him I needed less powerful. He prescribed 15mg oxycodone and I took two pills per day for the next month.

On the next visit, I handed over the remaining 15 mg pills, and he prescribed 10 mg Percocet. Next month 5 mg Percocet, but of these I only took one per day then one half per day, then skip a day.

Then I stopped taking them altogether. No withdrawals at all.

I'd weaned myself off oxycodone in less than three months. When I went back to Dr. S— I say I don't need any more pills. He says I'm the best patient he's ever had. I liked that.

And it felt good not to have that in my system anymore.

February 2014

Recovering from surgery quite nicely, six weeks later I was able to start touring with Hank Williams, Jr. Everybody was happy to see me again. I was happy to see them, too. I hadn't played the piano for almost five months since I was diagnosed with the tumor in September. I was a little rusty but got it back after the first show. It's amazing how muscle memory works.

I had a follow-up appointment with Dr. H— around this time. He came into the room. We exchanged pleasantries, then he asked how I was feeling. I was having difficulty opening my mouth. That would improve in time but, to help the situation, he recommended that every time I thought about it, I should open my mouth as far as possible and stretch it for fifteen seconds. The left side of my face and teeth were numb. That, too, he assured me, would improve in a couple of months.

Then he dropped the bomb: There's still part of the tumor behind my eye. He didn't remove it because he didn't want to take a chance of permanently damaging my vision, for which I was quite thankful. Still, there was good news: They could kill the rest of it with Gamma Knife Radiosurgery.

Dr. H— explained that the Gamma Knife is actually pinpoint cobalt-60 radiation. I'd check in, they'd put a brace on my head so I can't move it, do an MRI in order to plot exactly where the remainder of the tumor was, then put me in a tube bigger than an MRI tube where the cobalt-60 radiation could do its magic. Dr. H— assured me it would work, and he should know: He was part of the team who invented Gamma Knife surgery. His assistant says the appointment is April 21 and gave Kimberly a card with all the information.

I kept touring through the winter with Hank. The shows were going well, and my hair was growing back. I felt good just to be alive. But the Gamma Knife surgery was always in the back of my mind waiting for a moment to jump out and scare me.

When the numbness on the left side of my face left and I started feeling again, the pain hit like a flying brick. My face tingled, burned, and stung. It got so bad I couldn't sleep.

I called to make an appointment with Dr. B—. Luckily, he had a 1:00 p.m. opening that same day. Vitals completed, Dr. B— knocked and walked in. We talked music first, of course, then he asked what I was there for. I tell him about the tingling, burning, and stinging in my face, and he says that's simply the nerves waking up.

Had I ever tried Gabapentin?

Yes. It was prescribed along with the oxycodone to me to help kill pain from the Trigeminal Neuralgia. I had a few left over from the surgery and took some to see if it'd help with my face, but they didn't work.

Had I ever tried Lyrica?

That'd be a no.

He prescribed Lyrica and said we'd watch how I reacted to it. He handed over free samples for a tryout so that if it doesn't work I wouldn't need to fill the prescription.

That's great! Once in the car, I open the Lyrica and pull out a blister pack, push a pill through, wash it down with water, and drive home to Marietta. A couple of hours later the condition of my face improved greatly. The Lyrica was working.

I was so relieved that I prayed and thanked God. I felt so good I started writing a song on my Taylor Dreadnought acoustic. Later Kimberly got home from work. She says it seemed I was in a good mood. I was and told her about Lyrica. She was happy about that.

ALL GROWN UP: WHITNEY and JOEY Jr.

The Vault Makes Me Forget All My Troubles

Kevin Sellors and I opened The Vault Recording Lounge in April 2014. Soon we attracted many clients. It's a great studio with a great vibe. We had a Neve console and all kinds of analog gear including tube compressors, mic preamps, and EQs.

We were working on a project when Val called and asked if I was aware the Gamma Knife surgery was tomorrow morning. Damn, I'd forgotten. Hey, that's why they put Val in charge of such things and not me. There was no getting around it: Kimberly had to be out of town on business for several days at that time, so Val was to take me to the hospital.

The next morning Val was right on time. We made it to Saint Joseph's in twenty minutes. Nurse Kathy greeted me and took us back to a reserved room then came back with two Ativan. The ladies left the room while I changed into a hospital gown. Kathy put a peripheral IV in my arm. She came back in shortly asking if I knew this guy standing behind her.

I did! It was my good friend J.T. Williams. He'd come to give support. I gave him a hug and thanked him for coming. It sure meant a lot. Kathy came back in with a bag and hung it on the IV pole. What was in the bag? It's the good stuff, she said. I have a high tolerance to medication, but she knew that because Val had told her.

Kathy started the IV with a little saline solution to make sure it was working properly. Then the medicine started flowing. Yep. It's the good stuff. I would need it more than I ever could've imagined.

Remember earlier I told you about the medieval torture methods called the catheter and IPC? And you remember when I said those were the worst in the world at #1 and #2 respectively?

Well.

I.

Was.

WRONG!

Putting shame to the catheter and Intermittent Pneumatic Compression here came Dr. H— bursting into the room with Numero Uno Medieval Torture Device on a rolling cart carrying what looked like a box-shaped frame made of aluminum and weighing less than two pounds. Dr. H— says they're going to attach the frame to my skull. I shout What? He showed me the pins but they looked like drywall screws to me. I told Kathy I needed more medication. She left the room. Dr. H— says he's going to give me four injections of a local anesthetic. One on each side of my forehead and two in the back of my head.

Kathy came into the room with a syringe filled with the local anesthetic. Dr. H— gave me the first shot. It hurt like hell. Then he did the other three. It wasn't pleasant but maybe would make me numb so I couldn't feel those pins screwed into my skull.

Kathy! I need more medication!

I don't think she heard me.

Dr. H— picks up the frame and aligns it so the pinholes are over the injection sites. He starts screwing in the first pin. *It's very painful* doesn't even begin to describe the process. Teeth clenched I try not to scream. He starts the second. This time I screamed. He went to the back of my head and screwed in pins on the left and right. Then he put on what looked like a clear plastic space helmet that impeded head movement even more.

Please, please, please, please, Nurse Kathy, please, please! I need more medication.

Still no reaction from Nurse Kathy except to help me up and into a wheelchair and off to measure my head using an MRI. Kathy wheeled me into a corridor and left me around a corner where I waited my turn out of view until another patient finished.

This was way worse than the brain surgery. It's so painful all I could do was moan. I managed to call out Nurse Kathy! Nurse

Kathy! But to no avail. Finally, she comes around the corner and sees me in such agony she leaves and comes back with another bag of the good stuff and an IV stand.

As the meds flow, pain abates. By the time the IV bag was empty, I felt better. She wheeled me into the MRI theater and had me lay on the scanner table. It's cold, so the MRI technician gave me a blanket. They offer earplugs. I decline, choosing the periscope again.

Technicians picked up the scanner table and put me into the MRI. A voice comes through a speaker asking if I was comfortable. Same procedure as last time and it was done in less than an hour. Nurse Kathy wheels me to my room. I was still in pain, so I asked for more medication. In a minute, sweetie, was not the answer I wanted.

Now we wait for them to plot exactly where the Gamma Knife will kill the tumor without damaging surrounding tissue. That takes two hours. Kathy left and came back with another IV bag. That'd be the last one, she said, hung it up, and attached it to my IV. I felt it working right away.

Ooookay.

Joey goooood.

Val, J.T., and I sat around and waited. IV bag empty, I was feeling good and sing David Bowie's Space Oddity because I felt like I was wearing a space helmet.

Ground control to Major Tom!

Val started the countdown but started at number one.

That's not a countdown; you start a countdown at ten!

They were laughing their asses off, but I had a face of stone. I was taking this very seriously indeed. Val got it on video. It's on my FB page somewhere.

We talked for a couple of hours then it was time for Gamma Knife surgery. Val and J.T. wish me luck. Kathy wheels me down the hall to the Gamma Knife Theater. The Gamma Knife Tube was much bigger than the MRI chamber.

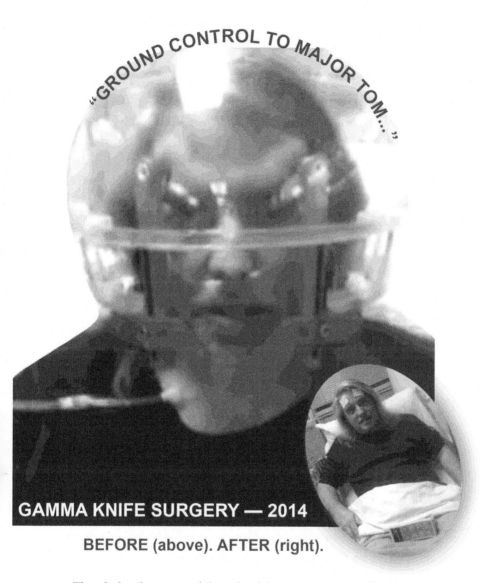

"GROUND CONTROL TO MAJOR TOM..."

GAMMA KNIFE SURGERY — 2014

BEFORE (above). AFTER (right).

They helped me out of the wheelchair and onto the Gamma
Knife Table. Snapped the head frame to latches so I couldn't move
my head and pushed me into the tube. None of this was good for my
claustrophobia, but I was full of the good stuff and Classic Rock was
playing inside the tube. Another disembodied voice says:

Are you comfortable? The procedure will start soon. Relax, we're starting the procedure now; please try not to move.

Like I could, latched in and all. Still, it wasn't so bad. I had the music to pass the time. I was relaxed. I think I even drifted off to sleep a couple of times. In any case, time seemed to pass quickly. Before I knew it, the technician was pulling me out of the tube and releasing the latches.

I'd been in the machine for an hour and forty minutes. I sat in the wheelchair where the tech took off my space helmet. He took out the pins from the head frame, too; that was painful but nowhere near as painful as when they went in. I felt so relieved, as if the weight of the world had been lifted off my shoulders. Kathy wheeled me back to the room where Val and J.T. were waiting.

I could get dressed now, so Val and J.T. left and I got dressed and walked out of the room where Kathy had documents about aftercare and a prescription for Percocet. Val took those and Kathy says we're free to go.

J.T. and I stood outside chatting for the five minutes it took for Val to get the car. Goodbye, J.T.! Then we headed for home. I was still loopy from the medication and made Val laugh at stupid shit.

Because Kimberly was still out of town on business, Val was going to spend the night at the house to make sure I was supervised. I was sore from the pins screwed into my scalp, so I took a couple of Percocet and sat at the kitchen table. We were both starving, so Val called in a pizza order, pepperoni with extra cheese.

While we waited for it to arrive, I told Val how painful it was to have the brace screwed into my skull. I was probably going to have nightmares from the experience. Soon the doorbell rang alerting us that the pizza had arrived. She brought it in. I opened the lid of the pizza box and drank in the aroma. It looked delicious. I hadn't had pizza in a long time and put a couple of slices on my plate, took a bite, and burned the roof of my mouth. It tasted so good. I let it cool and took another. We ate the entire pizza. Okay. I ate more than Val, but we both were so hungry we devoured it.

I called Kimberly and let her know I was okay and told her how painful the surgery had been and that I really wished she were home right now. She says everything's going to be all right. The Percocet is kicking in. I went upstairs, got ready for bed, and did my usual channel surfing in the recumbent position. Val joined me on the bed. I found an HBO movie wherein Al Pacino played Phil Spector. It's an interesting movie. I managed to watch the whole thing.

The movie ended and another started, but I was too tired to change the channel and Val had already drifted off to sleep in her clothes on top of the covers. I closed my eyes and drifted away. When I woke the next morning, I was alone. Val must have gotten up in the middle of the night and slept on the couch. I smelled coffee so guessed she was awake. My head hurt where pins had been screwed in, so I took a Percocet, put on my robe, and walked downstairs. Val was in the kitchen having a cup of coffee.

The coffee tasted good. But Val had to leave to catch up on work. Kimberly wouldn't be back from her work trip for another two days which meant I was going to be alone. I hadn't been alone since the surgery in January and fretted a bit. Val assured me she was just a phone call away, got ready, and left for work.

I was alone. Laid in the bed and found something to watch, but after a few minutes drifted off. When I awoke my head felt like it was burning where the pins had been screwed in. I was also hungry. I popped another Percocet and went downstairs to the kitchen. I opened the refrigerator but there was nothing to eat. I was going to have to go to the grocery store.

I got dressed and drove to Publix. Wheeled a cart into the store and stalked the aisles. I got three kinds of cereal, almond milk, vanilla Greek yogurt, a frozen peperoni pizza, mozzarella cheese, and Klondike bars. Back home, groceries unloaded, I was really starving now. Filled a bowl with Honey Nut Cheerios and almond milk and ate as if I'd never eaten cereal before.

Then had another bowlful.

Satiated and back in bed, I pulled covers up and channel-surfed but soon drifted away on a cloud of sleep. I woke up hungry and in pain, took a Percocet and ate, and did it all again. This was my existence until Kimberly got home.

I was incredibly happy to see her when she got back. I hugged her and kissed her and held her in my arms for a long time. I told her all about the Gamma Knife surgery and how it was more painful than the brain surgery.

2014: JOEY with MICHELLE MALONE AND PHIL ZONE AT GEORGIA MUSIC HALL OF FAME

MAY 5, 2014

Today was the day for the Gamma Knife surgery follow-up at Emory Saint Joseph's Hospital. Dr. K— had been involved with the Gamma Knife surgery, but I'd never met her. I had to have another MRI, though, before I'd be seeing her.

Kimberly and I woke early and drove to the hospital. We arrived, found the Imaging Department, and checked in. They put a band on my wrist, and we waited. Then off to the MRI and forty-five minutes later I'm dressing and putting jewelry back on. We waited in the cafeteria with a snack and coffee before my appointment with Dr. K—.

At appointment time, we checked in, but Kimberly filled out the paperwork only asking a question every now and then. A nurse called us back and documented weight and vitals. Fifteen minutes later Dr. K— came walking through the door. She's around thirty-five to forty years old with shoulder-length brown hair. She was a pretty woman. She introduced herself and asked questions.

How are you feeling? Any dizziness, vertigo, or blackouts? Your MRI looked perfect; the Gamma Knife killed all the tumor though some is still there, but it will eventually shrink and just leave a small hole in the brain where it had been; may take years for that to happen but we're very happy with the results.

So was I. I hadn't realized I'd still been carrying all this worry weight around and when Dr. K— said I was okay I felt it just roll off my shoulders. And there it was: A clean bill of health. One caveat: I had to get an annual MRI and checkup for the next ten years. I was more than okay with that.

And then...it was —

TIME TO START LIVING

Yes, now it was time to start living the rest of my life. I'm especially grateful for Val King. If not for her I'd never have made it through the brain surgery situation and that's a fact because I couldn't drive. How would I have gotten to all the doctors? She saved my life.

I'm grateful to everybody that prayed, sent positive energy, and generally wished me well. I'm grateful for all the people who supported me by donating to the aftercare fund.

John Lennon said all you need is love. But I think God says it best when He says These three remain: Faith, Hope, and Love; but the greatest of these is Love.

My faith remains though it sometimes wobbles.

My hope rises after each faltering.

And I now have a love in my heart that was not there before.

I don't think it was my time to go. God still has a purpose for me which I do not yet know. Maybe I never will. Maybe I'll be doing His will unbeknownst to me so as not to feed my big ol' ego. God has shown grace to this Kentucky country boy, Accidental Rock Star, ex-husband, and father who has floundered and burned bridges and sinned and repented and apologized and overcome and keeps on trying.

Even as I write this book, I'm still grateful for His grace.

PHOTO
ALBUM

Above: On tour with Lynyrd Skynyrd
Below: The Georgia Satellites

Joey: Always in the zone.

Chad Jackson, Joey (10), and Michael O'Neal are tearing it up and having a blast.

Joey and Greg Howson Pep Band

Joey Jr. with Dad

Joey and Eddie Moody

Cousin Tracy Huffman took this picture.
Joey was 13 and dreaming of the stage.

Early 80s:
Joey at Naples, Florida
band house.
Hey, is that Joey
making his famous
spaghetti recipe?
He was still a
baby, right?

1991: Joey on tour with
Michelle Malone and
Drag the River.

WHERE'S MY AQUA NET?

2013: Joey with Cleveland Willis

Joey and big brother Chuck

If you want to donate to Music Health Alliance you can do so by:

Venmo: @MusicHealthAlliance

PayPal: Paypal.me/MusicHealthAllilance

Or mail your check or money order to:

Music Health Alliance
2737 Larmon Drive
Nashville, TN   37204

Checks can also be made as Tribute Gifts honoring someone special, a special occasion, or the memory of a loved one.

ISBN: 978-1-950729-22-7
Blue Room Books
BlueRoomBooks.com

Made in the USA
Monee, IL
31 March 2023

30970348R00177